Jesus and the Exodus

Discovering the Key that Unlocks Scripture

Dr Tom Holland

Copyright

Jesus and the Exodus by Tom Holland

Copyright ©2023 Tom Holland

Apiary Publishing Ltd

34 South Street, Bridgend, CF31 3ED, UK

admin@apiarypublishing.com

All rights reserved. No part of this book may be reproduced or transmitted in any form or by any means, electronic or mechanical, including photocopying, recording, or by any information storage and retrieval system, without permission in writing from the publisher.

The views contained herein are not necessarily the views of the publisher.

Unless otherwise indicated, Scripture is from the ESV® Bible (The Holy Bible, English Standard Version®), copyright © 2001 by Crossway Bibles, a publishing ministry of Good News Publishers. All rights reserved.

Scripture quotations marked "NET" are taken from the NET Bible®. https://netbible.com copyright ©1996, 2019 used with permission from Biblical Studies Press, L.L.C. All rights reserved. Scripture quotations marked "NIV" are taken from THE HOLY BIBLE, NEW INTERNATIONAL VERSION®, NIV® Copyright © 1973, 1978, 1984, 2011 by Biblica, Inc.®. All rights reserved worldwide.

British Library Cataloguing-in-Publication Data

A catalogue record for this book is available from the British Library

ISBN: 9781912445196 (paperback)

ISBN: 9781912445417 (hard cover)

ISBN: 9781912445332 (epub)

Other Books by Tom Holland

Contours of Pauline Theology: A Radical New Survey of the Influences on Paul's Biblical Writings

Romans: The Divine Marriage: A Biblical and Theological Commentary, Volumes 1 & 2

Hope for the Nations: Paul's Letter to the Romans—A Corporate Theological Reading

Missing Lenses - How reading scripture with the first century church can help us find our lost identity.

Tom Wright and The Search For Truth, A Theological Evaluation, Second Edition Revised and Expanded

Prayer and the Goodness of God: Learning about prayer through Christians in discussion

For bulk orders contact sales@apiarypublishing.com.

Dedication

To Beniamin and Nora Faragau of Cluj, Romania.

Two dear friends whose fellowship and encouragement have meant more than they could possibly know.

Acknowledgments

As I come to the end of this book there are many people I wish to acknowledge. There are hundreds if not thousands of people with whom I have interacted over the years, and whose knowledge and understanding have enriched my search to know the Lord Jesus better. Many will not know the impact they made as I read their writings, listened to their thoughts and, on occasion, met with them. In this particular acknowledgement I would like to thank those who, in recent years, have encouraged me and done things for me that have made this particular book possible.

I want to thank Peter and Vrinda Isaac, who so kindly introduced me to their very special group of Indian medical friends and invited me to lead a weekly study for them throughout the days of lockdown during the COVID crisis. Meeting with them weekly by Zoom was a privilege I will always remember. They enriched me far more than I could have enriched them, and I am hugely thankful that I was able to meet with them over a period of about 18 months. This book was written during those dark days.

I want to thank Roy Harries, who patiently read countless draughts of this book, telling me bluntly but lovingly that what I was proposing was totally unsuitable for the average reader. His frankness drove me back to see how I could make the material more accessible, which I hope has been to some extent achieved.

And then, there is Bill and Ann Weaver in Chattanooga. I cannot count the number of times they have given their support when technical issues have been beyond my ability to solve. Without their support this book would not be in your hands. I thank them most sincerely.

And of course, there is Barbara, my wife for 50 years, who has been the glue as well as the love of my life. She has known all the frustrations of being married to a dyslexic husband who writes! She has checked the scripts of most of my books. For this and for countless other ways in which she has enriched my life, I joyfully thank her.

Endorsements

Normally, book endorsements focus only on the book being sold; but, in this case, they are not! The reason for this is that *Jesus and the Exodus* was written following requests from a range of readers in response to an earlier book written by Tom Holland, called *Contours of Pauline Theology*. Finding that this volume made such incredible sense, they appealed for a simplified version for the general public. *Contours of Pauline Theology* was first published in 2004. It was highly technical and beyond the scope of most to follow its arguments. It was revolutionary, bringing greater understanding to its readers about the person and work of Jesus. Because the reviews and endorsements of that earlier volume, from some of the world's leading scholars, were exceptional, it has been decided to include a selection of them after the endorsements provided for *Jesus and the Exodus*. This is so that the reader will have some idea of the intellectual credibility of the arguments that guide *Jesus and the Exodus*, which is written not for the scholar but for the average Christian reader.

The Missing Piece. This is a book for all Christians, regardless of their denominational affiliations. It reveals a new evidence-based understanding that confirms and enlightens the Church's great ancient creeds. The significance this book has for Christian teaching and experience is huge.

No one has explored the Exodus motif in the Bible as thoroughly and as well as has Tom Holland in this comprehensive book. I commend his work as worthy of prolonged consideration regarding this intriguing and provocative motif that attempts to unify the witness of the New Testament, presented by someone who has devoted years to its study and thoughtful consideration.
- **Stanley E. Porter**, President, Dean, and Professor of New Testament, Roy A. Hope Chair in Christian Worldview, McMaster Divinity College, Hamilton, ON, Canada.

Publishers make bold and unsubstantiated claims for their books. You know the kind of thing: "This book will change the church as we know it!" The subtitle of Tom Holland's book is certainly a bold one: "Discovering the Key that unlocks Scripture", but he presents plenty of evidence to substantiate such

a claim. This is no surprise to those who know him. He has spent a lifetime researching the Old Testament background to the theology of the Apostle Paul and he is the Senior Research Fellow at Union School of Theology.
 – **John Lewis**, (former manager of one of the largest Christian bookshops in Cardiff, Wales).

In an era where evangelical Christians seem to produce either detailed, scholarly, treatises, or overly generalised work, this book is a gem in providing important, and sometimes theoretical theological issues in a very readable and straightforward format. Using easy-to-follow narrative style writing, the reader is taken on a journey with the author to explore the apostle Paul's methodology, the Old Testament exoduses, and the culminating realisation of the new exodus, as discovered in the New Testament. In addition to this, we are invited to consider inter alia such matters as the corporate attitude of New Testament culture, the amazing use of Old Testament Scriptures by Paul, an analysis of the Biblical meaning of "flesh", and a fascinating bonus chapter on Rabbi Akiba. The content is presented in bite sized portions, so that one is able to easily grasp each ingredient before moving on to the next. As stated in the Preface, this is a book for Christians who want to dig deeper into the Bible. This is clearly true, but in my opinion, it is also a book that will demand a reappraisal of many previously unquestioned norms, leaving the reader with a greatly enhanced understanding of some important Biblical truths.
 – **Roy Harries**, Accountant.

I came to Christ in Germany. Most of my work was in the space industry with NGOs (Non-Governmental Organizations). Through this, I learned how communicating effectively with different languages and national understandings is very difficult, and failure to do it properly can easily cause serious confusion. In his book Jesus and the Exodus, Tom Holland shows by using simple language and examples, mistakes that have been made by gifted bible translators. By understanding this, Christians can possibly for the first time, understand incredible truths that are normally missed. This is a must-read book.
 – **Ian Schofield**, Scientist

In Jesus and the Exodus, *Dr Tom Holland presents an accessible and easy to read introduction to the importance of the Exodus motif in the Bible. The Hebrew worldview of the Old Testament writers is shown to be the Apostle Paul's also. This yields renewed insight into many aspects of Paul's teaching in the New Testament. Theological jargon is kept to a minimum in this concise exploration of the interwoven message of the Exodus book: that is the whole Bible.*

These observations in scripture grew out of Dr Holland's pastoral concern for the Bible's message to be open to all and not just the academic specialist. The Exodus is not just an ancient story, but the ongoing key to understanding the bold challenge the authentic gospel presents in an increasingly individualistic and alienated society.
    – Martin Waite

Jesus and the Exodus
Reviews of Contours of Pauline Theology

There is a remarkable thesis being presented here that demands scholarly attention. He has certainly produced a strong argument for a much greater influence of Passover typology than has generally been thought to be the case, and his arguments for the atoning sacrificial understanding of the original Passover sacrifice powerfully support the case argued by J. Jeremias and L. Morris. Dr Holland has produced a stimulating volume that deserves the most careful scrutiny from New Testament students. It is a remarkably fresh and creative study that makes one re-think familiar passages in new ways.
— **Prof H. I. Marshal**, Aberdeen University, *Evangelical Quarterly*.

This is a fascinating work that definitely requires thorough study, and it will certainly lead to serious debate regarding many aspects of Paul's theology. The author, however, time and again pre-empts us herein by engaging other important points in the discussion. This discussion will definitely (have to) be continued.
— **Prof H.J.B. Combrink**, University of Stellenbosch.

It is refreshing to read something radically new in such a popular area as Pauline studies. So often what promised new perspectives, new insights, turns out not to be essentially different. Tom Holland's original and creative approach to Paul does not fall into this category.

Here Paul is not the innovator of Christian doctrine–he received his theological model from his Jewish upbringing in which he was taught that Yahweh would bring about the promised New Exodus. Paul came to realize that this had been inaugurated by the paschal death of Christ. Thus, Holland maintains that there existed a common hermeneutical model for both Judaism and the New Testament church, i.e., the New Exodus. Justification is not a declaration of being in the covenant but refers back to the creation of a covenant between Yahweh and His people. This view of justification fits in with Paul's doctrine of corporate baptism, the washing of the believing community accomplished by the Spirit through the death of Christ. Paul's theology is not individualistic, but corporate, so it is believers collectively as the church and not the believer's individual body which comprise the temple of the Holy Spirit. I anticipate that if it finds acceptance, the proposals of this book should

provide a timely and fruitful alternative to some of the theological emphases that have guided the church for too long.
– **Dr William S. Campbell**, University of Wales, Lampeter.

In his Contours of Pauline Theology, *Dr Holland argues forcefully that the main contours of Paul's thought can only be understood when we understand Paul as an exegete and theologian of the Old Testament, with the hoped-for New Exodus now fulfilled in Christ at the centre of his reading strategy. This approach finds corporate and covenantal themes to lie at the very heart of Paul's concerns. In constant critical engagement with the whole range of contemporary scholarship Holland maps out for himself and his reader's new ways of understanding Paul and offers new insights into a range of absolutely vital issues from justification to Christology, and new insights into Pauline texts from Romans to Colossians. Challenging, unsettling, and infuriating, Dr Holland's tour de force cannot be ignored.*
– **Dr Peter Head**, University of Cambridge, UK.

It provides a fresh and useful treatment of Pauline theology, and many of its arguments offer corrections to widespread misunderstandings of Paul.
– **Prof Anthony C. Thiselton**, Nottingham University, *Expository Times*.

It should be compulsory reading for any who feel in any way seduced by the arguments of either liberal or 'New Perspective' theologians on the origins and content of Paul's theology. It presents compelling evidence that Paul's theology was thoroughly rooted in the Old Testament.
– **Dr Robert Strivens**, *The Banner of Truth*.

No one has helped me read and understand St. Paul more than Tom Holland. I find his work to be the near-perfect balance of creative yet careful, original yet faithful. While many talk about theological exegesis—Dr Holland actually does it, and he does it well.
– **Dr Dustin Messer**, www.kuyperian.com.

This is certainly radical, and it boldly pushes forward an idea that has not really been discussed in Pauline scholarship.
– **Tan Kim Huat**, *Trinity Theological Journal.*

A welcome and important contribution to the controversial area of Pauline theology.
– **Bill James**, *Reformation Today.*

Contours of Pauline Theology is a valuable tool for those in the Messianic movement who want to understand the New Testament, and those in the wider body of Messiah who are confused because they have been taught to read a thoroughly Jewish book through Greek lenses.
– **Richard Gibson**, *Chai Magazine.*

The strengths of the book are its robust challenge to many scholarly presuppositions and an impetus to new research on Paul's debt to the Old Testament…There is much that is very good and stimulating in this book.
– **Anthony Bash**, *European Journal of Theology.*

He has pointed to an interesting and important motif in the OT, in early Judaism and in Paul's theology, which needs to be studied more systematically and in-depth. Many of his challenges of recent scholarship on Paul and suggestions of his own are worth pondering.
– **Christoph Stenschke**, *Themelios.*

I am thankful to Dr Holland for he has renewed my desire to study Paul's writings and to understand afresh the glorious gospel that animated the life and ministry of this apostle.
– **Peter Misselbrook**, *Evangelicals Now.*

Generally speaking, conservative Reformed criticisms of the new perspective on Paul strike me as lacklustre and predictable. That cannot be said, however, of Tom Holland's new book, which is bound to shake loose some long-standing presuppositions in Pauline studies.

Holland's book raises enough questions about traditional assumptions to clear the way for ground-breaking research, and his approach does allow for a rigorous re-examination of the degree to which Paul is indebted to texts like Isaiah and the Pentateuch.
– **Mark Mattison**, *The Paul Page.*

If Tom Holland's conclusions are accepted, then it would mean a radical rethinking in the way we approach some of the well-known passages of Paul's letters.
– **Philip Eveson**, *Evangelical Times.*

Those who would seek to discredit Pauline theology will appreciate Holland's scholarship and the sound arguments on Paul's behalf. Those who ascribe to Paul as an apostle of Jesus Christ will appreciate Holland's apologetic prowess and find Paul's Jewish hermeneutic illuminating.
– The American Journal of Biblical Theology.

The present reviewer, an Old Testament specialist, finds Holland's arguments as largely compelling and would suggest that Holland has re-integrated the faith of Old and New Testaments in a manner that serves effectively to emphasise the unity of Scripture.
– **Stephen Dray**, *Evangel.*

The new perspective has both helpful insights and troubling implications – so we should do our best to reflect on it. To this end, Holland's book has been one of the best helps I have come across. It is readable, scholarly, imaginative, and stimulating. All in one book!
– **Chris Sinkinson**, *Congregational Concern.*

This is a book to be placed in the hands of serious academics, Jewish or Christian, who are interested in Pauline studies and the relationship between Christianity and Judaism.
– **David Bond**, *Laussane Consultation on Jewish Evangelism.*

Preface

Based on core themes from his ground-breaking work in reading the New Testament, Dr Tom Holland offers a fresh, accessible insight into the amazing storyline that unifies scripture. In addition to making the Bible easier to understand, seeing Jesus' mission in this context provides a breathtaking view of God's heart for humanity. This is a must-read for anyone who wants to know how to correctly interpret the bible.

Do you ever wonder how discoveries are made? They are normally made when, through careful observations, repeated patterns are identified. Once these are understood, numerous doors to a new understanding are then opened.

In this book Dr Tom Holland, who is acknowledged by fellow academics as the world-leading authority on Paschal New Exodus Theology, brings together the patterns he has observed which led him to discover that within the well-known exodus story was a previously unidentified exodus narrative that had been lost from the church's understanding. He explains what this means, not only for a clearer understanding of the Bible but also for Christian living and biblical confidence.

This is a book for Christians who want to dig deeper into the Bible.

Contents

Copyright 1

Other Books by Tom Holland 3

Dedication 5

Acknowledgments 7

Endorsements 9

Preface 17

Contents 19

SECTION 1 The Path of Disappointment 21

    Chapter 1 Looking for Paul 23

    Chapter 2 Theological Confusion 27

SECTION 2 Exploring History 35

    Chapter 3 Exploring the Terrain 37

    Chapter 4 Testing Observations 43

    Chapter 5 The Years of Research 51

    Chapter 6 Paul, His Message and Method 57

    Chapter 7 Paul and the Barrier of Language 67

    Chapter 8 Paul's Self-Understanding 75

    Chapter 9 Paul's Message about Adam 83

SECTION 3 Into the Exodus Narrative 91

    Chapter 10 Introducing the Egyptian Exodus 93

    Chapter 11 The Role of the Firstborn 101

    Chapter 12 The Predicted Babylonian Exodus 109

    Chapter 13 The Song of the Suffering Servant 117

    Chapter 14 The Problems of Evidence 125

Jesus and the Exodus

- Chapter 15 The Exodus Heritage 133
- Chapter 16 The New Exodus in the New Testament 143
- Chapter 17 Paul and the New Exodus 151
- Chapter 18 Back to Romans 6 159
- Chapter 19 Glorious Liberation! 165
- Chapter 20 Baptism and Freedom from Sin 175
- Chapter 21 A Baptism that Rings all the Bells 181
- Chapter 22 Baptism and Justification 191
- Chapter 23 The Second Marriage 201
- Chapter 24 The Law of Sin and Death 209

SECTION 4 Exploring Themes 215
- Chapter 25 The New Exodus and the Firstborn of all Creation 217
- Chapter 26 Checking This Out 221
- Chapter 27 Understanding the Biblical Meaning of 'Flesh' 231

SECTION 5 Checking Out History 237
- Chapter 28 Recovering Apostolic History 239
- Chapter 29 Introducing Rabbi Akiba 249
- Chapter 30 Conclusion 257

Hope for the Nations: Paul's Letter to the Romans 261

Bibliography 264

Author Index 269

Scripture Index 271

SECTION 1 The Path of Disappointment

Chapter 1 Looking for Paul

Many years ago, I began a journey of discovery, and its goal was to gain a better understanding of someone who would help me. Let me explain.

I had become a Christian a few days before my sixteenth birthday. It was one of those conversions that was resisted with shouting and screaming, not literally, of course, but the fierce resistance of my mind and will was very real.

My commitment was serious. I knew I had done things I was ashamed of, and the person who told me the gospel message didn't need to labour the point. I knew I had sinned and needed God to forgive me if I was to be accepted into heaven. Even as a teenager, I knew young people who had died before their time. These tragedies made me aware of the uncertainty of life, and I knew that, if I unexpectedly died, I wasn't ready to stand before my Maker and give an account.

A New Life

The change this commitment made was radical. I soon saw that the only thing that mattered in life was worshipping and serving this incredibly loving, caring, and forgiving God. I wanted to share what I had learned and experienced with anyone who would listen. I started to attend a local church in Liverpool where I lived and went regularly to its Bible studies and prayer meetings. These weekly events, which had been totally absent from my life, now became its highlights. Eventually, I experienced a strong sense that God wanted me to leave the profession I was training for to prepare to be a Christian pastor. After some time, the door opened to do theological training and for the next four years my time was spent working for a degree in theology from London University.

However, as I finished my studies there was a nagging concern. Most of my tutors, who were all believers, held differing views on how to interpret the scriptures. Which approach was I to follow?

This was a very serious issue for me. I saw the potential danger of following the most popular lecturer or the one deemed the cleverest. Fellow students had their favourites and built libraries of books reflecting the positions they'd embraced. I listened to their arguments; but what often caused me concern was that, while they quoted all the scriptures that supported their views, they often overlooked, neglected, or rejected texts that did not fit into the positions they had come to hold. This, I reasoned, was not taking the authority of scripture seriously. If I had come to understand and believe in the true God, then to dismiss crucial evidence in the scriptures, which He had inspired, was a denial of their authority.

Certainties That Are Dependable

I also reasoned that the God who was speaking through the writings and preaching of the apostles would not deliberately make His will complicated. He was not playing games, deliberately confusing His message to humanity. He wanted us to understand and obey it. I reasoned the same for the apostles. They, too, would have spoken in plain speech so that their listeners, including the uneducated, would have understood their message (2 Cor.1:13).

This deeply held conviction clashed with those who taught that the true message of God's word could only be accurately understood by highly trained academics. I found this view disturbing and could not countenance it for one minute for I had discovered that they often disagreed with each other! I became desperate to cut through scholarship and its presuppositions in order to come to a clear understanding of the teaching of the apostle Paul and what he taught about Jesus in particular. This made sense as he was the apostle with the largest collection of Christian teaching in the New Testament. Understanding Paul became the goal in those early years of my Christian journey, so that, through the truths he taught about Christ, I would be helped to serve and know Him better.

What I was very clear about as I graduated was that none of these good Christian leaders who had taught me had taken me to the real Paul. Their teaching and explanations had simply failed to satisfy.

Beginning with Doubts

It was with these doubts and concerns that I accepted a call to pastor a church-plant in Letchworth, a town equidistant from London and Cambridge. I had still not settled on a particular theological position and remained concerned with the many conflicting scholarly opinions I had encountered. Each seemed to have its own Achilles heel. I continued to be open-minded about the big issues of scripture and listened carefully to what others were saying, but Paul remained a stranger who dwelt in a fog of uncertainty. But I believed the apostle's preaching and teaching had to be clear and consistent. To achieve this, he had to communicate with the average believer. His letters were to teach such people and were not intended to be theological textbooks for the few who had the benefit of higher education. While it attracted the educated it was not exclusively for them, it had to make sense and have a powerful appeal to the average person. I longed to know why there was such confusion over his message.

Chapter 2 Theological Confusion

My move to the small town of Letchworth was very memorable. I met a young science teacher, and we married within a year. It was there we had our family of three daughters and gained all the memories that form a vitally important part of a family's treasury. But I was in Letchworth to pastor a community and to teach its believers from God's word, and these tasks dominated the next eighteen years.

Like most young pastors, I looked forward to the time when I began to preach a series of sermons from Paul's greatest letter, his epistle to the Romans. But I had a problem. A very famous preacher, whom I admired greatly, had said he refused to preach from Romans until he was confident that he had understood its message. I thought this was an excellent pattern to follow. However, I had a serious difficulty. I had studied the Greek text of Romans for a year while studying theology. I had learned all the arguments, issues, and problems concerning it and had passed the exam; but I knew that, while I had satisfied the examiners, I couldn't honestly say I understood the letter, and, more importantly, I had not satisfied myself. I had read many commentaries, written by some of the greatest theological scholars in the world, and had been disturbed by important disagreements between them. So how could I say that I understood Paul's letter?

A Change of Stance

I came to conclude that if I waited to understand Romans before preaching it, I would be with the rest of the redeemed community in heaven! So, it was this simple fact that persuaded me to lower the ideal I had thought was right. I began to preach on Romans six years into my pastorate in the evening services of the summer of 1976. The memories of those evenings stick in my mind. This was not only because this proved to be a vital step in the search I was on but also because it was one of the hottest summers recorded in the UK. I recall fighting to keep flagging members of the congregation awake!

The Predictable Pathway

Preaching preparation began in a very predictable and unspectacular way. I started by asking God to help me understand the passage I was going to preach from. Then, when I had read as many books as I could on the passage, I tried to structure my thoughts and wrote the notes I would use as a basis for my sermon. I hoped that I could effectively share the understanding I had acquired with the people who gathered. There was nothing special about this way of preparing, for tens of thousands of preachers around the world do the same thing week by week as they seek to teach their congregations.

Facing the Reality

But I still knew that I didn't properly understand what the letter was about. I knew it as a text with blocks of teaching, but I couldn't see how the original readers in Rome would have made much sense of them. Paul seemed, at times, to make sudden, unexplained changes of direction in what he was saying and, at times, seemed to contradict himself. Many scholars, in their attempt to make sense of a passage, would change the word that Paul had used and say he had meant something else! Most scholars devised their own explanations as to what was happening, but no scholar left me with the sense that their understanding was the one, reliable guide that would help people meet and understand Paul.

This failure to have arrived at a clear understanding of his teaching was magnified in my mind when I realized that if Paul was the greatest teacher of the early church and we cannot be sure what he was teaching, how can we rely on him to guide us to a proper understanding of who Jesus is and what He achieved? And if giants of the church had failed to do this, what hope did I have of breaking through this concrete ceiling? I concluded that I was destined just to have a passing knowledge of Paul and his Master, Jesus.

I was deeply disappointed. I was effectively a blind leader of the blind. I had seen that it was not enough to preach dogmatically, asserting that my understanding was the correct version of something that felt unknowable. So, my journey, even though I had been appointed to teach and lead others, was far from complete.

Defending My Territory

To deal with this sense of incompleteness, I had what I considered to be a satisfactory 'get-out clause' that provided me with some limited protection. I reasoned that I didn't know these things because I was not as spiritual as St. Paul. I convinced myself that if I had experienced Christ as he had done, it would have given me a better understanding. So, there was still hope that someday Christ would reveal Himself to me in a similar way as He had to Paul. I was not particularly looking for a theophany, a direct manifestation of God, but anticipated that it would come through some mystical experience, the sort that some Christians have claimed they had known.

Despite this position initially giving me some comfort, I came to realize that this hadn't solved my problem. There is no place in Paul's letters (or those of any of the other apostles for that matter) where he says that his readers had to seek such experiences, nor did he suggest that they were the key to Christian progress. Indeed, Paul asserted that his readers, many of whom he had never met, were complete in Christ (e.g., Eph. 2:4–6; Col. 2:10). So, he was not pointing forward and saying: 'This is what you are to strive for.' Rather, he was both explicitly and implicitly saying: 'Do not strive for this; you have it already!' What he longed for them and prayed for regularly was that they grew in their understanding of Christ and in their love for Him and His people.

Making a Start

So, I finally began to preach on the great opening themes of Romans: the gospel's power to save (Rom. 1:1–17); sin and judgement (Rom. 1:18–32); human pride and arrogance (Rom. 2:1–29); the justice of God (Rom. 3:1–20); the death of Jesus for our sins (Rom. 3:21–28); the faith of Abraham (Rom. 4:1–25); the grace of God (Rom. 5:1–11); and the roots of man's sinfulness (Rom. 5:12–21).

It was in this last section in chapter 5 that the penny dropped, or, perhaps better, a clue was given that was to change my entire understanding when I came to preach from chapter 6 onwards.

The clue was something the Cambridge New Testament Professor, C.H. Dodd, wrote.[1] He told his readers that to understand what Paul was saying in Romans 5, they had to put away their normal way of thinking. He explained that the chapter's teaching is structured in a totally different way from the thinking that modern Westerners employ, and, because of this, they often miss what Paul is saying. Dodd said that Paul was arguing in concepts of solidarity,

---

[1] C. H. Dodd, *The Epistle of Paul to the Romans* (London: Collins, 1946).

i.e., how a community functioned and the way its members related to each other. A strong sense of solidarity means that members put the community and its needs before themselves and their own well-being. I came to understand that this was, and still is, the natural way for Jews to think.

The Clash with Modernism

There are many today who reject this way of understanding because it challenges the authority or right of individuals to make their own decisions, irrespective of social or political norms or legal prohibitions. The modern and mostly prevailing views reject corporate solidarity and promote individualism, arguing that all human beings should decide for themselves. In addition, twenty-first century people follow what is called 'Post Modernism', which denies 'absolute truth' and promotes the idea that truth is whatever seems right to the individual, which is often defined by that which makes the individual happy.

All I want to explain at this point is that there are these two very different ways of thinking, and not appreciating this will leave people of one group totally missing the views of the other. All societies fall into one of these two classifications. Some try to combine what they think are the best features of both views, i.e., corporateness and individualism; but ultimately, there is no middle ground or common bridge that will allow a mingling of the two positions without essentially destroying the distinctives of both in one sweeping stroke.

A Modern Example

Sometime later, I talked with a teaching colleague who had taught in Africa. We discussed the importance of this concept of solidarity for understanding Paul. He said that, in Kenya, if he asked a student his name, he would tell him the name of his tribe. When he said, "No, it's your name I want to know", he would be told the name of his father. Finally, after explaining that what he wanted to know was the name his parents had given him, the student would state his own given name. "You see", my colleague explained, "in Africa, people can't think of their identities outside of their tribes or families. They cannot think of their existence apart from these controlling communities".

In fact, this way of thinking is widespread throughout the world, even though it's expressed in different ways. I've often asked overseas students who have come to the UK to study what the biggest difference is between the UK and their homelands. Almost always the answer is: "Everyone here is so individualistic". They were not all African students but came from countries around the globe. What was common was they came from countries that did not follow Western forms of education with roots in Greek thinking and emphasis on individuality.

The West Versus the Rest of the World

How different it is in the West. People just don't think corporately. They insist on their rights and freedom to think and act as they please. Our culture rejects (or thinks it rejects) the notion of solidarity and promotes whatever enhances the peoples' interests, i.e., it is committed to individualism.

It was as I came to understand this massive distinction that I began to appreciate my problems in understanding the Bible. I was reading it as though it was written to a post-Enlightenment readership, i.e., the time following the eighteenth-century, when a fundamental change in understanding overcame the controls of solidarity that had previously dominated Europe. From that time on, Western thought separated itself from the thinking patterns of the rest of humanity, which still tend to focus on solidarity as the basic building block of learning and understanding who and what people are.

When the World Changed

Most of the European nations were influenced by the Enlightenment.[2] This was an intellectual/cultural movement in the seventeenth and eighteenth centuries which produced a massive change in thinking. As a result, it not only began to challenge previous patterns of thinking but also the then universally accepted notion of the existence of a supreme being or power. From then on, it became important to claim to be enlightened and progressive; and this meant rejecting the existence of God. This was to have massive social consequences for, when people stopped believing in God, they stopped believing in heaven

---

[2] "The Enlightenment, also known as the Age of Reason, was a philosophical movement in Europe during the seventeenth and eighteenth centuries. At its core was a belief in the use and celebration of reason, the power by which humans understand the universe and improve their own condition. The goals of rational humanity were considered to be knowledge, freedom, and happiness". "Enlightenment Key Facts," *Online Encyclopaedia Britannica* (https://www.britannica.com).

and hell and so had no ultimate controlling inhibitions on their behaviour. If it is pleasurable, it is good; if it is good, it is, beyond question, correct. This new attitude was to increasingly characterize the mindset of following generations who were 'the children of the Enlightenment'. The fruit of such thinking is to deny that there is right and there is wrong, Moral absolutes are categorically denied to exist.

Now, while religion has been swept away by many communities, its absence has left a vacuum into which superstition and occult practices have emerged and flourished. Despite the rejection of absolutes, most people believe in an ultimate evil that they probably identify as the devil, but they refuse to acknowledge the existence of God! This sort of reasoning is coming from a position that claims all ideas are valid except belief in a Creator. Then, whenever the question is asked as to where this evil comes from, their inane reply is "God is responsible"! Clearly, such contradiction is ridiculous, and it screams out for them to re-evaluate their presuppositions.

This digression is to show that to understand others, we must understand their presuppositions and the mindset they have created or adopted. It is also given as a warning of presuming that our understanding is right and that of others is wrong. We have all inherited a set of beliefs by which we judge others and, to be true to ourselves, we ought to critically examine our own views as closely as we do the views of those we disagree with.

The World View of Paul

Paul lived centuries before these ideas and their consequences emerged. His message did not promote the worldly rights of the individual (although what he taught has contributed massively to the idea of 'human rights', which is rooted in the biblical doctrine of the equality of all people before God). He challenged and changed pagan understanding by focusing on the facts of the life, death, and resurrection of Jesus.

But even if Paul had been able to miraculously anticipate these later intellectual shifts, it would have been pointless for him to have used them for none of his readers would have understood his argument. It was simply not their worldview. The understanding of their identity was based on human solidarity and not individualism. It is because of this that, as we will see, when we hear Paul, we try to put him right because he does not speak our language or use our concepts of personhood.

So, in the coming chapters, I will consider some important examples of this approach, i.e., where we tend to impose our thought system(s) on Paul's letters. This, I believe, will bring us not only to the real Paul but also to the Hebraic roots of Christian teaching and to the God who sent His Son, Jesus, and commissioned Paul to be His Son's messenger to the nations.

The Exodus and Jewish identity

I was beginning to see that in order to understand Paul's way of thinking I needed to recognise that he stayed within the culture he was born into. Paul belonged to a nation that had experienced the Exodus event. This had Passover at its heart and defined the nation's very existence. It was through this event that God not only saved Israel from slavery in Egypt but established her as a nation. This event continues to this day to be at the heart of Jewish identity and its worldview, and Jews all over the world continue to celebrate it annually in their homes at Passover.

Conclusion

I was beginning to appreciate how important the Exodus with its Passover event was for Paul. I was beginning to see that this Exodus narrative was central to his theology and the foundation of much of his teaching. So, in order to know him and his teaching about Jesus better, I needed to engage with it in a way I had never done before. If we appreciate the centrality of the Egyptian Exodus, and the ones that eventually replaced it (i.e., the Babylonian and New Exodus as we will see later), we will hopefully come to a greater understanding of Paul, of Jesus, and of Jesus' ministry. At this stage of my journey, I was still very much in the dark, but I believed that these flickers of light concerning the corporate identity and the importance of the exodus had given me some hope of progressing to a greater understanding of the Bible's teaching and the importance of the Passover event for the apostle.

SECTION 2 Exploring History

Chapter 3 Exploring the Terrain

Having preached on chapters 1–4, and having gained a new understanding from chapter 5, I was now ready to progress. With this in mind, a close reading of Romans 6–7 led me to see some important points I hadn't considered before.

Discoveries That Made a Difference

Firstly, Paul was NOT talking about the individual believer's experience. I had always been taught that he was and accepted that as true. But now I was coming to see that what he was saying in chapter 5 had a historic perspective. It was about two groups of people: those whom Paul describes as being 'in Adam' and those he describes as being 'in Christ'. Obviously, as both communities are comprised of individuals, Paul's teaching applies to them individually as well as corporately. Yet, nevertheless, it is the group, and not the individual, that his focus was on.

Secondly, unless Paul has made the point in chapter 6 that he had stopped speaking about these two communities, i.e., those in Adam and those in Christ, then we should carry the way he has argued in chapter 5 into chapter 6. This suggestion becomes even more obvious when we recall that there were no chapters in Paul's letters. Neither the reader nor the listeners had any reason to think that a new subject had begun. In other words, the argument adopted in chapter 5 flows seamlessly into chapter 6 as one continuous narrative or statement. Consequently, the corporate, or group, context of chapter 5 is the bedrock of chapter 6. In addition, the letter was addressed to the church in Rome (Rom. 1:7) and it would have been read to the community there. It was not written to individual Christians but to the church, and it was to explain God's dealings with them and all His people.

Thirdly, only a few people would have been able to read the letter for themselves. Copying texts, especially deeply revered ones, was hugely expensive, so few would have owned them; indeed, when the scribes were copying a section of the Jewish scriptures, the entire document was destroyed if one mistake was made. (Not until the invention of modern printing and the wealth that resulted from ensuing industrialization did the average person have the wealth to secure their own copy of a Bible.) Paul's letters explained the scriptures and so it would have been important to have accurate authoritative copies. In fact, we find no example of large-scale copying of the letters, just copies to be read out to churches in other locations (Col. 4:16). Because of this, the only way the congregation in Rome could know what Paul was saying was by meeting together to hear his letter being read to them. This occasion was very important. It was when the church would hear Paul explaining how God had brought them, as a community, into a unique relationship with Himself, that was like, but far greater than, the corporate relationship the nation of Israel had with Him in times past.

I came to see that this way of approaching the message of Paul (and biblical understanding as a whole) is a key to a proper or, at the very least, a better understanding of what is being taught. Of all the letters he wrote, only four (the two pastoral letters to Timothy and the letters to Titus and Philemon) are to individuals. Thus, when reading Paul's letters to the churches, we should keep in mind that they were invariably heard simultaneously by whole congregations. Any exposition that fails to recognise this is *likely* to be out of tune with Paul's intended meaning.

His exhortation to Timothy supports the above: "Until I come, devote yourself to the public reading of Scripture, to exhortation, to teaching" (1 Tim. 4:13). That doesn't sound like an exhortation to train the church in the private reading of scripture. The public reading of these early Christian documents is underlined in the statement found in Revelation 1:3, that the one who reads the prophecy (i.e., to the congregation) is blessed. In saying this, I am not questioning for one moment the value for those who can engage with the text for themselves. I am merely pointing out that very few members of the early church could have done this; so reading publicly to the congregation was the key method of teaching. The accepted practice of reading the scriptures publicly would have meant that the reading of letters implied its message was to the community and not to explain an individual's experience and status.

Insight Confirmation

I recall visiting the University of Otago in New Zealand to give a lecture. I was collected from the accommodation that had been provided by one of the department's lecturers and, as we walked to the lecture theatre, he asked me what I had planned to speak on. I explained it was the corporate nature of the message of the New Testament letters, and I asked him what his subject was. He said he was a specialist in the Dead Sea Scrolls. These documents had been written before or about the time of Jesus and Paul by a non-Christian group of Jews who lived about 102 miles from Jerusalem, beside the Dead Sea. They were evidence of how these Jews saw the Old Testament scriptures and how they interpreted them. I immediately realized that he had the very expertise I needed. I asked him how the Qumran community would have read their scriptures "Oh," he replied, "not as we read the scriptures today. They'd always read them as documents to the community, never to individuals." He went on to say that this was normal for all communities throughout the world at that time.

So, here was the confirmation I needed and from an expert of that period of history. No one would see a document to be about themselves (unless, of course, it was individually addressed) but about the community that he or she belonged to. Having understood it in that way, they were then able to ask, "what does this mean for me?"

Thus, the letters were not individual instructions but broad general instructions on how Paul expected Christian communities to live. While an individual was addressed very rarely, occasionally groups within congregations such as slave owners, slaves, husbands/fathers, wives/mothers, and young men, were given general guidance on how they should live and serve as followers of Christ (1 Cor. 12:12–31; Eph. 6:1–9; Phil. 2:12–18; Col. 3:1–25).

The Origins of Paul's Teaching

Now it is clear that Paul's teaching did not come out of a vacuum. It was already there in the Old Testament, which he had known since childhood. In his letters, Paul was explaining to Gentiles how these new patterns of thinking and behaving were rooted in what God had already said to His people, the Jews. This is clear because Paul continually cites passages from the books that make up the Jewish scriptures as evidence.

We might be tempted to think that the Old Testament is a Jewish book and has no relevance for Christians, and even less for non-Christians; but that is far from the way Paul thought and taught. The Old Testament contains messages from God that were relevant specifically to Israel but, on occasion, also to the surrounding nations at specific times. Typically, many of the messages were delivered in times of Israel's spiritual disobedience to warn her of the consequences of offending God.

Lessons From Sacred History

Paul's reasoning is very clear. He says to the churches that the Old Testament tells them what God thinks about their understanding and practices. He shows that the Jews, with their special relationship with God, were taught and warned about what would happen if they forsook Him and followed other gods. Paul's message is that these events in Jewish history are examples to all who think they can play fast and loose with the God who has created them. He made this clear when he wrote: "For whatever was written in former days was written for our instruction, that through endurance and through the encouragement of the Scriptures we might have hope". (Rom. 15:4).

The Old Testament and its Purpose

Of course, earlier Jewish understanding was not identical to how the Christian leaders taught. The apostles taught that the Law had been fulfilled in Jesus; so, they held a different perspective from that of unbelieving (i.e., non-Christian) Jews. This difference was because the believers in Christ had come to see that Christ had removed the curse of the Law (Gal. 3:13) and that Gentile believers were not "under the law" (Gal. 3:23).

Such divine intervention gave the Mosaic Law new meaning and significance, and it is from this position that Paul applies the Law of Moses and the teaching of the prophets. He applies them to Christian Jews and Gentiles, both of whom together form the New Covenant Community.

My Change of Perspective

Thus, I began to realize that Paul thought differently from the way I had been taught. I had seen him as a very gifted young Jew, who was so bright that he comfortably held to his own people's culture as well as Roman/Greek culture. I had been taught, and never doubted, that Paul, as the apostle to the Gentiles, presented the gospel message by building Graeco-Roman spiritual and intellectual bridges through illustrations that his audience naturally related to. Many scholars continue to think that this was his practice, and so, in following

Paul (as they understand his method), they give Graeco-Roman explanations.[3] If this understanding is correct, then Paul effectively wrote a new Christian theology, which led the Church away from its Jewish heritage. But the understanding growing in my mind challenged all this. I was finding that Paul had not adopted these Greek ideas for explaining his message. His letter to the Romans began to change my thinking about his method of interpretation. I was finding that the Graeco-Roman illustrations that were normally appealed to did not bring clarity, but often greater confusion, and that Old Testament illustrations not only fitted what Paul was saying but were actually far more compelling than the extra-biblical illustrations.[4]

Conclusion

Reflecting on the way the original receivers of Paul's letters engaged with them led me to see that hearing them read as letters to believing communities was not only natural to them but, given their circumstances, it was inevitable. Reading his letters through this lens began to show me that the letters were not about the beginning of a new religion but that they formed the concluding chapters of the Old Testament as they explained how Christ had fulfilled the ancient promises. At the heart of the Old Testament was the story of the Exodus and God's saving work for Israel. Paul is showing how a new, loving, and obedient community had been brought into existence, and that it fulfils all that Israel had failed to do. The door was beginning to open in my mind as to

---

[3] For example, Chadwick says: "The eschatological and apocalyptic character of the primitive Palestinian Gospel was a grave liability in preaching the Gospel of Christ to an audience of Hellenistic intellectuals, he boldly reinterpreted the gospel so as to put into the background the concept of the end of the world and interpreted the supremacy of Jesus Christ in terms of Cosmic Wisdom, the agent of God in creation." Chadwick, H., *All Things to All Men (1 Cor. IX:22)*, NTS 1 (1955) 261-75, 73. Hengel, M. *The Atonement: The Origins of the Doctrine in the New Testament*, (Philadelphia: Fortress, 1981), says: "Any historical investigation which is to do justice to the New Testament cannot be content with stressing the tradition of the Old Testament and Judaism, important though that may be; it must also pay very close attention to the Greco-Roman world, where the problems become particularly interesting to the point where Jewish and Greek conceptions have already become fused in the pre-Christian period." Engberg-Pedersen, Troels, *Paul and The Stoic*, (Edinburgh: T&T Clark, 2000) argues that Paul cannot be understood without the help of the stoic philosophers.

[4] The evidence that Paul did not use Greek culture or events to illustrate his message is given in my book Tom Holland, *Tom Wright and the Search for Truth*, 2nd edition, (Apiary Publishing, London, 2020), pp 47-126.

the role of the Exodus; it was not a fading memory from history but the key for interpreting Israel's future experience. It became the narrative that showed the Old Testament had not been cancelled but had been fulfilled in Christ and His saving work.

Chapter 4 Testing Observations

I was beginning to see that Paul stayed faithful to his Jewish roots and scriptures. I was also beginning to see how the Exodus and the Passover were central to the nation's identity and how he could never abandon this identity. I needed to know if my new way of thinking was correct. I recognised that I needed solid evidence to support such a change in understanding Paul. I needed to see just how dependent he was on the Jewish scriptures when he wrote his letter to the Romans. He'd known these scriptures since childhood, and they had controlled his thinking and practice right up to his acceptance of Jesus as the promised Messiah. In what way did they continue to influence him as a follower of Jesus?

Also, I needed to see what reliance he had on Greek and contemporary Jewish thought. I had a Greek copy of the New Testament,[5] and, at the back, there was an extremely helpful index. It listed all the Old Testament texts quoted in the New Testament books, so it was easy to see what texts Paul had quoted in his letter to the Romans.

Old Testament Dependence

Looking at the index, it was clear that, while there were many quotations from a whole range of Old Testament authors in Romans, what stood out was that three books dominated these citations. These were Deuteronomy, Psalms, and Isaiah. I thought it was reasonable to assume that Isaiah, who provided the most (eighteen quotations), had a far greater influence than a book that had only one or two quotations. I found that the quotes from Deuteronomy mostly related to the covenant God had made with Israel, especially warning about what would happen if she failed to keep her part of the agreement. Then, when I looked at the quotations from Psalms, I found they were from those Psalms that rehearsed Israel's history and God's faithfulness, even though the nation had repeatedly failed to keep the covenant. Within this repetition of her history, there were Psalms that picked up on the promises God had made with David (2 Sam. 7:1–17, particularly v13; Ps. 18:50; 78:70–72; 89:3–4,20–29,35–

---

[5] The Greek New Testament, Third Edition (Corrected) United Bible Societies, Stuttgart, 1983

37,49; 132:1,8–12,17.) that one of his sons would always be on the throne of Israel. The Exodus was repeatedly appealed to as an encouragement to the worshipper that God was dependable and merciful in saving His people.[6]

The Unexpected Insight

The third book, Isaiah, which supplied the greatest number of quotations, was especially interesting. There was something very significant in the way that Paul used these eighteen passages. When I saw them listed in this tabulated way, something extraordinary dawned upon me.[7]

The list, read out in the order Paul cited them, summarised the history of redemption from the fall of man to the coming of the Messiah to bring judgement. In other words, if these eighteen quotations could be lifted from the scroll the letter was originally written on and left suspended in the air above the parchment, they give a summary of salvation history. They begin at the very beginning of biblical history with the Fall and give the skeleton of biblical history through to the rejection of the Messiah, His death, and finally His return for His people. They show God's incredible kindness in promising He would rescue not only Abraham's family but also the Gentiles. It was clear that the chosen quotes were the scaffolding upon which Paul built his argument. If we appreciate what these quotations are for, i.e., giving structure and authority to Paul's letter, then the influence of Isaiah is appreciated, and it is easy to understand why so many of the Patristic Fathers called Isaiah the

---

[6] For example, in Ps. 29:3-4; Ps. 29:10, and Ps. 78, the Exodus reminds Israel of how God rescued Israel, often in terms of the cosmos and nature as well as history: "He divided the sea and let them pass through it, and made the waters stand like a heap" (Ps. 78:13). See also the 'Exodus collect' i.e., Psalms 90–106. For further information see *PSALMS 90-106: BOOK FOUR AND THE COVENANT WITH DAVID*, Susan Gillingham, European Judaism: A Journal for the New Europe Vol. 48, No. 2 (Autumn 2015), pp. 83-101 (19 pages) Published by: Berghahn Books

[7] Rom 2:23 is from Isa. 52:5, Rom:3:15–16 is from Isa. 59, Rom 9:27–28 is from Isa. 10:22; Rom 9:29 is from Isa. 1:9, Rom 9:13 is from Isa. 8:14; Rom 9:33 is from Isa,28:16; Rom 10:11 is from Isa. 28:16 (LXX); Rom 10:15 is from Isa. 52:7; Rom 10:16 is from Isa. 53:1; Rom 10:20 is from Isa. 65:1; Rom 10:21 is from Isa. 65:2; Rom 11:8 is from Isa. 29:10; Rom 11:26 is from Isa. 59:20; Rom 11:34–35 is from Isa. 40:13–14; Rom 14:11 is from Isa. 45:23; Rom 15:12 is from Isa. 11:10; Rom 15:21 is from Isa. 52:15.

'Fifth Gospel'.[8]

The examination of books with only one or two citations was also very interesting. They all supported the overall theme that Deuteronomy, Psalms, and Isaiah were giving. They supported the Old Testament theme of humanity's sin (in Adam), and then Israel's sin and rebellion. Paul used the whole range of citations to show how Israel had been unfaithful to God and that she continued to be so. The nation had followed the same path of disobedience and separation from God that Adam had chosen, rejecting God's continual pleading and warning. Despite these warnings, she persisted and came under His terrible judgement. This was fulfilled when Judah was conquered by Babylon (597 BC) and her people were taken into exile.

The Message of the Minor Prophets

Both the major prophets and the minor prophets spoke into this tragic mess. Despite the later writings being shorter, and therefore less detailed than the major prophets (Isaiah, Jeremiah, and Ezekiel), they still spoke into the same situation of Israel's wanton rebellion and are as important as the material in the major prophets, adding to the same message of judgement in their own unique way. And, importantly, they fit perfectly to support the narrative of the major prophets, especially Isaiah, that Paul is constructing.[9]

---

[8] The mathematical possibility of these quotations being in the correct order by chance is 1 chance in 6×10^{15}, i.e., one chance in 6,000 million million. In other words, if you had this number of US dollar notes (or any other currency for the illustration, I have chosen the US dollar as most nations are familiar with it) and you gave every man, woman, and child on the planet an equal share in the money, then everyone would own just less than 1 million dollars! (Actually $800,000 each.) Now if one of these dollars notes was marked before being distributed, and then you asked someone to be blindfolded and to pick the marked dollar note out of all the dollar bills distributed throughout the world, that is the same possibility of Paul citing these 18 quotes from Isaiah in the correct order that forms this clear pattern. It is a 1 chance in 6,000 million million! (The population of the planet was 8 billion or 8,000 million on Nov 15, 2022, at 1.42pm according to the United Nations. Source Science News)

[9] There are in fact a total of 42 OT quotations in Romans that have not come from the book of Isaiah. These are also carefully placed in the argument that Paul is making to support the structure that his use of Isaiah gives. These are also used in the precise correct order, so supporting the theme of redemptive history that the quotations from Isaiah give. We have noted that the possibility of the structure of the 18 Isaianic quotations being an accident is 1 in $6 \times$

The Greater Perspective

Such a deliberate selection of texts ruled out the then-prevailing view that Paul quoted verses indiscriminately to bolster his arguments, even when they seemed to have no relevance. Indeed, it was the very opposite. In fact, it is not only the citation of Deuteronomy, Psalms, and Isaiah that are important for understanding Paul's message but also passages from the minor prophets as well. The web of associations that all these texts form with other Old Testament passages provides an even greater pool of evidence that feeds into Paul's argument, making it incredibly rich and authoritative. He is like a gifted composer, using the entire range of musical instruments available to him to enrich and support his work. So, Paul uses the whole range of biblical texts that were available to him, bringing texts from the minor prophets to support the main instruments, i.e., the three major books that he cites. So, while there are instruments that dominate the score, all, even those that have the weakest impact, are blended together to form an exquisite composition. As all the notes played by all the instruments harmonize to achieve the composer's goal, Paul expresses his insight into the 'divine symphony' by carefully selecting and merging the whole range of OT quotations. It is a masterpiece of theological understanding. Not one citation is in the wrong place, each one contributing to the majestic narrative Paul has produced.

The Repeat of Sacred History

Paul showed how this sacred history of rebellion, exile, and redemption was being played out yet again. The Jews continued to disobey God, ignoring His message now being preached by the apostles. Paul's entire storyline was

---

10^{15}. But the possibility of correctly placing 60 texts (18 + 42) in their correct order, so tracing Israel's history, is one chance in 8×10^{81}, or 8 with 81 zeros following, so adding another 66 zeroes to the example given in footnote 6. The number of dollar notes that each person would receive would be 1 million dollars with another 65 zeroes following! Such selection and order being the product of chance are in the realm of the totally impossible. To put this in perspective, the value of the world economy, global GDP in 2020 amounted to about 85.44 trillion U.S. dollars, two trillion lower than in 2019. (Source: www.statista.com/statistics/268750/global-gross-domestic-product-gdp/). Since a trillion is one thousand billion, the 2020 global GDP is about 1 million dollars with only 8 zeros following. Clearly, these sorts of numbers are beyond what our minds can cope with, but they give some idea of the impossibility of one chance in 8×10^{81} being fulfilled. (I am grateful to Kevin Taylor who is a retired mathematician for providing me with the statistics).

created by using appropriate Old Testament quotations and using them in their appropriate order. This was far from a haphazard use of irrelevant texts. Every text cited fit into this Old Testament redemptive story with perfect precision. Paul was skilfully creating an amazing narrative that was firmly rooted in all that God had promised, as well as the history of rebellion and failure that Israel was guilty of. Paul was showing how this amazing theme was still being worked out, not just for the Jewish people but for the whole of rebellious humankind.

A Question of Credibility

It's natural to ask, "Could this pattern really exist? After all, it sounds almost miraculous." I could respond by saying that the ultimate author was the Holy Spirit, and this is evidence of Paul's inspiration by the Spirit, but I do not need to. My answer is, "Yes, it does exist, but no, it's not unique and it's not miraculous". There is a more recent parallel example of this phenomenon, and it is found in the works of the composer Handel. In his 'Messiah', eighty-one texts (one more than what Paul used!) from fourteen books of the Old and New Testaments were used by Handel's collaborator, Charles Jennens, to present the history of salvation to Handel's audience. It was Jennens who selected the scriptures and Handel who wrote the music.[10]

Jennens who was a deeply religious man carefully chose and placed with precision these texts into the biblical narrative he was seeking to present. Undeniably, both Paul and Jennens were men who knew scripture and its magnificent theme of salvation. They both clearly selected texts that fitted perfectly together to present this majestic theme to their respective audiences. Interestingly, Jennens, like Paul, quoted Isaiah the most frequently, followed by Psalms.

The Prevailing Pattern

I found that this pattern of redemption was not limited to Paul's letter to the Romans. This same sub-framework of redemption history is also present in his other letters written to the churches. This was the theology that defined the

---

[10] See the article Wikipedia contributors, "Charles Jennens," *Wikipedia, The Free Encyclopedia*, https://en.wikipedia.org/w/index.php?title=Charles_Jennens&oldid=1114209331 (accessed July 15, 2023)

gospel, i.e., God loving rebellious people and acting in incredible ways to save them, whether they were Jews or Gentiles. Isaiah had written of God's coming judgement on Israel and His promise to her was of a Second Exodus from Babylon (Isa. 11:11–12) that would be a copy of the First Exodus from Egypt. But an important difference was that in the Babylonian Exodus, God would include Gentiles from the surrounding nations and they would be a true part of this new covenant community without surrendering their national identity or having to be circumcised (Isa. 19:18–24).

Identifying the Three Exodus's

I had come to see that three key Exodus events are mentioned in the Bible. The first was when God saved Israel from Egypt. Centuries later, after repeated rebellions and warnings of judgement, Israel (or to be more accurate, the nation of Israel less the two tribes of Judah, for the nation had divided and the much larger ten-tribe breakaway kingdom retained the name Israel) was taken into exile by the Assyrian king Sennacherib, This exile does not figure in the narrative of exile/promises we are following because breakaway Israel had rejected the rule of David and, in so doing, had cut herself off from the promises which were bound up with his promised descendant.

Judah herself did not learn from this act of judgement on Israel and argued that she was safe because she had the successor of David as her king. The leaders reasoned that the promise God had made to David that one of his sons would always rule over His people (2 Sam. 7:1-16) was their protection from judgement. Finally, Nebuchadnezzar II, the king of Babylon, destroyed Jerusalem in the 18th year of his reign (587 BC), and, because Judah refused to pay ongoing tribute money, a final invasion and deportation occurred in 582 BC.

This left Jerusalem and the temple destroyed, with only the aged and sick left to inhabit the ruined city. The rest of the population was deported to Babylon. It was in this period of utter darkness for the nation that God promised a Second Exodus, which would bring the Jews out of Babylon. This Babylonian Exodus was to be modelled on the Egyptian Exodus, but it would be far more significant. We will look more closely at the promises associated with it in the following chapters. (Isa. 40:1–5)

But there is a Third Exodus mentioned, and it is found in the New Testament. In this Exodus, the apostles collect all the lessons, imagery, and promises of the two Old Testament Exoduses to explain what Jesus has achieved through His death and resurrection. If we fail to understand how the first two Exoduses provide the details used to reveal the meaning of this third Exodus, which I will call the New Exodus, then we will miss vitally important details that will help us understand its incredible richness.

Postscript

Before moving on to the next chapter, a comment on the future of exiled Israel (the ten tribes) should be made. Ezekiel gave a prophecy (Ezek. 37:20-28) in which, directed by God, he took two sticks and stripped the bark from them. He wrote on one of them: 'Belonging to Judah and the Israelites associated with him'. On the other stick he wrote: 'Belonging to Joseph (that is, to Ephraim) and all the Israelites associated with him'. He was then told to bind the two sticks together and tell the people that the two nations would be reunited to form one nation, which would be ruled by the promised Son of David.

Like many prophecies of that period, it was not fulfilled in the expected time frame or way. But in God's good time, it was, and the New Testament church proclaimed that all the promises of God had been fulfilled in Christ (2 Cor 1:20). All believing Jews and all believing Gentiles have been united under one Head, Jesus, the Son of David, who is the King of kings. In this fulfilment, all the believing descendants of deported Israel have been united with all other believing Jews and believing Gentiles to form one covenant people of God.

Conclusion.

The Old Testament is the story of God, who is merciful, kind, and gracious to a point that is impossible to understand. Having been repeatedly rejected by His people, He warned them that He would have to keep to the conditions of the covenant and give the nation over to her enemies, so causing her to be exiled in Babylon. He planned for her deliverance and return, and this work of redemption is the core message of His dealings with Israel throughout the Old Testament. Importantly, this message continues into the New Testament. So, throughout the Old Testament, the Exodus theme keeps emerging, each time detail being added to earlier promises and expectations that enriched its significance and importance for Israel of what her coming King would achieve. In grasping this dominating, developing theme, we are moving steadily toward understanding The Exodus narrative.

Chapter 5 The Years of Research

As I was trying to make sense of Paul's statements in Romans, a new picture was emerging in my understanding. I began to see that Paul had not moved from his Jewish roots found in the Old Testament. The way he built up his arguments by citing Old Testament texts showed that he was mastered by the Jewish scriptures and could not make his argument without having them as his essential evidence. This was not the product of a man who thought himself free to consult or use a range of first century texts, but of a man who continued to revere, respect, and be ruled by Israel's scriptures. In other words, contrary to what many people argue, Paul was not a free thinker. My understanding was clarified after wrestling with what he was saying in chapters 5–7. Within weeks of starting to preach on these chapters, I found what had been incomprehensible for years was becoming incredibly clear. It became obvious that the whole presentation was a very Jewish message. What was thrilling for me was that what I discovered in these chapters brought me a greater understanding not only of Paul's other letters but also of other New Testament letters as well as the Gospels themselves.

Now, while my understanding advanced massively those months in the summer of 1976, it was to take many years of research to confirm that it was viable and likely to be the correct way to read Paul.

The Years of Research

I went on to research these issues during that intensive period of study and preaching, but it didn't end when I finished preaching that series on Romans to the Letchworth congregation. I would spend much of my spare time following this pattern of thought and wanted to know if I had correctly represented Paul's message.

I was fortunate to live only twenty-five miles from the world-famous theological library in Cambridge called Tyndale House. I went across to this incredible wealth of learning as often as I was able and read everything I could that related to this theme. I was eventually given sabbatical leave from the church and spent three months researching. During this time, I recorded my thinking to help clarify the evidence and arguments that were being made. I took advantage of asking people whose theological abilities I respected for their comments on the conclusions I was coming to.

An Invitation to Train Others

It was through my work being talked about and being passed around to others that I was eventually invited to become a lecturer in a theological school in Wales. This appointment (eighteen years after I had become a pastor and after I had read or consulted almost a thousand books and journal articles, which had anything to say on any theme related to this subject) led to the principal (president) of the college speaking to the university about what I had been doing. The professor (dean) requested I send him all that I had written (it had grown to a document of 220,000 words), and this resulted in an invitation to meet him in person at the university.

At the interview, I was told that the university was willing to register me for a PhD degree and that I could submit it in eighteen months. This was a huge concession for a post-graduate student to be given. Normally, a doctoral student must be registered for at least three years of full-time study. During this time, he/she must work intensively under two university-appointed supervisors to satisfy the university that the student's thesis was being scrutinized. This was to ensure that it had reached a standard where it could be examined. Even at the Even at the end of that process, not all students would be allowed to submit their work if it was judged unworthy of the award. For those that could submit, there was no guarantee that the examiners (one of whom was a leading expert in the subject area and who came from another university to ensure there was no favouritism) would award them doctorates.

Unexpected Kindness

And here I was, having broken the rules (for I should have done all my work under two supervisors), being told I could submit the thesis in eighteen months. In fact, during this period, the university was going to treat me as a part-time student and charge me a fraction of the normally high fee. This was a massive departure from the usual rules. I must confess that, at the time, I did not appreciate the enormity of the concession that the university was making.

What I'm seeking to share is how the understanding that emerged in those months of preaching transformed my understanding and gave me the framework for my later research. However, it was to take almost two decades to make the case that it was valid and intellectually robust. But it was those insights, gained in sermon preparation, that provided the foundation of the PhD study: *The Paschal New Exodus in Paul's letter to the Romans with Special Attention to its Christological Significance* that the University of Wales awarded me in 1996.

The Pressure of Study

In sharing the above, I have jumped the gun by telling you the outcome of those sermons. I want to share the experience of those months in more detail. I was doing none of this work with an eye to gaining a university research degree. My only concern was to understand the passage so that I could teach it faithfully to the congregation.

In the early days of preaching through Romans I had very mixed feelings about this process of discovery. I was excited over what I was uncovering; but, once a message was delivered, I had to prepare for the next sermon to be preached the following week. Throughout this period, I had to keep warning the congregation that, because I could not be sure that what I was saying was correct until the series was finished. I was aware I could hit a brick wall of understanding if the keys I was using ceased to make any sense. I didn't have time to study the entire passage using the keys I had identified, i.e., reading the text as written to the Roman congregation and from a Jewish mindset. But if this way of reading did unlock the meaning of chapters 5–7, I hoped I could be reasonably confident I was understanding what Paul intended to convey.

Trepid Progress

Thus, during this time of preaching, I repeatedly warned the congregation that I might have to say that Romans was no longer making sense to me and I needed to abandon the project. I would have to ask them to forget (and forgive!) all the suggestions I had brought them. I had previously explained what the normal understandings of the passages being considered were and why I had problems with following them; so, I feared I would have to tell them to ditch my suggestions and revert to the standard understanding(s) I had questioned. Because of this, there was incredible pressure as I studied the next section of the letter, namely chapters 6–7. So, it was a huge relief to discover that the understanding was not only possible but continued to open up new insights.

During those months of study and preaching, the whole project continued to hang by a very slender thread of possibly being correct. Though I was exhausted, I was excited in a way I had never been before. It not only made sense of the text but also of Christian experience, increasing my confidence in the authority of the Gospel itself.

The Time Factor

During that period, study time was limited. Like most pastors I was called on to preach three times each week: two sermons on a Sunday and a Bible study midweek. The series on Romans was being preached in the evening service and often it meant preparing into the early hours of the morning before going off to the morning service and coming back home after lunch to spend the afternoon finishing the preparation of the sermon on Romans to preach in the evening service. On top of preparation and preaching, there were the normal pastoral duties including visiting the sick and those shut in; dealing with everyday problems that inevitably arise in a community of people; taking funerals and weddings; and chairing meetings with elders and deacons. In addition to this, like many young pastors, I was a husband and father of a growing family. My weekly timetable during that period perhaps explains why eighteen years was needed to fully research what I had discovered. My motivation was solely so I could teach God's word more clearly and, hopefully, more helpfully; and it is still my hope that what I'm saying will help many more Christians understand what the Bible is saying.

Extended Research

The award of a PhD led to my appointment as head of biblical research at the college. This post allowed me not only to give more time to research but to teach at the Masters level and to supervise students working for PhDs in Biblical Studies. I supervised some twenty-five students, and over half of them developed the Exodus theme into other areas of study. Each student's work was built on my own but took the insights into texts I had not been able to study to PhD level due to time constraints. These students have made their own unique contributions to biblical knowledge.

Further Endorsement

This cohort gained their qualifications without their examiners knowing they were part of a project researching the extent of the New Exodus theme in the

New Testament. The result of these studies and their examination by independent experts, who all agreed that the students had brought new insights to their chosen segment. This has given a 'fingertip' standard of examination that few other research projects in one specialized area would have had. Along with the supervision I was involved in, I have had my own writing projects. For any who are interested in how these works have been received, they can consult the reviews displayed on the publisher's website.[11]

Because of my work, I was honoured with an invitation to give the triannual lecture in Biblical Theology at the Tyndale Conference in Cambridge in 2015. This is a conference that is attended by hundreds of scholars from around the world who come to hear lectures on the latest findings in theological research. I benefitted from the feedback that followed from those who attended the lecture.

Conclusion

The slow progress of my extensive research was finally bearing fruit. It was a tremendous privilege and honour that I was able to spend many years working with young scholars who added to the work I had done by taking their insights into a wide range of New Testament studies. It was especially satisfying that their totally impartial examiners, who were experts in their field of specialization and who knew nothing of the wider project, recognised that the New Exodus is the key to new insights being opened up on a whole range of New Testament passages. It is because of this very thorough examination and the endorsement given by the examining scholars, that I was able to conclude that The Exodus narrative is not a figment of my imagination but really is, at the present time, the most important key to a proper understanding of the New Testament.

---

[11] Apiary Publishing, http://www.apiarypublishing.com.

Chapter 6 Paul, His Message and Method

As I have explained, I came to see that Paul had stayed faithful to his Jewish roots and had never attempted to Hellenise the message of Jesus for the Greek world. I can imagine some thinking "That is impossible. As non-Jews, they would never have understood his message." I know that this response is likely because the same assertions have already been made to me.

Before I get back to the summer of 1976 and the messages that I was preaching based on the letter to the Romans, let me digress so I can explain why my position is not only possible but the only one that is reasonable!

A Man of Conviction

I hope you've seen from the earlier chapters that Paul was not a man who played around with the Jewish scriptures, and, because of this, I could not conceive he would ever have departed from them. My focus, therefore, was to understand what he, as a Jewish (Christian) follower of Christ was saying in chapters 5-7 of his letter to the Romans. I'm sure most readers who know his letters would agree that these chapters are some of the most difficult of his writings to understand. I was convinced that Paul never intended to confuse his readers, and, because of this, I concluded there must have been a story that they all shared. I reasoned that if this story could be identified, his teaching would become much clearer.

Questioning the Status Quo

I had been taught that Paul was responsible for taking the primitive Christian message and making it palatable to the Greek world. This assumption caused most scholars to believe that the message of Jesus had become layered in Graeco-Roman religious ideas or culture and that Paul was the person responsible for leading the early church away from its Hebraic heritage. But I was coming to question this because of the way he was so clearly controlled by the Old Testament scriptures, especially Isaiah.

So rather than seeing someone who brought Hellenism into the church, I was coming to see that he was a very conservative Jewish teacher and that he would not have borrowed ideas or practices from other religions or cultures. Indeed, I found that applying illustrations from the Graeco-Roman world to

Paul's statements produced greater problems than solutions. In fact, when I studied the sources of Paul's teachings, I realized that not once does he call on his rabbinical background to make or support his teaching or arguments. I had thought that he was doing this in Galatians 4:21–31 where he reasons about the status of Jews and Gentiles, but recent scholarship has shown that he was doing nothing of the sort.[12] He was doing what has become known as intertextual interpretation,[13] which happens regularly in his writings.

In fact, Paul expects his readers to be familiar with the Old Testament texts that he either quotes or even alludes to and expects them to reflect on the wider context of the cited verse so as to understand how the text's context supports his argument. From the number of examples scholars have found of this intertextual reading in the New Testament writings, it is clear that his readers were familiar with this method of reading. This familiarity enabled them to share in the argument he was making. This is borne out by the fact that he does not even have to explain to his readers in Galatia that he is using this method of reading the Old Testament when he makes his case in Galatians 4:21–31.[14]

Abandoning the Past

Now what is also very interesting, at least for me, is that in turning from the massive amount of learning that he had acquired in his rabbinical studies Paul has embraced the method of interpretation that Jesus himself followed. When asked by a teacher of the law a difficult question He simply responded, "What does the scripture say?" He would then take them back to the scripture and explain its meaning. And this is what Paul was doing! In other words, we have all the evidence needed to show us that Paul not only became a disciple of the Lord but when he became one, he surrendered his great learning for which he

---

[12] See Harmon, Matthew S., *She Must and She Go Free: Paul's Isaianic Gospel in Galatians. BZNW* (New York: de Gruyter, 2010)

[13] Intertextuality is the shaping of a text's meaning by another text, either through deliberate compositional strategies such as quotation, allusion, calque, plagiarism, translation, pastiche or parody, or by interconnections between similar or related works perceived by an audience or reader of the text. These references are sometimes made deliberately and depend on a reader's prior knowledge and understanding of the referent. From Wikipedia.

[14] See Hays, Richard, *Echoes of Scripture in the Letters of Paul* (New Haven: Yale University Press, 1989). who shows how this method is found throughout secular literature of all ages.

was so greatly admired and would know nothing but "Christ crucified". From this, I concluded that a man with such an attitude, leaving such lofty Jewish traditions, is never going to seek help from the writings of the Graeco-Roman world nor, for that matter, from the Jewish world which opposed Christ and the message of His death as the only source of salvation. The closer I examined the extra-biblical material that Paul was supposed to have used to build his theology, the more I realized he used none at all! All the evidence shows that he was controlled by the scriptures he believed his God had inspired.

Naturally, I had to think about this newly acquired understanding very carefully because it challenged the widespread assumptions that control scholarly opinion.

I've looked at the examples others have cited as evidence that Paul was the originator of the Christian Gospel and I have concluded that the claim cannot be sustained. Close examination has shown that the Greek illustrations he was supposed to have used are not from the Greek world but from the Old Testament.[15] If this is correct, then the whole argument for reading Paul as the creator of a mutated gospel, which was produced to satisfy a Gentile audience, has no foundation at all!

A Better Understanding

Everyone accepts that the early first century churches had been founded by Jews. Jesus, of course, was born a Jew, and He preached to the Jewish people for three years. His early disciples were Jews and on the day of Pentecost, thousands of Jews became His followers. Now Peter's message that persuaded them was a very Jewish one that was firmly based on explaining Old Testament texts.

Whenever Paul entered a town, he attended the local synagogue on the Sabbath where he was offered the opportunity to explain his message (Acts

---

[15] I deal with the examples normally cited for upholding the theory that Paul transposed the Christian message into a Gentile-friendly version in Holland, *Search for Truth*, pp 79-159. The evidence persuades me that Paul had little interest in Hellenism. His own Jewish resources equipped him with all the material he needed to conquer the darkest and hardest of hearts and minds. And the greatest of these weapons was the fact that Christ died for our sins according to the scriptures and that he had been raised from the dead (1 Cor 15:3-4).

13:5,14; 14:1; 17:2,10; 18:4,19). Often his message was essentially the same as that preached by Peter on the Day of Pentecost and like on its first presentation it often offended the leaders of the synagogue leading to and his colleagues being expelled from their buildings. This caused them to find alternative meeting places and new independent congregations were formed which could develop their own leadership. These were made up mainly of Jews who had believed Paul's message and had put their faith in Jesus as Lord. In addition to these Jewish believers were God-fearing Gentiles (Acts 13:48). They had previously worshipped with the Jews and, having learned the scriptures from them, they found that Paul's Hebraic message made perfect sense.

The Message Paul Proclaimed

The heart of Paul's message was twofold. Firstly, God, through the death and resurrection of Jesus, has created a New Covenant Community of believing Jews and Greeks who stand on an equal footing. Secondly, Gentile men were not required to be circumcised as demanded by the synagogue regulations. Paul told them that their membership in the New Covenant Community was possible solely because of what the death and resurrection of Jesus had accomplished for those who believed and repented.

The point is that there was no need to adapt the account of Jesus or His teaching. The early evidence, which is provided throughout the Acts of the Apostles, is that the 'primitive message' had all the clarity needed to draw not only Jews but also a fast-growing number of Gentiles into the faith. These Gentiles who had been taught in the synagogues were now being taught in the context of these growing, Jewish 'Jesus' congregations; and they continued to learn just as they had done in their synagogues.

Indeed, these new disciples continued to learn from the same Old Testament scriptures; and, in some cases, they were being taught by the same Jewish teachers who had taught them in the synagogues. So, the Gentiles did not experience problems in understanding a Jewish message as academia claims. They had already deliberately put themselves under Jewish teachers by attending synagogues and were used to being taught from the Old Testament. They had come to share the same reverence for these texts that their Jewish teachers exhibited. For Paul to have challenged this acceptance by introducing a more cosmopolitan version would have been madness! Such a history of the growth of the Christian community challenges the widespread view of Paul touring the Gentile world and preaching a Hellenised form of the message he had first received.

An Exceptional Later Case?

There was one notable occasion when Paul cited a Greek poet; it was when he preached in the marketplace on Mars Hill (Acts 17:16–34). He was in Athens waiting for Timothy, and he decided to attract the attention of the crowd he was in by quoting from one of their Greek poets. But there was no attempt to use Hellenistic thought to make, justify, or even illustrate his message. Having gained their attention, he immediately proclaimed the historic message of Christ crucified and risen.

Some scholars have sought to say that this example shows that Paul regularly engaged with the Greek philosophers on their own grounds, but this is highly speculative. The average Westerner, even from amongst those with the poorest education, can cite a line from Shakespeare without having any detailed acquaintance of his works and no concept of the context of the quote. That Paul cited a Greek poet is hardly evidence of him seeking to make a meaningful engagement with Greek philosophy. I will show later that Paul was certainly not alone in fiercely holding to his Jewish heritage. We have clear evidence that, within a generation or two, tens of thousands of rabbis were doing the very same thing and possibly as a result of Paul's example.[16]

It was Paul's refusal to enter a philosophical debate on Mars Hill that caused most of the crowd to leave, having earlier accused him of babbling about his strange teaching. In fact, the message had little hope of winning many, for a resurrection from the dead was the very last teaching Greek thought could accept. Greek thinking held that all material substance was evil and, therefore, a resurrection to a physical state was the return to a sinful condition!

Scholarly Oversight

The fact that Paul kept to his Jewish message, which was at the heart of the early church's teaching and outreach, is usually overlooked by scholars. Most

---

[16] See chapter 29 and for a fuller treatment t in Holland, *Search for Truth*, 424-435.

experts begin their reconstruction with the premise that Paul was leading a missionary movement that required a different presentation of the gospel, as well as illustrations to explain it. This understanding of the early days of Christian evangelism has dominated the academic explanation of how the church became numerically strong. It was due, they claim, to a repackaging of the Christian message so that it would attract Gentiles. I had been taught this in theological college and had accepted it. It was the basis of my previous reading of scripture and preaching. But the evidence I was seeing from my studies challenged this. I found that Paul preserved the primitive message. He did not change it or adapt it. I cannot say how deeply Paul may have studied Hellenism if he did at all. But what I do know is that if he had any such training, like his rabbinical training, he never utilized it in the way many assume that he did. What the evidence shows is that he preached to the Gentiles a fully Jewish message and it was powerful in affecting them, even affecting those who lacked its Old Testament background (Acts 13:44; 16:29–34).

A Strategy That Makes Sense

This evangelistic strategy makes perfect sense. Why would Paul revise his God-given message to reach people when there was already in place a widespread structure of Jewish teaching? Why go preaching to crowds that had no interest in his message when in the synagogues there were Gentiles who were seeking Israel's God? Even though Paul was preaching his Jewish message, the effect of his preaching even on the wider Gentile community that did not know the scriptures was on occasions even greater than on the Jews. We read:

> The next Sabbath almost the whole city gathered to hear the word of the Lord. But when the Jews saw the crowds, they were filled with jealousy and began to contradict what was spoken by Paul, reviling him. And Paul and Barnabas spoke out boldly, saying,
>
> It was necessary that the word of God be spoken first to you. Since you thrust it aside and judge yourselves unworthy of eternal life, behold, we are turning to the Gentiles. For so the Lord has commanded us, saying, I have made you a light for the Gentiles, that you may bring salvation to the ends of the earth." And when the Gentiles heard this, they began rejoicing

Jesus and the Exodus

and glorifying the word of the Lord, and as many as were appointed to eternal life believed. And the word of the Lord was spreading throughout the whole region. But the Jews incited the devout women of high standing and the leading men of the city, stirred up persecution against Paul and Barnabas, and drove them out of their district. But they shook off the dust from their feet against them and went to Iconium (Acts 13:44–51).

The message he preached to this Gentile crowd was exactly the same message that he had preached to the Jews. There is not one suggestion that the Jewish officials charged him with misrepresenting the scriptures for it was the same message to both communities. The statement "we are turning to the Gentiles" can be interpreted that Paul's mission no longer focused on winning Jews, but this understanding does not fit with what he is later found doing. In Acts 18, we read:

When Silas and Timothy arrived from Macedonia, Paul was occupied with the word, testifying to the Jews that the Christ was Jesus. And when they opposed and reviled him, he shook out his garments and said to them, "Your blood be on your own heads! I am innocent. From now on I will go to the Gentiles." And he left there and went to the house of a man named Titius Justus, a worshiper of God. His house was next door to the synagogue. Crispus, the ruler of the synagogue, believed in the Lord, together with his entire household. And many of the Corinthians hearing Paul believed and were baptized (Acts 18:5–8).

So, Paul had not ceased to make Jewish evangelism his priority. The earlier declaration of going to the Gentiles refers to his work in Pisidian Antioch only because the Jewish community of that city had heard his message and rejected it.

Profound Acceptance

What is clear from these two accounts is that the Gentile community became caught up with the preaching, and their incredible response was not because of any attempt to adapt the message. Gentiles embraced this very Jewish message with great eagerness. There's not even a hint that they were responding to anything but the Jewish message that Paul continued to be faithful to. When he went to the Gentiles, he simply changed the physical setting, keeping his message unchanged. We see an example of this in the passage above when he taught in the home of Titius Justus, who lived next to the synagogue (Acts 18:7). Here, many Corinthians heard and responded to the same Gospel.

Crucial Evidence

But further important evidence exists that shows that the apostles did not adapt their presentation but stayed faithful to the methodology of interpretation given to them by Jesus. It is found in the way Paul answered Felix and Agrippa (Acts 24:10–22; 26:32) both of whom had the power to free him or sentence him to death. In neither presentation is there even a hint of him appealing to any part of Graeco-Roman culture. Being mindful that Felix and Agrippa would have been trained for public office by receiving thorough Hellenistic training and that this was his first and probably only presentation he would ever make to them, it would have been natural for Paul to have emphasized any Graeco-Roman aspect of his message as a point of contact. But in these most critical moments, Paul shares nothing more than his original Jewish message. His presentation is completely compatible with Peter's message preached on the Day of Pentecost. And, when he spoke to Felix privately about righteousness, self-control, and the coming judgement, Felix was alarmed (Acts 24:25). Such a fact is hugely telling and must be answered by any who want to defend the prevailing view that Paul was multicultural and used anything at hand to teach his target audience. Here, the raw Jewish message of Paul cuts to the heart of this Roman official, and it disturbs him deeply (Acts 24:24–25).

Mistaken History Corrected

So, we can say that at this early stage of the story of the church, the supposed adaptation made to reach the Gentiles was not even thought of! The evolution of the Christian message awaited the second century, when Gentile churches began to appoint their own leaders who relied on the principles of their Hellenistic education. It was this development that caused the drift from the heritage of the Old Testament roots of the apostolic faith. The widespread assumption that the gospel message was amended by Paul to suit his Gentile audience is without foundation. Not one shred of evidence exists to prove that it had ever been present.

Jesus and the Exodus

I hope you have seen that the letter to the Romans, one of Paul's later letters, is incredibly dependent on a detailed knowledge and understanding of the Old Testament. After decades of missionary work, Paul still defined the focus of his ministry as:

> I am under obligation both to Greeks and to barbarians, both to the wise and to the foolish. So I am eager to preach the gospel to you also who are in Rome. For I am not ashamed of the gospel, for it is the power of God for salvation to everyone who believes, to the Jew first and also to the Greek. For in it the righteousness of God is revealed from faith for faith, as it is written, "The righteous shall live by faith." (Rom. 1:14–17).

At this late stage in his ministry, about AD 58, Paul still sees his ministry to be based on taking the Gospel to the Jew first. Indeed, even later, when Paul had reached Rome and was placed under house arrest while he waited to appear before Caesar, Luke records that the Jewish leaders visited him and:

> When they had appointed a day for him, they came to him at his lodging in greater numbers. From morning till evening he expounded to them, testifying to the kingdom of God and trying to convince them about Jesus both from the Law of Moses and from the Prophets (Acts 28:23).

So, just before his death, Paul continued to reason from the scriptures, just as he had done when he wrote his letter to the church in Rome. On the basis of this discussion, in which real evidence and not unsupported presuppositions have been considered, Paul evangelized and taught the growing congregations as a faithful Jew who expounded the Old Testament scriptures to all who would listen.

Conclusion

We have seen that Paul was not a reforming radical who rewrote the gospel to make it more acceptable to the Gentiles. There is not a shred of evidence that Paul did this, nor that he encouraged anyone else to do it. It is because scholars have uncritically accepted that Paul's sources were Graeco-Roman that they have missed his reliance on the Old Testament. It is only by following the major narrative of these writings, which is about the rescue of Israel from exile,

Jesus and the Exodus

that we come to see the importance of this theme in the New Testament, and by this focus we see the importance of The Exodus narrative.

Chapter 7 Paul and the Barrier of Language

The next few chapters are a slight digression. Up until now, I have tried to share what I discovered when preparing a series of sermons for the church I was pastoring. I am digressing to give details I didn't know then, but which have helped me further understand Paul's Jewish heritage. I hope that in providing them, you will be helped to understand better what Paul was saying in Romans 5–7.

The Jewish Understanding of Sin.

The reality of sin is a fact that blights all our lives. Even though humanists might not want to accept the Christian understanding of it, they accept the reality of something they call 'evil'. Language linking sin with flesh is found in Romans 7:5 ("For when we were in the realm of the flesh, the sinful passions aroused by the law were at work in us, so that we bore fruit for death"). Also, Romans 8:3 ("For what the law was powerless to do because it was weakened by the flesh, God did by sending his own Son in the likeness of sinful flesh to be a sin offering. And so he condemned sin in the flesh") is seen to be speaking about the innate evilness of man. This language has dominated the way most of Western Christendom interprets Paul's teaching on sin.[17]

It was biblical texts like these with their powerful language that influenced Augustine as he battled to make sense of his own sin. In particular, he focused on the guilt he felt for fathering a child as a teenager to a woman he was not married to. This event became an important lens through which he read scripture regarding its teaching on sin. The experience became a major influence on his doctrine of sin, which he bequeathed to the Western church. Because of this lens, sexual lust became, for Augustine, the key issue to understanding human sinfulness.

This Augustinian view of sex being sinful is despite the Old Testament's teaching that it is good and a natural expression of human reality, and that it

---

[17] See also Romans 7:18, 25.

calls not for its destruction or conquest but its intended practice in marriage. Hence, the ten commandments, when referring to sex, focus on the sanctity of marriage, warning against both adultery (Exod. 20:14) and coveting a neighbour's wife (Exod. 20:17). Thus, the Hebraic understanding of sex is not that it is sinful but natural and God's good gift to humans.

The Missing Anchor

Because Augustine didn't have this Hebraic anchor, he analysed his behaviour by the Graeco-Roman model, which taught that all physical things, including the body, are sinful. It didn't take long for this understanding to morph into the distortion that sex is sin and for it to become the key to understanding what happened at the heart of Adam's fall. This is the reason why nuns and priests in the Catholic Church vow to remain celibate, seeing it to be part of being married to Christ. This understanding of the Divine Marriage (a biblical doctrine we will consider later) has lost the biblical context of this metaphor, for as we will see it is not about the individual's relationship with Christ but the community's relationship with Him.

Different Traditions

In contrast, the Eastern Orthodox Church, which severed its relationship with the Western church, rejects several of the Western Church's understandings of biblical teaching, and this doctrine of human sexuality is one of them.

While recognising the importance of this sad division between the Eastern and Western sections of the church, I don't intend a detailed comparison between these two great traditions. Thankfully, I was kept from making the same mistake as Augustine in my adolescence, so I didn't have the same crippling guilt he experienced. My own understanding of the doctrine came through trying to understand the meaning Paul intended as he wrote about it in Romans 5–8. Until recently, it was assumed that when he spoke of his "sinful flesh", Paul was talking about his sinful nature, which somehow resided in his physical body.

The Source of Confusion

A major cause of the problems that many Christians experience with their understanding of sin is due to confusion over how language works and how words adapt to various cultures and situations. It is at the root of most of the problems we meet as we try to follow Paul's argument in Romans 5–7. Let me explain by means of an illustration.

Many are aware of Winston Churchill's famous observation that the USA and the UK are two countries divided by a common language. He knew from personal experience that a word could mean one thing in the UK but have a totally different meaning in the US. For example, in the UK we speak of pavements in front of buildings. Pavements separate them from the road where traffic travels and are reserved for people to walk along safely. But, in the US, they are called sidewalks, while pavements are the hard areas in front of or beside buildings where cars are parked. In the UK, it's illegal to drive on the pavement, but in the US, it is the very place where cars are driven onto and parked. There are many differences in the way words are used that will illustrate Churchill's statement about English-speaking countries being separated by a common language. The fact that we are separated from other countries by different languages hardly needs to be said. I recall a situation in my teens. I thought I knew the meaning of a foreign word and was totally wrong, with potentially very embarrassing results.

An Example from the English Channel!

I was fifteen and on a school trip to Germany. We were crossing the English Channel by ferry, and I needed to visit the toilet (the restroom). I looked along the deck for the most likely door and saw two signs that looked promising. I hadn't learned any German at school other than a few words given us for the trip, but then I saw a door labelled 'Herren' and reasoned that it was the room for women, and so proceeded to walk towards the door labelled Damen. Of course, they referred to the very opposite genders that I had given them. Herren is gentlemen and Damen is ladies in German!

Fortunately, a lady suddenly emerged, showing no sign of embarrassment at having been in the wrong room. This was enough to make me realize my mistake and change direction, very thankful that I'd been saved from an extremely embarrassing experience.

I was totally wrong in judging that 'Herren' indicated the room for women. It came from my ignorance of the German language. Likewise, most who read the New Testament effectively guess what the various uses of the word 'flesh' mean. In the West, it's generally a shorthand expression for sexuality; so, by 'the sins of the flesh' (a term who's commonly held meaning was probably inherited from the legacy left by Augustine) they assume they know what the New Testament is referring to; but, as we shall soon see, they are miles off understanding what Paul meant.

A Further Example

Another example of terms being misunderstood is the recent confusion over the word 'virus'. It traditionally referred to an inanimate 'particle' that spreads, infects, and causes disease in its host. Then the IT industry used the word to describe an internet file that was deliberately designed to damage computer programs and systems. The confusion between these two uses of the same word attached itself to the Covid 19 virus as it spread throughout the world. It just so happened that at that time, telephone companies in the UK were preparing for the coming of 5G and putting up relay stations in key places to provide the new service. There was some difficulty in setting up these relay stations, and the explanation that was given and published across the media was that a virus had damaged the IT system. Some people understood that these stations were the source of the Covid 19 virus! Being convinced that there was a conspiracy to reduce the world's population by its deliberate spread, they reacted by setting fire to the equipment. They confused the coronavirus with the IT virus and made an invalid deduction. Of course, there is no connection between the two meanings whatsoever!

The Importance of Context

So, it's vitally important to know the context of words in order to establish their meanings, such as the type of literature they're used in, the period of history and language in which they were written, and the people group they originate from. These and other issues need to be considered when interpreting the meaning of important words. I mention all this to stress that to understand the meaning of a word in the New Testament we need to know a little about the language of the Old Testament and what guided its translators. It was the Old Testament translation from Hebrew into Greek that had a huge influence on the writers of the New Testament. It has been shown that when the Old Testament scriptures were translated, its translators did their very best to convey the meaning of the Hebrew words into the Greek translation they were making. Scholars have recently shown that Paul deliberately kept to the Hebrew meaning of the Greek medium in which he taught.[18]

Losing the Past–The Reason for the Translation

The Old Testament was written mostly in Hebrew, the language of the Jews. But there came a time when, because of conquest and deportation to Babylon, their language was in danger of dying. Many of their descendants began to lose the use of their language in Babylon where the language of the host country displaced their ancient Hebrew. Because of this, those born in exile could no longer read their ancient scriptures.

At the end of their exile, a time of rapid change and turmoil followed when they came under the control of a range of new masters. Eventually, the Greek empire, which had been in control of the Jewish people and had imposed the Greek language on them, was conquered by the mighty Roman Empire. When Rome conquered the Greeks, it accepted that Greek was an effective international trading language and pragmatically chose to use it as the main international language of its Empire. The official language of Rome was, of course, Latin. Most of the Jews, even though they had returned to their own land, could no longer speak Hebrew, and found themselves using the language which Greece, then Rome, had given her.

The Search for Preservation

To give their people access to their scriptures, the Jewish religious leaders decided they had to translate the Hebrew scriptures into Greek, so that all Jews could again read or hear their sacred texts with understanding. This Greek translation of the Hebrew Bible, made about two hundred years before the birth of Jesus, is called the Septuagint. This is the Latin word for seventy because, it was believed, the translation was the effort of seventy Jewish scholars. You might have seen references to the LXX (seventy, in Roman numerals) in the margin of your Bible. It is used as shorthand for the Septuagint translation.

---

[18] See J. Ziesler, *The Meaning of Righteousness in Paul: A Linguistic and Theological Enquiry*, Society For New Testament Studies Monograph Series, (Cambridge: Cambridge University Press 1972), 20. See also Hill, David, *Greek Words and Hebrew Meanings Studies In The Semantics Of Soteriological Terms*, (Cambridge: Cambridge University Press, 1967).

So, here was the Hebrew Bible, the Old Testament, being translated into Greek to give the Jewish people a version they could understand. It was through this translation that differences in understanding arose. This is how two meanings of some words came into circulation. One meaning, preferred by the Jewish educated, emphasized the meaning of the Hebrew word that had been translated. In contrast, those who could not appreciate the subtlety of language translation accepted its commonly used meaning.

And as you might have suspected, this was a change that illustrates how words can have two meanings. It depends on which people were reading or hearing a particular Greek word in the translated scriptures as to what they thought the word's intended meaning was.

Re-establishing the Connection

Because scholars have the Old Testament in both Hebrew and Greek, it is possible for them to see what the translators of the LXX meant when they chose a particular Greek word to translate a specific Hebrew term or idea. For example, when the translators came to translate the Hebrew word for flesh, *basar*, they chose the Greek word *sarx* as its equivalent. The problem was there was no Greek equivalent of the Hebrew word *basar*. The Greek word *sarx* focused on the body and contained the idea that it was intrinsically evil. But the Hebrew word *basar*, while one of its meanings is the human body, had other meanings that were not in the meaning of the Greek word. These meanings made it very clear that the meaning of *basar* was very different from that of *sarx*. Thus, the translators of the LXX were stuck with *sarx* as there was no Greek word with an equivalent range of meanings as the Hebrew word had. But this choice introduced massive misunderstanding concerning the 'body' and 'sin'. Keeping the Hebrew meaning to the fore is clearly important, for the translation was not made for the sake of the Gentiles but for the Jews so that they could have access to their own sacred texts.

The Loss of Intended Meaning

Unfortunately, by not appreciating the original Hebrew words, which gave a distinct Hebrew meaning to the Greek words used to write the New Testament, many Christians experience serious lifestyle applications due to this 'rewording' of scripture.

The point is, we can all too easily draw conclusions about the meaning of words and be totally off-target. This sort of confusion, hopefully without the embarrassment I experienced on board the ferry, is repeated by many people who read the New Testament. There are many other words in the Greek New Testament that the average reader is left confused by. Without understanding the background of the translation of the Hebrew script into Greek just considered, many well-meaning translators of the Greek fail to either appreciate or consider the influence of the Hebraic text and so emphasise the Greek meaning in their translations. This secular Greek meaning unfortunately tends to dominate most English translations so adding considerable difficulty to gaining a correct understanding of the apostles' message.

Fundamental Differences

We will never appreciate this misreading of scripture if we fail to understand that the Greeks hold to an understanding of nature that is known as 'dualism' and that this is the very opposite of Jewish understanding. In the system of dualism, all physical things are inherently evil, and all spiritual things are good. In Jewish understanding, creation is good because God created it and, at the end of each day of creation, God looked at what He had brought into existence and saw that it was good (Gen. 2:10). It is because all physical things are evil and not good for the Greeks that they had a huge problem in accepting the resurrection of Jesus. In their system of thought, Jesus must have had an evil body, even when He rose from the dead. Because He had a physical body He was, by their definition, evil!

So, the Jewish understanding of creation is the exact opposite of the Greek understanding. Creation is not evil; it suffers because of the Fall when humanity became estranged from God. That event made it broken, but it did not make it evil. So, when Paul, who was a Jew, *appears* to speak of flesh being evil, we ought to pause and question what is going on. Was he using the Greek meaning or the Jewish meaning? If the Jewish meaning, then how does this reflect on how we read the statement? We have to decide if he meant the Greek meaning, or focusing on meanings of the original Hebrew word that was translated *sarx*? This can only be decided by carefully considering the context which the word is used in. This might seem irksome, but it must be considered whenever any translation of any literature is made, regardless of the languages involved and the type of literature that is being translated. If this consideration is not kept in mind, the meaning of the author of the original work can be confused and lost. What I am saying must be done is no more than what every good translator keeps in mind when making a translation.

A study of the way the Old Testament term *basar* was translated into *sarx* and the way the New Testament authors used this Greek transition needs to be considered. However, because it requires sifting through lists of passages to see how they are used, I will not deal with it here but in chapter 27.

Conclusion

Language confusion is extensive in reading the Bible. Most readers naturally assume that what they read has no other meaning, even though it might lead to gaps in their thinking and contradictions in their understanding. The only way to get over this invisible hurdle is to trace the meaning of the words back to their origins. This does not need to be done for every word we read, but it should be done when we reach the borders of our understanding and instinctively know that there is something that is not making sense or appears to contradict other biblical truths. When we have reached this position, we are beginning to understand that there is a paradigm that controlled how the New Testament writers thought and taught. When we get to this point, we hopefully are willing to consider the New Exodus narrative.

Chapter 8 Paul's Self-Understanding

As pointed out in the previous chapter, the translators of the Hebrew Bible into Greek had the task of choosing Greek words to express Hebrew meanings. So, for example, the Hebrew word for servant/slave is *ebed*, which means either, and mostly, servant or, less often, slave. This was translated *doulos*, a Greek word that referred mostly to classical slaves but, in a few limited cases, it also referred to servants who were not owned but were employed! So, while they had similar meanings, they could be read quite differently from what the translators intended. This is another case where the intended meaning can only be discovered by carefully observing the word's Hebrew origin and the new context in the New Testament where the translated word is used.

Unravelling a Case of Crossover.

There are certainly places in Paul's letters where he used *doulos* with the Greek sense of a person who was owned by someone, i.e., as a slave in classical terms (so, 1 Cor. 7:22; 12:13; Gal. 4:1 and Eph. 6:5); but these references are few and far between. Most of Paul's uses of *doulos* (as for the rest of the NT writers) echo the uses of *ebed* in the Hebrew scriptures, which are about special Jewish leaders such as kings or prophets. In fact, Israel herself was called God's *ebed* (servant).

Now the very last thing these leaders were was slaves in the classical sense. They were the people of God. They had been brought into a covenant relationship with Him and it had bestowed great honour upon them. So, the religious meaning of *ebed* was light years away from the Greek classical meaning of *doulos*. Thus, the translation into 'slave' completely devalues the Hebraic meaning and strips Paul of the incredible dignity he saw himself to have because of being a follower of Christ. He was not a slave of Christ, for he saw himself as a servant of Christ in the very same way as the prophets were servants of God.

But can we be sure that this is how Paul saw himself? And the answer is yes, we can. We can see how he applied Old Testament passages that referred to the prophets to himself. He clearly saw himself as walking in their shoes and with a similar relationship with Christ as they had with God.

Jesus and the Exodus

A Suffering Servant.

First, we see how Paul's biographer, Luke, viewed him. Luke was Greek, not Jewish, and his natural understanding would be to present Paul as a slave. Instead, he sees him as a disciple of Jesus, whose experience matches that of his Master. He wraps Paul in the mantle of the work of Jesus, being separated to do the messianic covenant work spoken of by Isaiah in being a light to the nations (Acts 9:15; 13:47). He is rejected, especially by his countrymen, as was Christ (Acts 9:29; 13:50; 14:19; 17:13; 23:17–21). So, we can see that there is a parallel in the offence caused by the work they both do.

Christ was rejected because He sought to win sinners; Paul was rejected because he sought to win Gentiles, who to the Jews were utter sinners. The preaching of Jesus and Paul produced the same effects on those who did not believe, i.e., blindness and hardness of heart which are both outcomes that were predicted by Isaiah (Isa. 6:9–11). Paul's vision in the temple (Acts 22:17,18) is acknowledged to be based on Isaiah's own vision (Isa. 6). Paul's journey to Jerusalem is certainly paralleled by that of Jesus, for Paul set his face to go to Jerusalem (Acts 20:22), knowing that he would be betrayed. This paralleled Jesus Himself who had previously set His face like a flint to go up to Jerusalem and be betrayed (Lk. 9:51; 13:22; 18:31). Both were subject to similar exhortations to consider the unreasonableness of their missions (Lk. 13:31; Acts 21:10–14). And, finally, like Christ, Paul was misrepresented by the leaders, hounded by the mobs, and tried by the governor of Jerusalem. Here the parallel ends, for Christ's death at Jerusalem was foreordained but Paul's was not to be there. What was predetermined for Paul was that he would eventually stand before kings and rulers (Acts 9:15). This he eventually did when he arrived in Rome to be judged by the emperor.

Paul as a Servant of Christ

The picture of Paul as the servant in the Hebraic theological sense is no coincidence. It is supported by Paul's own description of his ministry. He described his call, found in Galatians 1:15, as being set apart from birth, a call which parallels those of the Old Testament prophets (Jer. 1:5). In 2 Corinthians, Paul was forced to defend himself regarding his calling to be an apostle. In 2 Corinthians 3:7–11, he compares the Old and New Covenants and their ministries. In 4:1, he says, "Since through God's mercy we have this ministry, we do not lose heart." Paul then proceeds to develop his comparison between the two covenants with reference to the motive of his ministry. He says, "Christ's love compels us, because we are convinced that one died for all, and therefore all died. And he died for all, that those who live should no longer live to themselves but for him who died for them and was raised again" (2 Cor. 5:14–17).

This reference to the death of 'once for all' echoes Romans 5:12–19, a passage accepted by many scholars as referring to Isaiah 53: That the Corinthian passage reflects the same prophetic message is borne out when Paul proceeds to speak of the New Creation (2 Cor. 5:17), which is brought about by Christ's representative death (2 Cor. 5:21). This is the very theme of Isaiah, for he also goes on to speak of all things being made new in the context of the promised New Covenant that the Servant's death established (Isa. 65:17). Thus, Paul sees his ministry as one that proclaims the fulfilment of all that Isaiah predicted. He is elevated above 'the evangelical prophet', in that what Isaiah predicted Paul proclaims has now been fulfilled.

Clear Evidence

Perhaps the most important passage that shows Paul saw himself as God's servant and not His slave is 2 Corinthians 6:3. He starts the section, which describes the sufferings his work has brought him, by quoting from the Servant Songs of Isaiah. He concludes with a further quotation from the Songs (Isa. 49:8).

> Working together with him, then, we appeal to you not to receive the grace of God in vain. For he says, "In a favourable time I listened to you, and in a day of salvation I have helped you. Behold, now is the favourable time; behold, now is the day of salvation." (2 Cor. 6:2)

And then Paul says at the end of the chapter:

> What agreement has the temple of God with idols? For we are the temple of the living God; as God said, "I will make my dwelling among them and walk among them, and I will be their God, and they shall be my people. Therefore go out from their midst, and be separate from them, says the Lord, and touch no unclean thing; then I will welcome you, and I will be

a father to you, and you shall be sons and daughters to me, says the Lord Almighty." (2 Cor. 6:16–18)

Paul as the Servant of the New Covenant

Thus, it is evident that Paul sees his ministry as a servant of the New Covenant just as Moses, Isaiah, and all the prophets, and Israel herself, were servants of the Old Covenant. As the prophets addressed Israel and appealed for fidelity, so Paul appeals to the church at Corinth. Paul's credential for the genuineness of his ministry is that he shares in the suffering that both the Old Testament servants and Jesus himself had experienced.

The question is, does Paul see himself as a suffering servant because he was an apostle or because he was a Christian? The importance of the question is this: if it was because he was an apostle, then it follows that his experience of suffering is part of his apostolic calling and does not necessarily apply to Christians in general. If, however, it is because he was a Christian, then all Christians are called to experience suffering as part of their discipleship. If this is the case, then, importantly for our study, being called *douloi* in Romans 6 does not refer to them as being slaves in the Hellenistic sense but as servants of God in the Hebraic sense.

Suffering and the Church.

The fact is, Paul never saw his sufferings as limited to the apostles for it related to the consequences of the messages effect on unbelievers. This aspect of 'servant-suffering' included all members of the Church of Christ which (just as Israel in the Old Testament) was the Lord's corporate servant.

> For you, brothers, became imitators of the churches of God in Christ Jesus that are in Judea. For you suffered the same things from your own countrymen as they did from the Jews, who killed both the Lord Jesus and the prophets, and drove us out, and displease God and oppose all mankind. (1 Thes. 2:14–15).

Paul warned the churches he visited to encourage that they must, through much suffering, enter the Kingdom of God (Acts 14:22). Clearly, he presupposed the inevitability, if not the necessity, of suffering. This suffering was not something to be merely endured, for it actually formed part of the will of God (2 Thes.1:5-6).

The Nature of Paul's Suffering

This suffering is not vicarious, as was Christ's passion, but it is essentially the same as the suffering Christ experienced during His ministry of proclamation. Because of this, Paul frequently links his sufferings and that of other believers, with Christ's. To be God's servant means being rejected by those who insist on walking in darkness.

> Now I rejoice in my sufferings for your sake, and in my flesh, I am filling up what is lacking in Christ's afflictions for the sake of his body, that is, the church, of which I became a minister according to the stewardship from God that was given to me for you, to make the word of God fully known, the mystery hidden for ages and generations but now revealed to his saints. To them God chose to make known how great among the Gentiles are the riches of the glory of this mystery, which is Christ in you, the hope of glory. (Col. 1:24–27)

Such suffering is not endured in isolation, for the believer is part of Christ's body and Christ is the head of His Church. He said to Saul: "I am Jesus, whom you are persecuting" (Acts 9:5). Again, Paul says concerning the Church: "that there may be no division in the body, but that the members may have the same care for one another. If one member suffers, all suffer together; if one member is honoured, all rejoice together." (1 Cor. 12:25–26).

More than a Sign

For Paul, suffering is not merely a sign of being part of the kingdom of God, it is a means of spiritual maturing and preparation for the glory and splendour of Christ's appearing.

> Not only that, but we rejoice in our sufferings, knowing that suffering produces endurance, and endurance produces character, and character produces hope, and hope does not put us to shame, because God's love has been poured into our hearts through the Holy Spirit who has been given to us. (Rom. 5:3–5)

This parallels the theme of Isaiah, who saw Israel's suffering as necessary for bringing in the Messianic Kingdom (Isa. 40:1-10; 54:1-14).

Jesus and the Exodus

and if children, then heirs—heirs of God and fellow heirs with
Christ, provided we suffer with him in order that we may also
be glorified with him. For I consider that the sufferings of this
present time are not worth comparing with the glory that is to
be revealed to us. (Rom. 8:17-18)

This passage is not the first reference to suffering in Romans. In Romans 4:25, Paul has affirmed that Christ "was delivered over to death for our sins and was raised for our justification". In fact, some see Romans 4:25 and Romans 5:2 to be reflecting Isaiah 53. Now, if this is so, and Paul links all believers (as he does in Romans 5:12ff) with the suffering of their Representative, they will not only be His servants (Rom. 6:13) but will also share His rejection and suffering. This was the theme of Romans 5:3–5 and Romans 8. In chapter 8, Paul emphasizes the relationship and its blessings. Believers are in Christ. They have no condemnation (Rom. 8:1) but they do share in His sufferings as the Suffering Servant.

The Suffering of the Wider Community

We may also note how Paul links his own suffering with those of other believers. "I consider that the sufferings of this present time" (Rom. 8:18); "Likewise the Spirit helps us in our weakness" (Rom. 8:26); "If God is for us, who can be against us" (Rom. 8:31); "we are more than conquerors through him who loved us" (Rom. 8:37). This is very different from that which Paul adopts towards the Corinthians and the Galatians, who had moved from the truth of the gospel because of intellectual or religious offence. There, he set his sufferings against their allegedly superior positions (2 Cor. 10–11; Gal. 2:17–3:5). He relates to the Thessalonians and the Philippians as he does to the Romans, because they are also partakers of the suffering of the gospel (Rom. 8:22–34; 1 Thes. 2:14ff; Phil. 1:29-30).

Also, Paul, in Rom. 8:36, quotes from Psalm 44:22. Examination of this Psalm shows that it summarises the message of Isaiah 40–66, its message being to those in exile. The same historical background is alluded to, and even the same language is used, not in relation to an individual, as in Isaiah 53, but in relation to the nation. Paul seems to be deliberately linking the experience of the Church, as she waits for the

Jesus and the Exodus

consummation of her salvation, with the faithful Jews, waiting for their deliverance from exile so they could return to the place of promise.

Old Testament Links

It is no coincidence that Paul selects Psalm 44, shown by the fact that in Romans 10, where he describes the work of the Church in proclaiming her message, he quotes from Isaiah 52:7. This is a passage that presents a similar picture to that painted in Psalm 44, but which describes the work of the faithful remnant who had waited for God's redemptive act. They are God's servants, chosen to proclaim the message of deliverance and renewal.

> How then will they call on him in whom they have not believed? And how are they to believe in him of whom they have never heard? And how are they to hear without someone preaching? And how are they to preach unless they are sent? As it is written, "How beautiful are the feet of those who preach the good news!" (Rom. 10:14–15)

The original context of the cited text from Isaiah sees the ones who were left behind in Jerusalem waiting to welcome the remnant, whom Jeremiah and Ezekiel had said would one day return. The faithful Israelites, who were released from Babylon by the Persian king Darius, made their way through the desert back to the smitten, devastated, and seemingly abandoned city. All the while the citizens of Jerusalem watched from the city walls, looking to see if God's promise of deliverance had begun. Seeing the pilgrims in the distance and hearing them singing that their God had delivered them was the news they had waited for seventy long years.

The Key Source of Paul's Thinking.

Thus, Paul is not only quoting but is drawing his theology from the prophecy of Isaiah. This book not only provides him with themes but also dominates his thought processes. Isaiah is a book that focuses on the promises of Yahweh to Israel and explains how the expectation of fulfilment of those words provided comfort and encouragement.

Because scholars have locked Paul's use of *doulos* into a Greek understanding, comparing his and our status to that of slaves, who were despised and valued only for what they could do for their owner, it has stopped the Christian understanding that being God's *doulos* was not something that took personal dignity and freedom away. Rather, it elevates believers to the highest place imaginable. They are God's representatives to all nations, and nothing on earth can compare with the privilege and dignity of that calling.

A Servant Like the Prophets

Thus, Paul does not describe himself in Graeco-Roman terms as being a slave; he confidently insists that he is a servant of the living Christ, just like the prophets were servants of the living God throughout the Old Testament. The very last thing Paul would have done would have been to present himself as a mere slave when he had this incredible commission from his Lord.

This insight, I suggest, gives us every confidence we are dealing with a man who would surrender life itself before becoming disloyal to the One who had saved him. The last thing he would do is risk this message being confused by overlaying truths with a web of illustrations from the Greek world that would confuse his Jewish listeners as to the origins and meaning of his message.

We shall go on to see how deeply his Jewish heritage controlled his description of humanity.

Conclusion

Our consideration of the meaning of the Greek term *doulos* has shown that Paul's intended meaning is not that believers are slaves of Christ but that they are His servants. This realization clarifies the source of Paul's theological vocabulary and roots his thinking patterns firmly in the Old Testament. A key part of that sacred document is the story of how God repeatedly saved His wayward people by involving Himself at great cost in rescuing them from the results of their wilful disobedience. Each of these rescue events was an Exodus. As we bring this pattern into our reading of the New Testament texts, we will discover that God again rescues His people, this time through the final Exodus, the New Exodus. And when we see this link and how all the riches of the Old Testament events merge to give us a greater collective understanding through which we should consider the Exodus of Jesus and its achievements, we have touched The Exodus narrative in our thinking.

Chapter 9 Paul's Message about Adam

One part of Paul's message was:

> So then, just as sin entered the world through one man and death through sin, and so death spread to all people because all sinned. (Rom. 5:12 NET)

The typical western (individualistic) response to the apparent unfairness of this statement is: "Why should we suffer because of Adam's sin?" But Paul's Jewish listeners to the letter would have had no difficulty in accepting this because their scriptures taught it to them (Exod. 34:6–7). Throughout its history, the fate of their entire nation had depended on its leader or king. Effectively, his victories were their victories, and his failures were their failures. In fact, this simple principle is worked out in the history of every nation on earth. To deny this intergenerational relationship would be unwise. It even applies to families. The failure of a father is carried by his family as they struggle to recover from his mistakes. Likewise, the business success of a father produces the wealth from which his family benefits. This applies to nonmaterial issues as well. The good name that a father acquires enriches his family and gives it standing in its community. The Old Testament, however, made it clear that children do not inherit the guilt of their parents (Deut. 24:16; see also Jer. 31:29–30 they are punished only for their own sins.

And Paul says that in Adam, the whole of humankind, which is his family, share in the condition of death to God and have been sent into exile from Him and His blessing because the father of humanity sinned!

The Western Mindset

Despite the absence of these ideas in most Western nations, it is vital we understand that the ideas of solidarity are far more important to Western thought than most appreciate. Before looking at its presence and influence, let's just remind ourselves of Paul's argument.

He says that Adam, as the father of humanity, was given a vital role, and, with it, a huge responsibility. He was not 'his own man'; he was God's man. He was responsible for the future of the family he was going to father. He could not step outside that responsibility if he found it too irksome and, if he rejected God's commands, he would bring the most serious consequences on his family, i.e., the entire human race.

Adam's Fatherhood

This is the very nature of fatherhood. The father is responsible for his offspring, and it is mandated by God that he carries out that responsibility with love, care, and dignity. If he fails, his family will suffer. If Adam, the father of the human family, chose to disobey God, he would not be put out of God's presence alone for his wife and his future family would be put out with him. They will all die with regards to their relationship with God. They will all have "died (to God) in Adam". Indeed, they would not only be separated from God because of Adam's sin, but they would also, by their own choice, share the guilt of Adam's sin because they all individually chose separation from God as their way of life. This is the same as what John says when speaking about the condition of man:

> Now this is the basis for judging: that the light has come into the world and people loved the darkness rather than the light, because their deeds were evil. For everyone who does evil deeds hates the light and does not come to the light, so that their deeds will not be exposed. But the one who practices the truth comes to the light, so that it may be plainly evident that his deeds have been done in God. (John 3:19–21 NET)

This is very strange to Western minds, but it is very natural to Jewish/Semitic ones and to those of people in many other parts of the world.

Now, it is interesting that Paul, when writing to the church in Rome (a city he'd never visited and capital of the Roman empire), did not attempt to tell this story in culturally acceptable terms. It was about God saving humankind from the consequences of Adam's momentous act of disobedience. It could not be dressed up in a more acceptable narrative. For Paul to tell it in any other way would, more than likely, cause his readers to miss the point of the Christian message, i.e., that the whole of humanity is estranged from God because of its common ancestor's rebellion. It needs to be rescued from the judgement, which is the ultimate separation from Him. There are no exceptions. All, not some, died (to God) in Adam.

Outdated thinking?

For most in the West, the idea of the solidarity of a people group is archaic. Indeed, living within such a notion is considered the reason why some nations cannot break through into the modern world with its freedoms, intellectual insights, skills, and opportunities.

But is this an outdated way of thinking? Or are there issues that we, in the West, need to reflect on to recover important insights that are part of this ancient heritage? Does twenty-first century Western society need to renew this ancient understanding to make sense of its predicament of lostness and hopelessness?

Solidarity is not Dead in the West.

There are events that suggest that the concept of solidarity is far from dead in modern Western societies. The crowds at a football match forget their individualism and become one screaming, shouting, chanting mob of supporters as they urge their team on to victory. Not one of the supporters did anything on the field, but their eleven representatives achieved a victory that was owned by them all. For the entire game individualism was taken over by the reality of corporate solidarity. And when they lose? A leading BBC football commentator told how, as a boy, he'd attended an FA cup final at Wembley. The team he supported was playing for the most coveted football trophy in the UK in one of its most prestigious stadiums. His team lost, and he cried for the entire 100-mile journey home! He shared their pain in defeat as well! No amount of reasoning that he did nothing wrong changed the pain of failure. The team's loss was his loss! So, solidarity isn't controlled by the mind or reason. For this little football supporter his team's defeat was like a bereavement, and no amount of reasoning could change that for him. This experience is not limited to children. Ask any sports supporter whose team is beaten how they cope with the depression that follows after seeing or hearing the dreaded result!

Solidarity and Western Democracy

Solidarity is also alive in politics throughout the world. Elections give the leader of the victorious party massive power that, if handled poorly, can lead an entire nation into tragedy. The quality and success of the victorious candidate will not only affect the lives of millions of his people but possibly hundreds of millions of others.

An Example from Recent History

An example of this principle of solidarity took place on 22nd January 1972, when the British Prime minister, Edward Heath, went to Brussels. By one signature he took an entire nation into a relationship with the other nations that formed the European Economic Community at that time. By signing that treaty, Britain surrendered a range of distinctive British positions covering our independent nationhood. This impacted our laws, travel control, the authority of Parliament, and many other issues. Of course, Brexit has since reversed this; but the principle was still the same. It was the letter from Boris Johnson who was the new prime minister and appointed representative of the British people that removed the UK from that former relationship, and it happened despite 48% of the UK population being deeply unhappy. Again, the old principle of solidarity was at play.

The year before the UK joined the European Community, I got married. My wife and I had not started our family when the signature was penned, but all three of our children, who were yet to be born, were on that day taken into the European Community. They would be born European citizens and live under its laws. This, of course, was true for all other yet-to-be-born children whose parents were British. Their parents may not have agreed with entering the European Economic Community, yet, because the United Kingdom, through its representative head, signed the accession document, they became Europeans. Even if their parents did not live in the UK, their passports determined what identity they had.

Solidarity and the Financial System

And what about financial institutions? When people open bank accounts, they commit themselves to the demands that the banking institutions make on them. In becoming 'customers' they unwittingly surrender complete control of the money they deposit. Legally, they have no claim on their banks' assets if they go into bankruptcy. Their deposits are technically loans, allowing the banks to use the money as they wish to benefit their shareholders rather than depositors! If the banks fail, all the deposited accounts are treated as assets of the bank and can be claimed by creditors to pay the banks' debts. I know most readers will be surprised that this is their relationship with their bank, but I assure you, it is a fact throughout the USA, the European Union, and many other 'developed' nations. We live in an economic reality that makes individuals victims of the failures of managers who have been responsible for reckless banking practices.

So where is individualism when such events have happened in financial history? When the great stock market crash happened in 1929, many millionaires became penniless the moment their banks failed. There, in that catastrophic event, the modern principle of solidarity was displayed in all its raw reality and power. And, to this day, it remains the cornerstone of the banking industry!

And what about when war is declared? The legal head of a nation can declare war on another, and in that declaration, the two nations become foes, regardless of their citizens' wishes. An entire nation becomes part of the declaration of war because the principle of corporate solidarity is universal. Just look at Putin to see how this works out

Solidarity and Human Existence

There are many other examples of solidarity. They function as the essential backbone of the nations of the world and the systems they have devised to give meaning and order. From the birth of humanity to its closing generation, people will have been bound in solidarities of one form or another. But, regardless of what political system we live under, Paul's message is that, because every human lives under the consequences of Adam's rebellion in the Garden of Eden, all have been taken from the realm they were intended for, which is fellowship with God.

So, when Paul speaks of humanity being in Adam, he means that our forefather determined our future. If Adam had obeyed his Creator, his offspring would have been born into a loving and fruitful relationship with the One who had brought them into existence. But Adam did not obey; and his one act of disobedience caused countless millions of people to be taken out of that perfect kingdom with its joy and incredible blessings. [19] Adam's

---

[19] We will soon see that this act of disobedience is not to be compared to a naughty child disobeying its parents, it is of infinitely greater significance than any other decision made in human history, see chapter 22.

disobedience made them members of a kingdom whose king was not God but Satan. It was the opposite of everything they had been created for. By that one act, Adam brought his offspring into alienation from God, and this meant death to God.

That is what Paul was writing about when he wrote: "sin came into the world through one man, and death through sin and so death spread to all men because all sinned." (Rom. 5:12)

The World View of Paul.

Paul's own worldview, contrary to the thinking of many eminent theologians, was not Roman/Greek with its heavy dependence on Greek philosophers. It was Jewish, which was, and still is, strongly rooted in the concept of solidarity. I believe it can be shown that Paul held to a very strict Jewish worldview; thus, to understand Paul we must explore his concept of human relatedness. We will explore this later. Meanwhile, I am satisfied with making this one very important point. If we wish to 'find' Paul, we must step outside our secular models and seek him in his own cultural/intellectual environment. Importing ideas from outside this mindset will cause a loss of clarity in his arguments. Because this is the normal practice when interpreting Paul, much confusion and disagreement exists among scholars.

The Critical Difference.

This picture of the apostle is contrary to the understanding of many professors and pastors who hold that Paul was comfortable with, if not immersed in, Hellenism. They reason that his wider cultural identity, which they assume he had, gave him the perfect set of credentials for his work as a missionary. It is this clash of perspectives that must be resolved if we are to be confident that we have 'found' Paul.

My studies have persuaded me that Paul never abandoned his Jewish heritage, even after his acceptance of Jesus as the Messiah. His heritage was rooted in the Jewish scriptures and nothing else. The scriptures remained his authority throughout his life as a servant of Christ. They were the foundation of his evangelism and teaching to the infant church. If we bring anything into his teaching that is not from this unique heritage, we are constructing a gospel that he never preached. The Old Testament writings are the source of many of his illustrations. However, because the Graeco-Roman world has been seen to be a/the key to understanding the New Testament, confusion and conflict have been introduced. Failure to recognise this fact is at the heart of so much misunderstanding of Paul's message.

I know I have made sweeping, controversial claims in this chapter; but if they are correct, they massively alter the way we should interpret Paul.[20]

Conclusion

We have seen how ancient understanding of humanity is essential for a balanced understanding of its present condition and status. In the West, we are taught that we are individuals who are responsible to no other person than ourselves. History shows that such a view is extremely limiting and deprives us of the experience of our ancestors and the insights they and others have gained. It is this understanding of solidarity, of the interconnectedness of one generation with another as well as with the rest of our own generation, that is essential to understand what I have described as The Exodus narrative. The Exodus stories throughout the Bible are not primarily about individuals but about the communities they belong to. So, to understand The Exodus narrative we need to take a far greater view of humanity than it being about how individuals secure their own deliverance from sin, for no one can achieve this by their own efforts. As Paul says in Romans 3:23: "for all have sinned and fall short of the glory of God". To escape from this condition of guilt and separation, humanity needs a Saviour.

---

[20] I have explored this in Holland, *the Search for Truth*, 29-126.

SECTION 3 Into the Exodus Narrative

Chapter 10 Introducing the Egyptian Exodus

Having considered a range of topics that are significant and which we need to grasp regarding Jewish understanding, we now return to consider the Exodus events of the Bible. We saw in chapter 4 that the letter to the Romans is controlled by citations from the book of Isaiah. At the heart of that book was teaching about the promised return of Israel, which was exiled in Babylon, to Jerusalem. This deliverance would be similar but far greater than the Exodus event that brought Israel out of Egypt.

In this and the next two chapters we'll examine the three main Exoduses that comprise The Exodus narratives of the Bible. The Egyptian Exodus event contributed insights that the prophets of following generations used as the basis of their preaching to Israel because she had come under judgement for playing the harlot and had been punished with exile. This led to Israel needing God's mercy and forgiveness afresh. They preached that without repentance she would be left in her state of separation from her God and her homeland. Appreciating this unfolding Exodus narrative with its accumulating insights will help us to understand its climax, i.e., What Jesus achieved for His people through His death and resurrection, i.e., through His Exodus event.,

Naming the Different Exoduses

Discussing three Exoduses in the same book causes a problem in knowing which one is being referred to. To overcome this, the first Exodus will be called the Egyptian Exodus and the second, the Babylonian Exodus, because God rescued His people from captivity in Babylon 'a second time' as Isaiah predicted:

> In that day the Lord will extend his hand <u>yet a second time</u> to recover the remnant that remains of his people, from Assyria, from Egypt, from Pathros, from Cush from Elam, from Shinar, from Hamath, and from the coastlands of the sea. (Isa. 11:11, emphasis added)

The Third Exodus is found throughout the New Testament. To distinguish this from the predicted Second Exodus from Babylon, I call this, as already mentioned, the New Exodus. This is hinted at in Luke's Gospel, where he writes about Jesus's transfiguration saying:

> And as he was praying, the appearance of his face was altered, and his clothing became dazzling white. And behold, two men were talking with him, Moses and Elijah, who appeared in glory and spoke of his departure, which he was about to accomplish at Jerusalem. (Luke 9:29–31)

The word 'departure' is the Greek word ἔξοδον (Exodus); so, Jesus spoke with Moses and Elijah about His coming Exodus. As we will see, this is far from being the only reference to Jesus' Exodus.

The New Exodus would fulfil all the promises that the two earlier events failed to deliver. Paul declared that, at last, all the promises of God were fulfilled in Jesus Christ: "For all the promises of God find their Yes in him. That is why it is through him that we utter our Amen to God for his glory" (2 Cor. 1:20).[21] The Exodus fulfilment of these promises was noted by C.F. Moule who as the Cambridge Professor of New Testament theology, without indicating that he knew just how profound he was, wrote:

> To a unique degree, Jesus is seen as the goal, the convergence point, of God's plan for Israel.... The Passover gathers up into itself a large number of strands of covenant promises: to speak of 'its full realization' is to use the root we are considering in a highly significant manner.[22]

I shall consider the three Exoduses separately so we can better understand the development of this important narrative.

The Egyptian Exodus Prophesied

The Egyptian Exodus was mentioned hundreds of years before it took place when God made His covenant with Abraham. He warned that his descendants

---

[21] Note the NIV which stresses the scope of this fulfilment, 'For no matter how many promises God has made, they are "Yes" in Christ. And so, through him the "Amen" is spoken by us to the glory of God.

[22] Moule, C. F. D., Fulfilment-Words in the New Testament: Use and Abuse, NTS 14(1966), 293-320.

would be taken into captivity but promised that He would redeem them and return them to the Promised Land. We find these details at the end of Genesis 15:

> As the sun was going down, a deep sleep fell on Abram. And behold, dreadful and great darkness fell upon him. Then the LORD said to Abram, "Know for certain that your offspring will be sojourners in a land that is not theirs and will be servants there, and they will be afflicted for four hundred years. But I will bring judgement on the nation that they serve, and afterward they shall come out with great possessions. As for you, you shall go to your fathers in peace; you shall be buried in a good old age. And they shall come back here in the fourth generation, for the iniquity of the Amorites is not yet complete. (Gen. 15:12–16)

In fact, an earlier, but less explicitly stated exile, could be said to be in the Genesis creation narrative when Adam was put out of the Garden and cut off from intimate fellowship with God and access to the tree of life. Despite his disobedience and imminent expulsion, God made the promise that the seed of Eve would bruise Satan's head. The context suggests that this action would put right the tragedy of the fall and return man to the garden and fellowship with God:

> The Lord God said to the serpent, "Because you have done this, cursed are you above all livestock and above all beasts of the field; on your belly you shall go, and dust you shall eat all the days of your life. I will put enmity between you and the woman, and between your offspring he shall bruise your head, and you shall bruise his heel." (Gen. 3:14–15)

The requirement for restoring humanity to God's presence and the tree of life was the bruising of the heel of Eve's descendant. This descendant would suffer; but in doing so He would crush the serpent's head, robbing Satan of his authority and power.

The Rite of Circumcision

As we have noted, God required that all males were circumcised (Josh. 5:3–4), as had been required of the family of Abraham (Gen. 17:10). But the

Jesus and the Exodus

performance of this rite was postponed until after the Exodus, when the nation was safe from attack and her men could recover from the physically debilitating procedure. Circumcision continues as a key requirement of the Jewish faith to this day, and no man is a Jew unless he has received this ancient rite. Paul will eventually discuss its significance at length, as we shall see.

What is also interesting about this requirement is that no one is allowed to eat of the Passover unless he has been circumcised (Exod. 12:48). But we know from Ezekiel 20 that the Jews had ceased to follow the God of their ancestor, Abraham, when in Egypt. They had given themselves over to the gods of Egypt. Even Moses had failed to observe this rite and almost lost his life for not circumcising his son (Exod. 4:24–26).

So, Israel was far from an innocent community on the night of the Passover. She was as guilty as the Egyptian people on whom the judgement was about to fall. By remaining in Egypt after the death of Joseph, Israel had chosen the protection of Pharaoh over the protection of the God of Abraham no doubt hoping that the privileges that Joseph had been able to secure for her would continue. But this is not how it turned out; the people had to follow the faith of the Pharaohs and worship their gods. This subjugation by the gods of Egypt is evidenced in that, even at Sinai, they reverted to worshiping the Egyptian golden calf (Exod. 32).

The Strange Story

So, Israel was in a serious predicament despite the provision of the lambs because she had not continued the practice of circumcision. No one in the nation could eat the Passover, so all would have been barred from the protection given by the death of the lambs unless a way out of the predicament could be provided.

This is probably the significance of the strange story of the circumcision of Moses' son in Exodus 4:24–26, when Moses was returning to Egypt from his exile in Midian. It says:

> At a lodging place on the way the LORD met him and sought to put him to death. Then Zipporah took a flint and cut off her son's foreskin and touched Moses' feet with it and said, "Surely you are a bridegroom of blood to me!" So he let him

alone. It was then that she said, 'A bridegroom of blood,' because of the circumcision.

The fact that Moses' life was threatened by the Lord suggests it was required because he'd failed to circumcise his son. The circumcision of the boy by Zipporah (who seems to have known of God's requirement concerning this rite), appears to have been a vicarious act to save the nation's firstborn, for they, along with the rest of the nation's males, were uncircumcised. Technically, the firstborn were excluded from the one event that could save them, i.e., the Passover! The vicarious (i.e., substitutionary) circumcision of Moses' firstborn son seems to have allowed Israel to partake in the Passover until such a time as all her men could undergo the rite.

God's Power and Appointment of Moses

Any man can claim he is God's servant and appointed to lead people to a greater knowledge of Him. This has happened throughout history in almost every religion. Moses claimed he had met with Yahweh, who had commissioned him to lead Israel into freedom. But such a claim, while it was true and convinced Moses of his call, was witnessed by no other person. Certainly, Pharaoh was having no truck with the claim and, at times, even the Jewish people (including his family) challenged his authenticity (Num. 12:2).

So, what was the evidence that this deliverance was of God and not just the aspiration of a powerful leader? The Exodus event proved that the claims of Moses were genuine for God bathed the event in supernatural manifestations. He demonstrated His power over the gods of Egypt by a series of plagues and miracles culminating with the slaying of the Egyptian firstborn on the night of the Passover. As we will see, the manifestation of God's power and its significance for marking out God's appointed servant, chosen to lead His people out of captivity, was to become a common feature of future such saving events, i.e., of future Exoduses.

The Purpose of Deliverance

In the Egyptian Exodus, Israel had been delivered from Egypt and led by Moses to Mount Sinai, where God made a covenant with her. The making of this covenant contained all the elements of a marriage ceremony, and this was no accident for God was taking Israel as His bride. The Old Testament is full of references to the Sinai event (Exod. 20:2–4; Deut. 4:20; Ps. 78:12; 106:7;

Jer. 2:20; Hosea 2:14–20) and later, when Israel broke the covenant with God by worshipping other gods, she was called an adulteress (Duet 31:16; 2 Chron. 21:13; Ps. 106:39; Isa. 1:21; Jer. 2:20; Ezek. 16:30; Hosea 9:1). Throughout her history, God reminded Israel of her unique relationship and called her to come back and be the loving obedient bride she'd promised to be (Isa. 62:1–5; Hosea 2:14–23; 14:1–7). This divine marriage imagery was possibly not a uniquely Jewish concept, for other gods from the surrounding nations took their adherents as their bridal people as well.[23]

The Scope of Deliverance

As we saw, when God made a covenant with Abraham, He promised that when his descendants were taken into exile by an enemy, He would rescue them from their enslavement (Gen. 15:13–14). But there was something else going on when that covenant was made, and it was to show that God was concerned not just for the descendants of Abraham but also for the entire human family. We find that God had previously said: "I will bless those who bless you, but the one who dishonours you I must curse, so that all the families of the earth may receive blessing through you." (Gen. 12:3). God had never rejected the Gentiles; His intention was always to use Israel to bless the nations of the earth. This is made clear, for Gentiles were allowed to join the Jewish people as they escaped from Egypt: "The Israelites journeyed from Rameses to Sukkoth. There were about 600,000 men on foot, plus their dependents. A mixed multitude also went up with them, and flocks and herds—a very large number of cattle." (Exod. 12:37–38). As we will see, this inclusivity would be a growing feature of all future exoduses.

The Vindication or Justification of God.

God had sworn on oath that He would redeem the offspring of Abraham when they were removed from the Promised Land. This was an important part of the covenant, for it was effectively a promise that God would maintain it. Sadly, Israel was incapable of keeping her vows. Like Adam she preferred the

---

[23] This is a conclusion I draw from the fact that Israel joined herself to other gods and related to them in the same way as they had previously related to her own God, as the bridal partner. Of course, the nations may not have seen themselves as having this relationship with their gods, but the prophets of the Old Testament saw that Israel had entered into this illegitimate relationship and this is what is significant for a proper understanding of their message.

seductions of other gods. God's character was being questioned. Would He be faithful to Israel even in the situation where she had betrayed Him? He would prove that He could and would and in this He was justified as the covenant keeping God, We will see that this aspect of justification would develop more fully as the Exodus narrative developed throughout Israel's history. It would become the seed of a far greater understanding of God's faithfulness that would one day be fulfilled in the giving of His Son. But this justification was not only about God's character being vindicated. Each saving event was evidence that Israel's claim to be the people of God, which was ridiculed by the nations that conquered her, was true. God's mighty act of deliverance demonstrated to the nations that Israel continued to be His firstborn son (Exod. 4:22) and thus vindicated (justified) her claims to be heir of the promises and truly God's people. Thus, we see that the seeds of the great New Testament doctrines of redemption, justification, adoption and atonement are not found in the practices or beliefs of other people but in the history of the Exodus. They are part of The Exodus narratives which guide us to a better understanding of God's dealing with His people in salvation history.

The Way of the Lord

On the journey through the wilderness the nation was led by God, symbolized by the pillar of fire at night and the cloud by day (Exod. 13:21). During this journey, God provided daily bread (Exod. 16:35) and water (Exod. 17:6). He instructed the nation to construct a tabernacle, i.e., a tent, where they could worship Him and He could come to meet with them (Exod. 26). He ordered the institution of a priestly community to represent the people before Him (Exod. 32:25–29). Vestments were made for them according to the instructions that God gave Moses and as instructed, they offered daily sacrifices. They were to keep a range of memorials or remembrances/feast days throughout the year so that the nation's history and God's mercy and kindness to her were regularly remembered. These were the essential details of the arrangements God designated for the nation to keep. This theme of the Lord guiding His people was to be embedded in future acts of deliverance or exoduses.

Conclusion

We have seen how the Egyptian Narrative was linked to the promise that God gave to Abraham of delivering His offspring from captivity. We also found that the firstborn played a vital role in the Exodus and that they would have died but for God instructing the families to slay lambs in their stead. When Israel arrived at Sinai, God made a covenant with the nation that she would be His bride and He would be her husband. Although Gentiles could not have a part in this unique relationship, God allowed Gentiles to leave Egypt with the Jewish community and live amongst them as long as they respected God's laws and did nothing that offended Him. They could become privileged members of the Jewish community if they submitted to circumcision and kept not only the moral laws of God but also the feasts and the prescribed rituals. In allowing this, God showed that He welcomed the Gentiles and that it was His intention to win the nations so that they could share in the blessings that the Jewish people had inherited.

Chapter 11 The Role of the Firstborn

In this chapter, we are going to look at the Passover in some depth and probably at a level you have not considered before. We will find important details that are not normally discussed or written about. These important details will become the key foundation stone upon which the New Testament doctrine of atonement is built.

The Lamb and the Firstborn.

So, the rescue of the Israelites from Egypt was God fulfilling the promise He had made to Abraham. The details of the rescue are, of course, well known. Essentially, they centred on a lamb dying in place of the firstborn son of each Israelite family and its blood being smeared on the lintel and doorposts of the home (Exod. 12:7). But it must be emphasized, for it is often missed, that to achieve this act of salvation the firstborn sons were appointed to die for the sins of their families. The lambs were merely substitutes for them.

The firstborn son was the key member of his family. When the father died, he was given twice the inheritance his siblings received. This was not out of favouritism but because he had to act as the family's redeemer. He would be responsible for settling any of its debts that had got out of hand and was expected to ensure that the family's property and land were kept within family ownership (Lev. 25:8–34; Ruth 4:4). Also, if any member of his family was the victim of an injustice, he was the one to pay to have the injustice rectified (Gen. 4:14–15,23f; Num. 35:22–29; Deut. 19:4–10). He was even appointed to be the one who, if one of his brothers died and his widow had no children, would take her as his own wife and have children by her (Deut. 25:5–10; Ruth 3:13; 4:1–8). These children would then be treated as those of his dead brother. This arrangement was known as 'Levirate marriage'. Such an arrangement was not unique to the Jewish community.

The Provision of a Redeemer.

The firstborn was at the heart of this incredible set of family relationships. The redeemer gave his family members someone who was always looking to defend them and keep them secure from harm. So here, on the night of the Passover. Unless a lamb was slain on his behalf, the firstborn son was going to be the victim and his life taken so that his family could be protected, forgiven, and freed.

This practice of the redeemer figure was soon to be enshrined in Israel's law, given by God at Mount Sinai as we saw above. While the firstborn was the appointed redeemer figure, a near kinsman could take his place if he was unwilling to fulfil the role at a social level. But there was one role the firstborn could not abdicate, and that was the giving of his life on the night of the Passover. Unless a lamb took his place as prescribed by God, he would die.

But why did the firstborn of each Israelite family have to bear this death sentence? It was because they represented families that had abandoned Yahweh in favour of the Egyptian gods. Sadly, this was not a relationship the Israelites loathed. They'd become devotees of these gods while living in Egypt (Exod. 32:1–6; Ezek. 20:4-20) and were in willing bondage to them. However, their initial favourable circumstances changed when a new Pharaoh came to the throne. He had not known Joseph and he feared the growing numbers of Israelites in his kingdom. He put them into state servitude, and they were made to provide slave labour for his magnificent building projects. Their bondage was much deeper than physical slavery, for their acceptance of the gods of Egypt meant that the Israelites had become their property. Liberation from such spiritual bondage could only come through death, a sentence that all the firstborn redeemers must bear on behalf of their families.

The Protection of the Firstborn

But the firstborn sons of the Israelite families were spared because God allowed lambs to die in their place. This idea of saving people through the substitution of an innocent victim is a major theme throughout the Bible. Each household was to protect its firstborn by slaying a lamb.[24] This imagery had huge significance for the New Testament writers as they explained what Jesus' death had achieved.

---

[24] See Exodus 12:1-30.

Jesus and the Exodus

Even before we get to the New Testament, the role of the redeemer develops to describe Yahweh's relationship with Israel. He called Himself Israel's Redeemer: He would rescue her from danger and bring her out of captivity (Isa. 43:3–4,14–15, see also Exod. 40: 1–5; 49:25–26); He would pay her debts (Isa. 51:11; 52:8–10) and take vengeance on her enemies who sought to harm or destroy her (Isa. 34:8; 35:4); and He would take her as His bride and have children by that marriage (Isa. 54:5).

So, from the role of the firstborn, Israel was learning about the depth of commitment God had made to her. We will discover that God's commitment to be Israel's Redeemer was at a level that no Old Testament Jew could have ever dreamt. Prior to the night of the Passover, the night of deliverance, God demonstrated to Pharaoh His power over the gods of Egypt. He performed miracles, which were miracles of judgement (Exod. 7–11) and, by these, He demonstrated that He was the Almighty God that no other god could equal. The final plague, the tenth (Exod. 12), judged Pharaoh himself and the Egyptian nation with the death of their firstborn.

The Death of Firstborn and Atonement.

Most scholars claim that there was no atonement in the Passover event; they claim it was solely about redemption and that atonement was dealt with on the Day of Atonement. I understand this argument; but I believe it misses vitally important evidence that challenges this claim. I will discuss this later in chapter 15. Here, it is sufficient to point out that the angel of death passed over the Jewish homes when he saw the blood. So, blood was turning away judgement. Now if this is not atonement, then the definition of the word needs to be rewritten.

But it is what is said about the Levites, who after the Exodus were substituted for the firstborn, that is important. Because God spared Israel's firstborn, He claimed them all to be priestly people unto Himself (Num. 18:15–16). But rather than God taking the firstborn from their families, He made provision for them to stay in the care of their parents and took the tribe of Levi to minister in their place (Num. 3:11–13). Thus, the Levites became the substitutes of the firstborn, just as the lambs had been, but without the shedding of blood. The nature of this substitution was made clear in that the number of firstborn who were spared death in the Passover was counted, and the number of Levites that were separated to represent them was counted. However, the number of Levites needed for man-to-man substitution fell short by 273 (Num. 3:39,43). This shortfall was rectified by redeeming the remaining number of firstborn. Half a shekel of silver was put into the treasury for each unredeemed firstborn who did not have Levitical representation (Num. 3:46-47).

The Levites were separated to do the work of the temple, serving as support workers to those of the family of Aaron who were called to function as priests by making sacrifices. Now the Levites were not allowed to offer sacrifices, but some very unexpected statements were made about their role. In Numbers 8:19, it says: "I have given the Levites as a gift to Aaron and his sons from among the Israelites, to do the work for the Israelites in the tent of meeting, and to make atonement for the Israelites, so there will be no plague among the Israelites when the Israelites come near the sanctuary." This seems to be a contradiction, for the firstborn never offered any sacrifices, never mind atoning sacrifices. Another unexpected statement about the Levites and their role in relation to the tabernacle is found in Numbers 1:53, where it says: "But the Levites must camp around the tabernacle of the testimony, so that the LORD's anger will not fall on the Israelite community. The Levites are responsible for the care of the tabernacle of the testimony."

So, what do we make of these two statements? The only explanation that makes sense is that as the lambs had kept the angel of death from the firstborn on the night of the Passover, so the Levites, representing the firstborn, now keep the anger of God from falling on both the family of Aaron and the nation generally, by coming between them and God. So, their very presence functions as an atonement, not because they are somehow special but because they represented the firstborn whom God had spared.

The Firstborn and Ongoing Atonement

So, the very presence of the firstborn or their representatives functioned as the death of the lamb did on the first Passover night. They turned God's wrath away from Israel and allowed her to continue in fellowship with Him.

Other Old Testament passages speak of the atoning significance of the firstborn. The Psalmist, recalling the Exodus, says: "Yet he is compassionate. He forgives sin and does not destroy. He often holds back his anger" (Ps. 78:38).

The passage speaks of God forgiving the nation's sins on the night of the Passover. It goes on to say:

> His raging anger lashed out against them. He sent fury, rage, and trouble as messengers who bring disaster. He sent his anger in full force. He did not spare them from death; he handed their lives over to destruction. He struck down all the firstborn in Egypt, the firstfruits of their reproductive power in the tents of Ham. Yet he brought out his people like sheep; he led them through the wilderness like a flock. (Ps. 78:49–52 NET)

It might be argued that atonement is not specifically mentioned as it only says "forgiveness". But this is to take the term out of its Old Testament context, for God, who is holy, must exercise justice and judgement when His law is broken. So, there must be a sacrifice to cover the sin committed, in other words, atonement must have been made. This implied appeasement is so evident to the translators of the English Standard Version that they translate Psalm 78:38:

> Yet he, being compassionate, *atoned for their iniquity* and did not destroy them; he restrained his anger often and did not stir up all his wrath. (Ps.78:38, emphasis added)

Another Example

Another example of the atoning significance of the Passover is given when Ezekiel, speaking of the degraded state of Israel's worship, says in ironic tone:

> I also gave them decrees that were not good and regulations by which they could not live. I declared them to be defiled because of their sacrifices—they caused all their firstborn to pass through the fire—so that I might devastate them, so that they would know that I am the LORD.
>
> Therefore, speak to the house of Israel, son of man, and tell them, "This is what the Sovereign LORD says: In this way too your fathers blasphemed me when they were unfaithful to me. I brought them to the land that I swore to give them, but whenever they saw any high hill or leafy tree, they offered

> their sacrifices there and presented the offerings that provoked me to anger. They offered their soothing aroma there and poured out their drink offerings. So I said to them, 'What is this high place you go to?' (So it is called "High Place" to this day.)"
>
> Therefore say to the house of Israel, "This is what the Sovereign LORD says: Will you defile yourselves like your fathers and engage in prostitution with detestable idols? When you present your sacrifices —when you make your sons pass through the fire—you defile yourselves with all your idols to this very day. Will I allow you to seek me, O house of Israel? As surely as I live, declares the Sovereign LORD, I will not allow you to seek me!" (Ezek. 20:25–31 NET)

The passage is ironic in tone and mocks the idea that God has given to Israel a law that could not be fulfilled (v25) and sacrifices that, instead of purifying her, were intended to defile (v26). This is because they have replaced the appointed sacrifices with those offered to the pagan gods and have argued that these are what God has appointed. These were the sacrifices offered to Molech and involved his devotees offering their sons as atonements to avoid the god's judgement: "when you make your sons pass through the fire". The Jewish leaders do this to appease the anger that God has toward Israel because of her infidelity. The sacrifices offered to Molech were definitely of an atoning nature.

Further evidence that the firstborn was seen to be an atonement is found in Micah, where it says:

> With what should I enter the LORD's presence? With what should I bow before the sovereign God? Should I enter his presence with burnt offerings, with year-old calves? [7] Will the LORD accept a thousand rams or ten thousand streams of olive oil? Should I give him my firstborn child as payment for my

rebellion, my offspring my own flesh and blood for my sin?"
(Micah 6:6–7 NET)[25]

The final mention of a Passover theme in the Old Testament is found in the prophecy of Zechariah, where it says:

> I will pour out on the kingship of David and the population of Jerusalem a spirit of grace and supplication so that they will look to me, the one they have pierced. They will lament for him as one laments for an only son, and there will be a bitter cry for him like the bitter cry for a firstborn. (Zech. 12:10 NET)

I will consider this statement further in chapter 14 where the relationship between Passover and the prophecy of Zechariah and that of Isaiah are considered.[26]

The third feature that would be carried over into all future acts of deliverance was the circumcision of all of Abrams sons and his male servants. Paul will make it clear that Abram was not justified.

Conclusion

We have considered aspects of the Passover event that are normally not considered. They are important, and their absence from Christian understanding has left the Church impoverished in its appreciation of the wonder of Christ and His work. We have seen that the sacrifice of the lamb in place of the firstborn, who should have died, was an atoning sacrifice as well as a sacrifice for redemption. Understanding the Passover in depth will help us identify the significance of the Jesus' Exodus narrative.

---

[25] For a discussion on how a range of scholars view this and the case I am making see Holland, T. S., *Contours of Pauline Theology: A Radical New Survey of the Influences on Paul's Biblical Writings* (Fearn, Ross-shire: Christian Focus Publications, 2004), 248f.

[26] For a range of interpretations on this verse and how they fit into my proposed interpretation see Holland, *Contours*, 249-251.

Chapter 12 The Predicted Babylonian Exodus

The Second Exodus in the Old Testament was when Israel was delivered from her captivity in Babylon. Like the Egyptian Exodus, the predictions of the Babylonian Exodus included a range of events that the servant, who would lead them, would accomplish. While in the Egyptian Exodus the miracles were mostly events of judgement, those of the Babylonian Exodus would be about healing and mercy and would be the crucial sign that the servant's ministry was authentic. The prophet who focused most on this predicted event was Isaiah. As we have seen, it is this section of the Old Testament that Paul especially used as the scaffolding to write his letter to the Romans around. It was this prophet who said:

> I am the LORD; I have called you in righteousness; I will take you by the hand and keep you; I will give you as a covenant for the people, a light for the nations, to open the eyes that are blind, to bring out the prisoners from the dungeon, from the prison those who sit in darkness. I am the LORD; that is my name; my glory I give to no other, nor my praise to carved idols. (Isaiah 42:6–8)

Need and Failure

The need for an Exodus from Babylon arose because of Israel's repeated unfaithfulness earlier in her history. At Sinai, she had accepted the terms of the covenant that made her the people of God, the bride of Yahweh; but while she formally accepted them, she had no intention of keeping them. This is apparent in that, while Moses was on the mountain, the people pressed Aaron to make them a god of gold to worship. It was also true that, just as Abraham was commanded to circumcise his entire family (Gen. 17:11), so Israel accepted circumcision, but never lived out the meaning of the rite in her life as a nation. Circumcision was intended to symbolize a pure, contrite, obedient, heart (Deut. 10:16); but that is the last thing the nation and her people had or wanted. She threw herself into the godless lifestyle of her neighbours to such a degree that even they were shocked over what she sank to. So, rather than being the faithful bride that Yahweh had rescued her from Egypt to be, she became the most shameful of brides, and Yahweh's name was blasphemed among the nations because of her behaviour (Isa. 37:23; 52:5; 65:7).

Rejection of Her God

Instead of rejoicing that God was her King and she was His bride, the people asked for a king like other nations. Saul, the Benjaminite, was the first to rule; but, after his death, David of Bethlehem was appointed king. Solomon inherited David's throne, and when he died the throne passed to his son Rehoboam, who caused unrest among his people because he increased their taxes. In time, there was a rebellion against the king and the nation divided into two kingdoms. The larger northern kingdom, which retained the name Israel and consisted of ten tribes, made Jeroboam its king and built an alternative temple. This breakaway section was soon to be judged when the Assyrians invaded and took the people into exile (740 BC). The southern kingdom, known as Judah, wallowed in satisfaction that the breakaway kingdom had suffered. She believed she was safe because her king was a descendant of King David with whom God had made a covenant, and this covenant contained a promise that David would always have a descendant ruling over His people.

Theological Abuse

Rather than the covenant restraining Judah's behaviour, it became the grounds for thinking she was exempt from any judgement. The people went from bad to worse and continued in the false understanding of what the covenant with David would give them. But the last thing God was doing was turning a blind eye towards their behaviour. They sank so low that they sacrificed their own children to the gods they committed themselves to (Jer 19:5). The book of Hosea is a commentary on this tragic situation, lived out in the agony of the prophet. His wife, Gomer, was as rebellious and wayward as the nation.

This constant disgracing of God before the nations resulted in Him warning that His incredible patience and pleadings were not going to last. A day of judgement was set when her enemies would not be held back but allowed to take Jerusalem, destroy it, and deport the nation. So, the sacking of Jerusalem took place, and the people were deported as God had warned.

But He had not abandoned Israel. His intention was that the exile would be remedial rather than destructive. Israel had to learn the seriousness of her unfaithfulness, and this was the only way for her to learn. Even before it took place, prophets were predicting the exile and saying that Israel would return to Zion and worship God in truth and joy.

But there was a problem with God dealing with Israel in this way. Israel had broken the covenant by giving herself to foreign gods. By 'putting her away', God was acknowledging the marriage was over. She belonged to other gods and her covenant was now with them. So even if God wanted her, His own law would not allow Him to marry her again for it instructed the Jews that if a man divorced his wife and she remarried and eventually her new husband died and her old husband wanted to take her back, the marriage was forbidden (Deut. 24:1–4). Clearly, God could not take Israel back to Himself without being a lawbreaker! But, as we shall see, there was a costly way through which God could receive Israel back to Himself, and this was a price that He was prepared to pay!

The Song of the Suffering Servant

Isaiah 52:13–53:12 is one of a series of four passages from the book of Isaiah called the Servant Songs (Isa. 42:1–4; 49:1–7; 50:4–9; 52:13–53:12). Because of the clear theme of suffering in the last song, it is called the Song of the Suffering Servant.

Scholars hold different opinions on who this suffering servant was. They include suffering Israel, an unidentified king, and the prophet Isaiah himself. If we're to get a better understanding of who he was, we must recover all relevant indicators, not only in the Song but also from the immediately preceding and following chapters. All too often, scholars have taken the Song of the Suffering Servant as an isolated unit; but, of course, it was part of an ongoing narrative. To fail to recognise this leaves us guessing, something which the author would surely not have intended. The various documentary theories scholarship has offered have had the disastrous effect of fragmenting the book and thereby destroying not only its unity but also its message.

Contrasts of Events

Isaiah compared his predictions of this Second Exodus with the Egyptian Exodus, and assured Israel that, if she repented, her return would be more glorious and meaningful than it had been when the nation was rescued from Pharaoh's control:

Jesus and the Exodus

In the Egyptian Exodus, the people were led by Moses; this time, they would be led by a descendant of David. (Isa. 9:7; Jer. 30:9; Ezek. 34:22–24).

In the Egyptian Exodus, they were guided by the cloud, a symbol of God's presence; this time, they would be led and equipped by the Holy Spirit Himself (Isa. 32:15; 42:1; Ezek. 36:27).

Then, they were given a covenant that required physical circumcision (Lev. 12:3); this time, God would circumcise their hearts (Deut. 30:6; Jer. 4:4; Ezek. 36:26).

Then, they ate manna in the desert; this time, they would feast at the marriage table (Isa. 25:6; 55:1; Jer. 31:14).

Then, they had the tent of meeting; this time, they would have a glorious temple that the son of David (the prince) would sanctify and order (Ezek. 45:17–25).

Then, there was a covenant engraved on stone; this time, there would be a new covenant engraved on the people's hearts (Isa. 61:10–11; Jer. 31:31–33; Ezek. 36:26).

Then, they experienced the opposition of the nations; this time, the nations would flock to worship God in Jerusalem (Isa. 2:2; 11:10; 60:11).

Then, they drank water from the rock; this time, the presence of God would transform nature, and food and drink would be in abundance (Isa. 12:3; 32:2; 33:16; 41:18; 44:3).

Then, there were miracles of judgement; this time, there would be miracles of healing, mercy and forgiveness (Isa. 29:18; 35:5–6; 61:1–5).

Then, it was a relationship that was exclusively for the Jewish people; this time, all the nations would be invited to seek the Lord and know Him and His blessings (Isa. 2:2; 19:19–24; 34:1; 43:9).

Then, it centred on the death of the firstborn, delivered by the substitutionary death of lambs; this time, there would be no substitute, it would centre on the death of the Lord's Firstborn, the King (Isa. 53:1–12).

Then, the Spirit was given to a select group of people; this time, He would come on all people (Isa. 32:15; 44:3; 59:21; 63:14; Ezek. 11:19; 36:27; Joel 2:28)

Then, their arrival was with conflict and scarcity; this time, with joy and feasting (Isa. 54:18; 61:9; 62:1–9).

Then, the nation was made Yahweh's bride, but utterly failed to keep her vows; this time, she would be taken with changed (circumcised) hearts and be devoted to the One who had redeemed her (Isa. 41:14; 54:5; Hosea 2:16–20; 14:1–9).

Then, a specific tribe represented Israel before God; this time, all would know Him (Isa. 61:6; Jer. 31:34).

Isaiah's predictions about the events surrounding the Exodus from Babylon must have been staggering to hear as they were glorious compared to those of the Egyptian Exodus. But, as we know from history, these marvellous promises and predictions were not fulfilled. It seemed that God, speaking through His prophet(s), had failed to keep His promises but, in truth, it was the returning remnant's hardness of heart and apostasy that nullified them (Zech. 7:10–11).

However, ancient texts tell us that these promises never died in the hearts of Jewish people. Indeed, they are there to this day. They still hold on to the hope that, one day, the predictions of Isaiah and the other prophets will be fulfilled.

But these unfulfilled promises were to provide the rich material upon which the apostles based their message of the redeeming activity of God. At last, it was coming to fruition, and in a reality that far outshone the Old Testament's hope and that of Israel today!

Jesus and the Exodus

The Importance of Context

While we are focusing specifically on chapter 52:13–53:12, the preceding narrative, (Isa. 52:1–12), has two vitally important details we need to note. The opening of the chapter reminds Israel of her past exile and predicts that the next exile will be ended, as the former one, through the death of an innocent victim.

> Awake, awake, put on your strength, O Zion; put on your beautiful garments, O Jerusalem, the holy city; for there shall no more come into you the uncircumcised and the unclean. Shake yourself from the dust and arise; be seated, O Jerusalem; loose the bonds from your neck, O captive daughter of Zion. For thus says the LORD: "You were sold for nothing, and you shall be redeemed without money." For thus says the Lord GOD: "My people went down at the first into Egypt to sojourn there, and the Assyrian oppressed them for nothing. Now therefore what have I here," declares the LORD, "seeing that my people are taken away for nothing? Their rulers wail," declares the LORD, "and continually all the day my name is despised. Therefore my people shall know my name. Therefore in that day they shall know that it is I who speak; here I am." (Isa. 52:1–6)

Chapter 52 goes on to tell the Jews to prepare for their departure from exile and to comfort their distraught brethren in desolate Jerusalem by telling them that God has kept His promise and delivered them (Isa. 52:7).

When the people in desolate Jerusalem receive this news from a group sent ahead of the delivered pilgrim band, they burst out in songs of rejoicing, describing those who bring the news as having beautiful feet! Isaiah 52:7 is quoted by Paul in Romans 10:15, where he asks how can unbelieving Jews and Gentiles know that New Covenant membership is open to them if no one tells them.

The Message of the Pilgrim Band

The advance party will assure the struggling people that, unlike their ancestors' flight from Egypt, the exiles returning from Babylon have not fled in fearful haste (Isa. 52:12). God will return to Jerusalem (Zion) with them, protecting the returning remnant as they travel, and His deliverance will comfort the nation and lead to its cleansing.

> How beautiful upon the mountains are the feet of him who brings good news, who publishes peace, who brings good news of happiness, who publishes salvation, who says to Zion, 'Your God reigns.' The voice of your watchmen—they lift up their voice; together they sing for joy; for eye to eye they see the return of the LORD to Zion. Break forth together into singing, you waste places of Jerusalem, for the LORD has comforted his people; he has redeemed Jerusalem. The LORD has bared his holy arm before the eyes of all the nations, and all the ends of the earth shall see the salvation of our God.
>
> Depart, depart, go out from there; touch no unclean thing; go out from the midst of her; purify yourselves, you who bear the vessels of the LORD. For you shall not go out in haste, and you shall not go in flight, for the LORD will go before you, and the God of Israel will be your rear guard." (Isa. 52: 7–12)

So, Isaiah 52:1–12 is full of references to the Egyptian Exodus, and it is used to describe how God will bring about a far greater deliverance of Israel from Babylon.

Conclusion

Here, once again, we see the progressive development of The Exodus narrative. As it is passed on through the pages of Jewish history, it gathers expectations of a more glorious fulfilment than the previous Exoduses either gave or envisioned, and it eventually gave the Church her message of God's saving activity through the reality of the New Exodus of Jesus and His people. In reaching this point, we see how the original Exodus events seeded the understanding of the saving events that were to come and would supply the categories that became the source of the Church's doctrines. This is The Exodus narrative, and its details are what we will go on to consider in coming chapters.

Again, we have found heavy dependence on the Egyptian Exodus to make sense of the events of the Exodus from Babylon. The former event, however, lacked much of the hope that the prophet gave for the Babylonian Exodus when he anticipated a glorious outcome of deliverance. However, these two events together would seed the understanding of Jesus and His disciples as to what Jesus' Exodus, the New Exodus, would achieve – an Exodus far more glorious than Isaiah could have imagined!

So, the emergence of the silent but powerful existence of The Exodus narrative is being revealed.

Chapter 13 The Song of the Suffering Servant

Then, in Isaiah 52, comes the unexpected mention of the death of an unknown figure:

> Look, my servant will succeed! He will be elevated, lifted high, and greatly exalted – (just as many were horrified by the sight of you) he was so disfigured he no longer looked like a man; his form was so marred he no longer looked human so now he will startle many nations. Kings will be shocked by his exaltation, for they will witness something unannounced to them, and they will understand something they had not heard about. (Isa. 52:13–15 NET)

These verses are key to understanding who the suffering servant is. He deals prudently (v13, NIV), i.e., he is wise, sensible in action and thought and is beyond reproach, yet he suffers, for his visage was marred more than any man's.

Isaiah 52:14,15 yields a sure pointer to his identity. The nobility and the powerful of that age were used to seeing multitudes of innocent people suffering unjustly, and they didn't give them a second thought. But here they are stunned to silence; their mouths are closed, unable to speak about what they have witnessed. This can mean only one thing. The servant is one of their own. They are watching another king, a righteous king, being caused to suffer so much that his form is marred beyond that of any other person.

An Example from Recent History

The stunned silence of the rulers of the earth at the suffering of Israel's king is parallel to what took place in 1918, when the Bolsheviks murdered the Russian royal family. One doesn't need much imagination to grasp what the other royal families of Europe would have been thinking and feeling: "If it could happen to them, it could happen to us". Only the violent, unjust death of someone of equal standing could explain the reaction of the royal observers Isaiah refers to. The mysterious suffering servant must be of the royal household, a descendant of David.

Jesus and the Exodus

But, in his suffering and death, this king will sprinkle many nations (v15). The previous sentences say that 'many were horrified by the sight of him, he was so disfigured that he no longer looked like a man, indeed, his form was so marred he no longer looked human', suggesting that what is sprinkling the nations is the blood of this greatly abused servant. This has clear Paschal overtones because earlier in the passage Isaiah predicted an Exodus event (Isa. 52: 1-15). Here, the sprinkling is not with the blood of lambs but with the blood of Israel's suffering deliverer, her Messiah, her King, who elsewhere is called the 'Lord's firstborn' (Ps. 89:27).

The Passover/Exodus Background

Throughout, the language is borrowed from the Egyptian Exodus event, when 'Israel' was sprinkled with the blood of lambs to purify her and allow her to become the people of God (Exod. 24:8). Here, in Isaiah's predicted Babylonian Exodus, the purification is not for the Jews alone but for believing members of all nations (Isa. 52:15), allowing them to become the new people of God (Rev. 5:9–10).

So, in Isaiah 52:12, Isaiah tells of a community which has been called out of exile to be led on a pilgrimage by the one who redeemed and saved it through the sprinkling of his own blood (Heb. 12:24). All this is possible, he predicts, because a righteous king will die, releasing his people from their wretched, self–imposed separation. Does this not echo a future King who will do the same?

In chapter 53, Isaiah's focus continues to be on the sufferings of this righteous servant king. His suffering causes him to be described as a "man of sorrows" who people reject. They do not realize that his sorrow has been caused by them and they are the cause of his rejection.

> Who would have believed what we just heard? When was the Lord's power revealed through him? He sprouted up like a twig before God, like a root out of parched soil; he had no stately form or majesty that might catch our attention, no special appearance that we should want to follow him. He was despised and rejected by people, people one who experienced pain and was acquainted with illness; hid their faces from him; he was despised, and we considered him insignificant. But he

lifted up our illnesses, he carried our pain; even though we
thought he was being punished, attacked by God, and afflicted
for something he had done. (Isa. 53: 1–4 NET)

In chapter 53, Isaiah describes the servant king as being led like a lamb to the slaughter and one whose death redeems the people from exile.

The King Identified

So, who was Israel's king? Clearly, he was the son of David; but, for the Jews, there was a massive problem. They didn't expect the son of David to die. They expected him to be victorious and exalted after rescuing a disgraced Israel. In other words, the suffering servant's exaltation was not what they expected or wanted. Clearly, the humiliation of their king being treated like a common criminal and dying at Passover echoes a future event when a King was rejected. The apostles had no difficulty in drawing out the obvious parallel exalting Jesus high as the crucified King, who led His people out of death and who calls the nations to be His subjects. The Jewish community was ashamed of their deliverer; but the Christian community glories in His suffering and rejoices to make it the very centre of their preaching.

This all points to the death of the Servant being a Passover sacrifice. The strong Exodus themes of release and pilgrimage in Isaiah 52:11,12, together with the death of the firstborn (a name given by the Psalmist to speak of Israel's king in Psalm 89:27), are clear strands of a tradition that recalls Israel's flight from Egypt, when the son of Pharaoh died and his death became the reason for Israel's urgent expulsion from Egypt.

My understanding is that, unless Isaiah had made it very clear that he intended to write of a far-off event involving a future king, his suffering servant was contemporary with the predicted, redeemed community in Babylon. It is my opinion that he was an unknown son of David, i.e., a Davidic king. I will seek to support this shortly by considering the book of Zechariah, a text that scholars seem to have mostly overlooked in regard to this enquiry. Such an understanding in no way denies a future, far greater fulfilment of the text, which God, who inspired the prophet, obviously knew, but of which the people of that generation appeared to know nothing. In other words, rather than Isaiah 53 being a prophecy, it was s type of a far greater event that would one day happen.

Types as Prophecy

In looking for an answer to the fact that an event is called a prophecy, we must recognise that the apostles viewed 'types' as prophecy (Acts 2:28–30).[27] Types, such as prominent patriarchs and certain Old Testament events, helped the fledgling early church understand the salvation story. They were prophecies, but less defined than precise oral proclamations of future events or people. The people of the Old Testament who were part of such events did not understand that they were either a type or prophecy e.g., during the time of exile understanding that it was a picture of humanity's condition, but this became clear to the apostles as they eventually considered the Old Testament scriptures.

So, again, I think it's incorrect to see Isa. 53 as a direct verbal prophecy of what would happen seven hundred years into Isaiah's future, for it would have had no relevance to the generation he was speaking to. Nevertheless, I think the apostles saw that his statement foretold of a far greater act of deliverance, where the unknown Davidic king, spoken of in Isaiah 53, was identified as a type, and its fulfilment is seen to be no less than the Son of God Himself. I believe it is from this perspective that the early church interpreted it. As noted earlier, the apostles clearly used this sort of exegesis when dealing with other Old Testament events, so what I am suggesting is not violating apostolic methodology.

The content of Isaiah 53 stresses the innocence of the servant and the guilt of those who reject him (Isa. 53: 4–6). He did not fight against his execution even though he was perfectly innocent. His death, being like that of a slaughtered lamb, places it within the identified Exodus theme, so it is a clear reference to the Paschal lamb of the Egyptian Exodus that was sacrificed in place of the firstborn of each family.

More Than Redemption

In some apparently indescribable sense, the suffering servant was not only redeeming his people but restoring them to a place of innocence (Isa. 53: 4–9). The innocence of the servant is stressed throughout, and the outcomes of

---

[27] For a fuller explanation of types see chapter 20.

his death were that "the will of the Lord" was done (Isa. 53: 9) and that many were made righteous (Isa. 53:11). Throughout the description of the outcome of the servant's death held in chapters 52–53, there is the suggestion that it secured redemption and atonement. However, we must be careful not to draw this conclusion. The death of the servant is not about suffering for his people's sins as normally interpreted. I say this for two reasons. The first is that Isaiah 40:1–2 says:

> "Comfort, comfort my people," says your God. "Speak kindly to Jerusalem and tell her that her time of warfare is over, that her punishment is completed. For the LORD has made her pay double for all her sins." (NET)

This statement is normally overlooked by those who exegete Isaiah 53. The passage gives us the doctrine of atonement in that period of Israel's understanding. God did not close His eyes to her sin, He punished her through exile as He had warned when He took her as His bride (Deut. 30:11–20). Thus, the nation was sent into exile, God making her pay double for her sins. By this we see that Israel was not freely forgiven as in the Christian doctrine of justification. And because she had been punished, no further atonement was required. But if we insist on saying that the servant's death was an atonement for Israel's sins, it would be saying that God was not satisfied with the punishment He had inflicted on Israel. To argue that God now required a second atonement through the death of His servant, is to argue He changed His requirements and demanded more! Now, if we hold that this is what the text is saying, we have destroyed the biblical doctrine of justification and the belief that God can never go back on His word, something which Hebrews 6:18 says He cannot do. This is all the fruit of reading a later, fully developed Christian understanding back into the passage and completely ignoring the historical context of Isaiah with his limited Jewish doctrine of justification.

And the second reason for rejecting the imposition of the Christianized version on the text is that the Hebrew word for atonement is not used. (The KJV implies its use in Isaiah 53:10, "Yet it pleased the LORD to bruise him; he hath put him to grief: when thou shalt make his soul an offering for sin, he shall see his seed, he shall prolong his days, and the pleasure of the LORD shall prosper in his hand"). The fact is, the term Isaiah uses does not speak of atonement for it is אשם, *'asham*, which means reparation. It means that the servant's death in some way returns Israel to her previous status of being the bride of Yahweh. In this term, there is no suggestion of atonement. It means nothing more than an injured person or community being repaid for something they have lost on account of someone, possibly innocently, doing something that has caused them loss. After the first World War, Germany was required to pay reparation to the countries she had gone to war with. This was nothing to do with criminal punishment as that was dealt with separately. The reparation was solely to pay the cost of rebuilding the cities that had been destroyed.

Thus, because Israel had already been punished for her sin by God (who had handed her over to her enemies to be exiled for 70 years), her sin had been paid for. But now the servant must die to make redemption and reparation possible, and that latter element will be about Israel being restored to her former status so that Yahweh can receive His bride back (Isa. 61:10; 62:5),

If we do not submit to the clear meaning of the text and accept its divinely given authority, then we are taking control and forcing our preferred reading on it. Such a method of reading the text will not bring us to a better understanding of its intended meaning but will take us further away from it. We will see shortly that there are regular examples of this rejection of the explicit meanings that New Testament texts contain and where unsupported meanings have been imposed by well-meaning translators.

Conclusion.

The death of the suffering servant is a vital part of the New Exodus story we are about to consider. The death of the servant replaces the lamb that died in the Egyptian Exodus and, unlike the benefits of the death of the lamb, which provided both atonement and redemption, the death of the servant of the Lord, the descendant of David, secures only redemption. This leads to reparation, according to Isaiah 53. Through the death of the servant, the provision is made for the bringing forth of a New Creation in which all things are made new. This is a vital element of the final New Exodus of Jesus and an essential element for understanding the emerging, completed Exodus narrative.

What we have also discovered in this chapter is not only the need for a reinterpretation of what the death of the suffering servant of Isa. 53 achieved, but that we must be careful not to impose later, more developed Christian understanding on Old Testament texts. Also, we have found that we must not alter the clear meaning of the words found in scripture so that they fit into our preconceived understanding. We will soon see that this latter mistake is repeatedly made as scholars try to make sense of the message of Paul concerning what the death of Christ has achieved.

Chapter 14 The Problems of Evidence.

The Prophecy of Zechariah

The problem with the reading I am suggesting is that we don't know of a Davidic king who suffered death at the hands of his people. But this objection is overcome when we consider the prophecy of Zechariah, one of the prophets who ministered to those who had returned from exile. Despite opinions differing over the dating of Isaiah, what is not questioned is that the writing of the book of Zechariah follows that of Isaiah. So, it is possible, and probably likely, that Zechariah knew of the content of the book of Isaiah and faced the conundrum of the absence of a king who died as a result of what his people did to him when they rejected him as stated in Isa. 53. It is surely significant that Zechariah follows the same theme of the rejected king who suffers violence by the hands of his people.[28] Zechariah speaks of a Davidic king who suffers, saying:

> And I will pour out on the house of David and the inhabitants of Jerusalem a spirit of grace and pleas for mercy, so that, when they look on me, on him whom they have pierced, they shall mourn for him, as one mourns for an only child, and weep bitterly over him, as one weeps over a firstborn. On that day the mourning in Jerusalem will be as great as the mourning for Hadad-rimmon in the plain of Megiddo. (Zech. 12:10–11).

The suffering of this "only child" will open a fountain for the cleansing of the entire house of David. "In that day, there will be a fountain opened up for

---

[28] The following scholars have noted this link between Zechariah and the second Exodus theme of Isaiah, Petterson, Anthony R. *Haggai, Zechariah, Malachi* (Downers Grove: IVP, 2015); Hengel, Martin. "The Effective History of Isaiah 53 in the Pre-Christian Period". pp. 75–146 in *The Suffering Servant: Isaiah 53 in Jewish and Christian Sources*. Edited by Bernd Janowski and Peter Stuhlmacher. Translated by Daniel P. Bailey. (Grand Rapids: Eerdmans. 2004). Satterthwaite, Philip E. (ed); Hess, Richard S. (ed); Wenham, Gordon J. (ed), *The Lord's Anointed: Interpretation of Old Testament Messianic Texts,* (Cambridge: Tyndale Fellowship for Biblical Research, 1995)

the dynasty of David and the people of Jerusalem to cleanse them from sin and impurity." (Zech. 13:1)

It would appear that Zechariah expects the people to know who this victim is, for although he doesn't name him, he does provide statements that identify him. He has already spoken of Israel's longings being fulfilled:

> Rejoice greatly, O daughter of Zion! Shout aloud, O daughter of Jerusalem! Behold, your king is coming to you; righteous and having salvation is he, humble and mounted on a donkey, on a colt, the foal of a donkey. I will cut off the chariot from Ephraim and the war horse from Jerusalem; and the battle bow shall be cut off, and he shall speak peace to the nations; his rule shall be from sea to sea, and from the River to the ends of the earth. As for you also, because of the blood of my covenant with you, I will set your prisoners free from the waterless pit. Return to your stronghold, O prisoners of hope; today I declare that I will restore to you double. For I have bent Judah as my bow; I have made Ephraim its arrow. I will stir up your sons, O Zion, against your sons, O Greece, and wield you like a warrior's sword. (Zech. 9:9–13)

The descendant of David will be like his ancestor, not only a king but also a priest (Ps. 110:4; Zech. 6:13). Zechariah clearly sees that the promises of Isaiah are yet to be fulfilled. He uses the outline of Isaiah's message about the suffering servant to remind Israel that her salvation will, in time, be completed in the way predicted by his predecessor. As in Isaiah, Zechariah provides enough hints that the suffering servant is a descendant of David, (Zech. 12:7,8,10,12; 13:1). He also follows other themes of the earlier prophet(s). The king will be the true and faithful shepherd of his people, putting his own life forward for their protection (Isa. 40:1; Jer. 49:19; Ezek. 34:12; see Zech. 13:7) and he will be the fulfilment of Israel's hopes of being delivered from her enemies (Zech. 14:4–11).

The question that surely must be asked is why did God fail to fulfil His promises? The answer is clearly that Israel did not walk in the fear of the Lord but followed after other gods as her ancestors had done. Despite all she had suffered for doing this very thing, once delivered from exile she returned to her previous life of idolatry (Zech. 13:2), which brought further judgement.

Also, and inevitably, following their turning away from the Lord (Haggai 1:2,3) who had redeemed them, they failed to build the temple of the Lord and to give Him their tithes (Malachi 3:8) What is certain is that the four writers of the New Testament Gospels saw the importance of these passages were acting as witnesses to the events of the closing hours of Jesus' life, being predictive of the sufferings of the Son of God.[29]

Returning to Isaiah 54–66 and the Suffering Servant.

Isaiah 54

The redemption theme then continues into chapter 54, with the prophet calling on Israel to leave her barren state. She has a redeemer who has rescued her (v1). She is to have her own family and must, therefore, enlarge her tent (v2). Her Maker has redeemed her to be His bride (v4). Israel is to be rebuilt with an amazing beauty that all nations will acknowledge and in which she will be safe from her enemies (v11–17). Thus, the achievements of the Egyptian Exodus will be greatly exceeded when the Lord redeems her a second time to be His bride. Here, in the predicted return from Babylon (the Babylonian Exodus), the marriage will be witnessed by the nations and the matrimonial home will be beautiful.

Isaiah 55

The section begins with an appeal to all who are thirsty to "come to the waters." Again, there is a distinct echo from the Egyptian Exodus when Israel complained of a lack of food and water. In the Babylonian Exodus, the prediction was that this would not happen; indeed, the pilgrims would be supplied with the richest of fare, without cost and in abundance. Such provision is in stark contrast to the one given in the Exodus from Egypt. This Second Exodus also has a divine marriage promise that will come about through the covenant God made with David, i.e., to re-establish Israel and

---

[29] Texts from Zechariah are quoted in the New Testament in the following passages: Zech. 9:9 "the king comes to Zion humble and riding a donkey" is cited in Matt. 21:5 and John 12:15; Zech. 11:13 "30 pieces of silver thrown into the house of the Lord" is cited in Matt 27:9; Zech. 12:10 "looking on him whom they have pierced" is cited in John 19:37 and Rev 1:7; and Zech. 13:7 "the shepherd is struck, and the sheep are scattered" is cited in Matt 26:31 and Mark 14:27.

make her a blessing to the nations, indicating that it is correct to identify the suffering servant with his descendant. God says of David:

> Incline your ear, and come to me; hear, that your soul may live; and I will make with you an everlasting covenant, my steadfast, sure love for David. Behold, I made him a witness to the peoples, a leader and commander for the peoples. ⁵ Behold, you shall call a nation that you do not know, and a nation that did not know you shall run to you, because of the LORD your God, and of the Holy One of Israel, for he has glorified you. (Isa. 55:3–5)

So, this predicted Babylonian Exodus fulfils the promises made to the son of David; and it is the king's suffering and death that have brought about a deliverance in which the Gentile nations are summoned to share.

The Exodus theme is taken up again when Isaiah describes the great joy felt in Jerusalem on learning that God had redeemed the captives from Babylon. She "shall go out in joy and be led forth in peace". Nature is transformed, and the mountains and the hills burst into song, and the trees clap their hands (v12). For the argument I am making, i.e., the central importance of the Exodus motif for biblical understanding, the words of Isaiah in chapter 55 are most interesting:

> For you shall go out in joy and be led forth in peace; the mountains and the hills before you shall break forth into singing, and all the trees of the field shall clap their hands. Instead of the thorn shall come up the cypress; instead of the brier shall come up the myrtle; and it shall make a name for the LORD, *an everlasting sign that shall not be cut off.* (Isa. 55:12–13 emphasis added)

So, the redeeming activity of God in delivering His people from captivity will be an everlasting sign. It will endure forever, for it is a sign "that shall not be cut off". Can the importance of Exodus be stated more clearly?

Isaiah 55 is about how God keeps covenant with David. The passage does not stand alone as a new subject. It is linked to the Babylonian Exodus theme found in chapters 52 and 53, endorsing the suggestion that the servant is the promised Davidic king who, instead of being exalted with pomp through military conquest, establishes a far more glorious spiritual kingdom based on truth and peace.

Isaiah 60 The Call to Repentance

The following chapters in Isaiah are full of calls to repentance, not only to Israel but also to the nations which were sprinkled with the blood of the servant. The theme of the Babylonian Exodus returns in chapter 60, with the call:

> Arise, shine, for your light has come, and the glory of the LORD has risen upon you. For behold, darkness shall cover the earth, and thick darkness the peoples; but the LORD will arise upon you, and his glory will be seen upon you. And nations shall come to your light, and kings to the brightness of your rising. (Isa. 60:1–3)

The chapter lists how the nations respond to God's call to join Israel in being God's people. And the outcome of this salvation will be:

> The sun shall be no more your light by day, nor for brightness shall the moon give you light; the LORD will be your everlasting light, and your God will be your glory. Your sun shall no more go down, nor your moon withdraw itself; for the LORD will be your everlasting light, and your days of mourning shall be ended. Your people shall all be righteous; they shall possess the land forever, the branch of my planting, the work of my hands, that I might be glorified. The least one shall become a clan, and the smallest one a mighty nation; I am the LORD; in its time I will hasten it. (Isa. 60:19–22)

The Servant's 'Other Work'

Chapter 61 starts with the servant of the Lord explaining his message. He says that:

> The Spirit of the Lord GOD is upon me, because the LORD has anointed me to bring good news to the poor; he has sent me to bind up the brokenhearted, to proclaim liberty to the captives, and the opening of the prison to those who are bound; to proclaim the year of the LORD's favour, and the day of

> vengeance of our God; to comfort all who mourn; to grant to those who mourn in Zion— to give them a beautiful headdress instead of ashes, the oil of gladness instead of mourning, the garment of praise instead of a faint spirit; that they may be called oaks of righteousness (Isa. 61:1–3)

In the rest of the chapter, Isaiah foretells the final completion of this redemption, i.e., the lives of people from all nations will be transformed as they come out of the darkness of the rule of foreign gods into the light of the one, true, living God. The greatest transformation that takes place is that:

> he has clothed me with the garments of salvation; he has covered me with the robe of righteousness, as a bridegroom decks himself like a priest with a beautiful headdress, and as a bride adorns herself with her jewels. (Isa. 61:10)

Isaiah foretells that, as the community of exiles is rescued from captivity in Babylon, it will leave its sin and shame and be presented as a bride fit for her husband. This is the reparation event spoken of in Isaiah 53! He predicts that the Divine Marriage motif (the goal of the Exodus from Egypt) will at long last be achieved! This will be the pinnacle of the New Creation when all things will be made new. The theme continues in Isaiah 62:4–6.

Space does not allow an adequate exegesis of chapters 54–66. Indeed, Isaiah 40–66 deserves the closest reading. I have merely sought to show how powerful the Exodus theme, achieved through a descendant of David, is throughout the book of Isaiah. It is this rich theme that the apostles wove into their own writings to reveal the most glorious Exodus of all. This is the New Exodus; and it was this narrative that John the Baptist, Jesus, and the apostles followed.

Conclusion

We have seen how Zechariah, the prophet of Israel's faltering return from exile, takes up the themes of Isaiah's Babylonian Exodus promises and shows why they have been delayed and how they will eventually he fulfilled. He adds to the material that Isaiah has left and contributes imagery that will become part of the New Testament presentation of Jesus' work of saving His people from the kingdom of darkness. These passages, which are quoted in the New Testament, show how the Old Testament material concerning the promised

Jesus and the Exodus

New Exodus is the foundation stone that the message of the New Testament is built on. Also, we have traced the importance of the Second Exodus theme, found throughout Isaiah, and asked the question why this was not fulfilled as promised. Our answer was that, yet again, Israel chose other gods in preference to the God who loved her and rescued her at great price. This is the pattern of Israel's behaviour throughout the scriptures, and it again brought judgement on her with the promised blessing being withheld. She did return from exile but was not blessed with all those glorious predictions that Isaiah and the other prophets had made. What we have seen is that the promises of a second exodus continued to be the centre of Israel's hope and that it would bring to fruition all the unfulfilled promises. Tragically, it laid dormant because she has continued to be under the covenant curses warned of in Deuteronomy 32:23–25. Thus, The Exodus narrative remains to be completed, and we will see how powerful and essential this paradigm is to understand the completion of God's salvation. This will be achieved through the Good Shepherd who gave His life for His sheep, Jesus, the Christ, the Son of David (Rom. 1:1–6).

Chapter 15 The Exodus Heritage

As I have explained, the Egyptian Exodus event is like the DNA of scripture. It is from the unique encounter Israel had with her God that the course of biblical revelation flows, and all aspects of this amazing process and the teachings they bequeathed to both the Jews and the Church have their roots in what God did in those incredible days. I want to survey the extent of the heritage that the Exodus event bequeathed to the nation, then to the Church, and then to the wider world.

God had, of course, revealed Himself to different individuals throughout the book of Genesis, but none of those events came anywhere near to the significance of the Exodus revelation. This one event revealed truths about God that no previous disclosure had given.

God had revealed Himself to Abraham and promised him a son; but his descendants were totally disloyal to God, worshipping the gods of Egypt and rejecting Him by not circumcising their children (Ezek. 20). Yet God still comes to their rescue. No previous event had revealed God to be so patient, forgiving, and loyal as this event did. Without the Exodus event, our knowledge of Him would have been the bare minimum. In fact, the nature of the new relationship that Abraham had with God had not been defined other than that He had made a covenant with him and promised that his offspring would be protected. It is the Exodus event that clarified this relationship for, in preparation for it, God told Moses to command Pharoah: "Israel is my son, my firstborn, and I said to you, 'Let my son go that he may serve] me" (Exod. 4:22–23). From this we can see that the nature of the covenantal relationship, established in Genesis 15, is one of adopted sonship. By this relationship, Israel became God's firstborn, the one who is honoured to carry his Father's name. This is a term that was henceforth to be used throughout Israel's history to describe people who are called into a special relationship with God, so the king is God's firstborn (Ps. 89:27, see also Jer. 31:9; Zech. 12:10; Rom. 8:29; Col. 1:15; 18:23; Rev. 1:5).

The Law and the Honor of God

It was also in the Exodus event that God disclosed His character in a way that made His nature clear, disclosing what He despises and what He loves. The ten commandments do this in a way that had never been done before. God revealed that He is jealous over how people view Him. He hates idolatry, and He said that those who worship idols hate their Creator (Exod. 20:3–6). This jealousy carries a meaning not often assigned to the word. It is the right kind of jealousy, like how any husband would be expected to feel if someone sought to seduce his wife. It is jealousy based on love and it does not seek to control as the normal meaning of the word suggests. It wants to give love and receive love from the one to whom he has given his oath. He promises to take no other woman but to love and protect his wife until death.

God's name is holy and must not be used in vain (Exod. 20:7). This is not focusing on the way the ungodly speak of God, offensive as it is, but about misrepresenting Him and swearing falsely by His name. The name that is so sacred is the Hebrew name Yahweh, which is normally translated into English as LORD. When you see this capitalized term in the Bible, it is translating this sacred name. It is so sacred that the Hebrew scribes added consonants to the name when it occurred in scripture, making it impossible to pronounce so that no one could speak the name by mistake. They believed that even taking this name upon their lips defiled the name, taking it in vain. Something else that is sacred is the seventh day of creation. This is the day that God set apart for His people to rest and worship, and it must be honoured and practiced (Exod. 20:8–11).

The first five commandments are all elaborated on, explaining why they are important. Why breaking these commandments offends God has to be explained to the people, for other gods have no concerns over how their devotees behave. The Jews had been in Egypt for 400 years and had not held to the traditions of their ancestors' faith. They had lived under the control of Pharaoh and his gods. The generation that was rescued from Egypt had to be taught from scratch about the God who had saved them. Sadly, even though they had experienced this mighty act of salvation, they soon turned from Him to serve the Egyptian gods again.

The Law and Human Relations

The second section of the ten commandments is about human relationships, especially those that protect families. You shall honour your parents (Exod. 20:12), you shall not murder (Exod. 20:13) or commit adultery (Exod. 20:14). The next command is you shall not steal (Exod. 20:15) and you shall not commit false witness (Exod. 20:16), nor shall you covet your neighbour's wife (Exod. 20:17) nor any of his possessions that he has worked to acquire for his family. This preservation of the family, its resources and reputation, is an expression of God's concern that the family is sacrosanct and is an institution given by Himself.

The rest of the Decalogue displays His concern for the protection of people's rights and safety. They are laws that are aimed at protecting and caring for vulnerable people. So, in an age when the spoils of war included the taking of slaves, laws were given to protect these unfortunate people (Exod. 21; Deut. 20:1,10). Young girls who became pregnant could not be deserted by the man responsible; he had to marry her and care for the mother and child (Exod. 22:16). Individuals were protected from wilful gossip (Exod. 23:1). The poor had to be cared for and not exploited in their weakness (Exod. 23:6; Lev. 25:35). The immigrant must be treated with care and respect. The Jewish community should be eager to do this because they had suffered when they were aliens in Egypt, so they of all people should understand the needs of the foreigner (Exod. 19:33–34). Public health is an issue for all communities, especially those on a long pilgrimage; so how to deal with lepers was specified (Lev. 14:1), as were bodily discharges (Lev. 15:1). The management of the land is important for all communities, especially those living in places prone to drought. Boundaries must be respected (Deut. 19:14) and the land must be rested (Lev. 19:23). The land, out of concern for the environment, was so important for the wellbeing of families and the community as a whole that, if it had to be sold to raise finances to support the family, it could not be bought outright; it was effectively leased and had to be returned to its rightful owner when the year of Jubilee was reached (Lev. 19:23). Finally, guidance was given on relationships within the community. They were to love one another (Lev. 19:9). A young bridegroom was not allowed to go to war in his first year of marriage (Deut. 24:5) so that he could build the strong foundations required for a lasting marriage and to father a child in case he was killed, leaving his wife a childless widow. Men were not to have sex with men (Lev. 20:13) and they were not to consult with mediums (Lev. 20:6). The reason God gave these regulations was given in Leviticus:

> You must be sure to obey all my statutes and regulations, so that the land to which I am about to bring you to take up residence does not vomit you out. You must not walk in the

statutes of the nations which I am about to drive out before you, because they have done all these things and I am filled with disgust against them. (Lev. 20:22–23 NET)

In other words, the Lord is not like other gods, and Israel is to be like Him and not like them. It is not that other religions did not have their sacred traditions and teachings, but no other nation had been given them through the direct intervention of the living God, who acted in redemption in history and through verifiable evidence. Israel's very birth and continued existence is evidence that in the Exodus something profound and eternal took place. It is said that Queen Victoria asked one of her bishops how we know that God exists, and he answered, "The Jews, Mam".

Israel's Law and the Nations

Up until now, we have been looking at the theological heritage that the Exodus has bestowed and how it is the prism through which redemptive history should be understood. But, in the giving of the Law, a gift was given that was not only for Israel but for the rest of humanity. It was this legal framework that has guided the Jews for the past 4,000 years. Its moral principles moulded the ethics of the early church and, as the gospel spread and nations embraced its message, it influenced the way their national laws were reframed. So, vast numbers of the world's population, even nations that had never embraced Christianity, were indirectly blessed with that gift given to Israel. International law was mostly framed by nations that had accepted the truths of biblical Law, i.e., every person is valued by God and justice is the right of every human being. We still have to trace the theological development of The Exodus narrative, but its judicial value can be taken as established by the widely accepted fact that the Law of Moses, given to Israel during her Exodus from Egypt, shaped the recognition of the dignity of all human beings like no other document.

The Exodus and Modern Culture.

The Law's influence on culture and human consciousness has been huge, and it has equipped people across the world to believe that change is possible.

It was the story of the Exodus that galvanized countless thousands of black people who had been sold into slavery. It gave them hope in their desperate plight as leaders taught them that, as God had delivered Israel from bondage under Pharaoh, so He could deliver them from the oppression of their owners. Their hope was expressed in their songs, which spoke not only of Israel's experience but also of the salvation they believed God would bring them into. They came to understand that He hates oppression and wants all people to dwell in freedom and peace.

The Exodus story became the inspiration of Liberation theologians as they articulated the injustices of the political, financial, social, and religious systems that millions lived under. Israel's experience became the paradigm that gave not only their teaching authority but also their call to the underprivileged to stand together and use their combined voices to make their dissatisfaction known. Some of their leaders were assassinated by those who saw the movement would rob them of their power and authority. This biblically inspired movement has transformed nations around the world and given birth to a new hope for countless millions of ordinary people who live under oppression.

These social and political changes have been massive; but the greatest impact of the Exodus is in it being a model of the birth of a new community of people who have looked to Jesus as their Redeemer and been subsequently transformed by Him.

Sacrificial Truth in Two Parts.

The next part of this chapter would naturally have fitted into chapter 11, where we considered the Egyptian Exodus and the nature of the Passover. I indicated then that there was further important evidence that would support the case I was making, for it being not only an event of redemption but also one of atonement.

I have kept this section for now and not included it in the section dealing with the Egyptian Exodus because its historic location is the Babylonian Exodus. The prophet Ezekiel tells of the construction of a magnificent temple that not only replaces the temple of Solomon destroyed in the Babylonian invasion but also overshadows it in terms of size and significance.

As we have seen, Israel forsook Yahweh when she was in Egypt. She went after other gods and became an adulteress. She, as much as the Egyptians, needed atonement to protect her from judgement. And that is what the blood of the lambs did; it diverted the anger of the Lord from the firstborn of Israel.

Many scholars claim there was no atoning significance in the lambs' blood. They claim that the sacrifice was about redemption and nothing more. But the blood was displayed on the doorposts and lintels of their homes and, when the angel of death saw it, He passed over their houses and did not visit to take the lives of their firstborn. Now, if that is not propitiation (i.e., atonement), then the word needs to be redefined, for averting wrath is at the heart of the meaning of the word. For this reason, I hold that there was atonement in the original Passover sacrifice. However, after the Egyptian Exodus event, the Law separated what was achieved in the Exodus into two strands (i.e., redemption and atonement). The annual Passover was celebrated as a memorial for the Exodus redemption, and nothing more; but the Day of Atonement became the prescribed annual feast to make atonement for Israel's ongoing sin.

Passover Changes

It was Ezekiel who foresaw that the temple, which had been totally destroyed prior to the Babylonian exile, would be rebuilt by a descendant of King David (Ezek. 45:8,17–22, see also Zech. 6:12, who wrote later than Ezekiel). This king would not only build the temple but would provide all the sacrifices needed to sanctify it. The final (eschatological) Passover that the Davidic prince would celebrate would have a far greater significance than the original Passover. Ezekiel said that the Day of Atonement sacrifices, in greater abundance than was normal, would be offered during the celebration of the Passover, not on the Day of Atonement as would be expected. So, the prophet of the exile predicted that the Messiah would bring the elements of the two feasts back into one feast, and the Passover would once again achieve atonement and redemption in the same event. However, the event that fulfilled this prediction was going to be far greater than Ezekiel could ever have appreciated; for the sacrifice would be the Lord's Firstborn, the Messiah Himself.

Ezekiel predicted that:

> In the first month, on the fourteenth day of the month, you shall celebrate the Feast of the Passover, and for seven days unleavened bread shall be eaten. On that day the prince shall provide for himself and all the people of the land a young bull for a sin offering. And on the seven days of the festival he shall provide as a burnt offering to the LORD seven young

bulls and seven rams without blemish, on each of the seven days; and a male goat daily for a sin offering. And he shall provide as a grain offering an ephah for each bull, an ephah for each ram, and a hin of oil to each ephah. In the seventh month, on the fifteenth day of the month and for the seven days of the feast, he shall make the same provision for sin offerings, burnt offerings, and grain offerings, and for the oil. (Ezek. 45:21–25)

This passage describes how, after the Jews had returned from exile, the Son of David would provide all the sacrifices for the promised temple. These would be needed to purge it from pollution. He provided "seven young bulls and seven rams without blemish. On each of the seven days a male goat was offered for a sin offering". This was an offering far greater than the normal sin offering on the Day of Atonement. Indeed, it was many times greater; for not only was it more than what was offered on the one Day, it was offered on seven consecutive days. This overlooked text is laying a vitally important foundation for our understanding of what Jesus' death achieved.[30] Ezekiel, who had preached to the nation that her judgement was the result of disregarding the Law of God, is doing the very same thing. He takes it upon himself to change the Law concerning the sacrificial system and moves the sacrifices for atonement from the Day of Atonement to the Passover. He can be intending only one thing by this action. He is saying that the final Passover will be like the first, an event when Israel's sins are atoned for. If this is correct, then the first Passover was an atoning sacrifice as I have suggested.

Josiah and the Passover.

But it is possible that Ezekiel was not the first to bring the two feasts together again. In 2 King 23, the account is given of Josiah learning about the discovery of the book of the Law and responding to its instructions. He had led a great

---

[30] This merger was noted by J.D.G. Dunn, "Paul's Understanding of the Death of Jesus" in *Reconciliation and Hope, Essays presented to L. L. Morris on his 60th birthday*, ed. R. Brooks (London: Paternoster, 1974)125-141, but without recognising its significance. In fact, Dunn's observation made in an academic paper is completely missing from his commentaries where he seeks to understand the significance of Christ's death. The merger was also noted by R.E. Nixon, *The Exodus in the New Testament*, (London: Tyndale Press, 1963) 1ff.

reform in the land, putting away all the things that were an abomination to the Lord. It would be natural for this reform to conclude with a celebration of the Day of Atonement as an acknowledgment of the nation's sins; but we don't find this. What we do find is that:

> ... the king commanded all the people, "Keep the Passover to the LORD your God, as it is written in this Book of the Covenant." For no such Passover had been kept since the days of the judges who judged Israel, or during all the days of the kings of Israel or of the kings of Judah. But in the eighteenth year of King Josiah this Passover was kept to the LORD in Jerusalem. (2 Kings 23:21–23)

From this account, it is possible that the atoning element of the Passover was identified by the reforming king, or one of his predecessors, and his action had some influence on the understanding of what the Davidic king of Ezekiel 45 was to achieve.

Conclusion

We have seen that the gift of the Law to Israel in the Exodus event blessed not only her but all the peoples of the earth. Understanding the development of key elements of the Exodus from Egypt will help us to see how these themes are found in future national redemptive (Exodus) events. In the Egyptian Exodus, the Gentiles were welcomed if they repented of their sins and sought to live under the Law. This allowed them to live within Israel but not as full citizens. To receive the status of citizenship, they had to accept circumcision. We also saw that an important feature of the promised Second Exodus, which took place when God rescued Israel from Babylon, was that Gentiles would be welcomed into the New Covenant Community as equals with believing Jews without circumcision and without having to convert to the Jewish faith. We also saw that the Exodus event justified God as the promise-keeping God. This was yet a further step in the unfolding of the great doctrine of justification. We also saw that, while atonement and redemption were eventually separated into two feasts, the Exodus shows us how in both the Egyptian and Babylonian Exoduses they dwell together as one salvation event. We will see that none of these themes remain static but will grow and gather greater meaning and significance, always pointing forward to a far greater Exodus and a far greater Day of Atonement that took place in the final Passover sacrifice. These historical events, with their developing theological insights, are the essential elements of The Exodus narrative, which is the mega-narrative of biblical teaching and understanding.

Chapter 16 The New Exodus in the New Testament

As we have seen, the dominant theme of the prophecy of Isaiah was that of a promised deliverance of Israel from Babylon. Amongst the promises associated with this deliverance were the promises that Yahweh would take Israel as His bride. This salvation would lead to a new creation, where the effects of man's sin on creation, which came as a result of the curse, would be removed.

We have seen Zechariah, who ministered to those who returned from exile, was faced with explaining why the glorious predictions of transformation and exaltation of Israel had not been fulfilled. His message was that they had not been fulfilled because of Israel's continued hardness of heart. Despite this, Zechariah proclaimed that Isaiah's predictions would still be fulfilled.

The New Exodus and the Gospels

The uncompleted fulfilment of the promises of the Babylonian Exodus were taken up by the New Testament writers who showed how Jesus was their fulfilment. This fulfilment is the New Testament Exodus it is the Third or New Exodus, and it differs from the Egyptian and Babylonian ones in that it was not about a future event, but they declared that it had already taken place.

John the Baptist and the New Exodus

John the Baptist began his ministry citing Isa. 40:3, which was Isaiah's call to Israel to prepare herself for the coming, redeeming, visitation of God.

> A voice cries: "In the wilderness prepare the way for the Lord;
> make straight in the desert a highway for our God." (Isa. 40:3)

John was saying that he was the messenger appointed by God to tell Israel that the day of fulfilment had arrived! The nation had endured great pent-up pain and disappointment for over 400 years (since before the last book of the Old Testament canon); so, crowds, in their thousands, gathered to hear him. By linking himself to Isaiah's promise of a servant who would prepare the way for the coming of the Lord (Luke 3:4–6), his message focused on one of Isaiah's promises which reignited hope of rescue from the nation's Roman occupiers. This Old Testament text is so important for understanding the message of Jesus that all four gospels cite it at the beginning of their respective presentations (Matt. 3:3; Lk 3:4–6; Mark 1:2–3; John 1:23). As shown by the way the people responded, the citation of the statement encouraged their hearts and minds to expect that the Servant of the Lord was about to come and bring to completion the promised New Exodus. The fact that Isa. 40:3 is the only Old Testament text to be quoted by all four gospels at the start of each narrative shows how important it was not only for them as writers of biographies of Jesus but also for the Church for whom they wrote.

But John was not claiming that he was the agent of this coming transformation; he was only "the voice", the messenger, preparing the way of the Lord. He made it very clear that the Messiah was Jesus, and He would become their Lord and Master. John stated that he was not even worthy to act as the servant of Jesus who undid His sandals (Matt. 3:2) or to be baptised by Him (Matt. 3:14). But Jesus insisted that he did, and when He came up out of the water the heavens opened, and the Spirit came down and rested on Him. The words rang out: "This is my beloved Son, with whom I am well pleased". These echo the words of Isaiah 11:2 and Isaiah 42:1, making it clear that Jesus was the One designated to bring the New Exodus to its completion.

John the Baptist Questions Jesus Concerning the New Exodus

When John was in prison and facing imminent death, he could not understand why judgement had not come. So, he sent disciples to Jesus to ask Him if He really was the Messiah. John seems to have expected that judgement would come with the appearance of God's Messiah, as suggested in some of the prophets. Understandably, facing imminent death for his criticism of Herod, John expected the day of judgement would be the event through which God would vindicate him, with Herod himself becoming the focus of judgement. He could not understand why Jesus' message was not about this imminent event. But Jesus, quoting from Isaiah 42:7, replied:

> Go and tell John what you have seen and heard: the blind receive their sight, the lame walk, lepers are cleansed, and the deaf hear, the dead are raised up, the poor have good news preached to them. (Luke 7:22).

In this response, Jesus was telling John that the miracles He was doing were evidence that He was the expected Messiah. He endorsed His role as the Son of David when He told Jews who wanted Him to give them a sign: "Destroy this temple, and in three days I will raise it up" (John 2:19). In saying this, Jesus was claiming to be the King who Ezekiel had predicted would build the eschatological temple (Ezek. 34:24; 45:17, see also Zech. 6:12).[31] Again, like the prediction of Ezekiel that the Son of David would provide the sacrifices for the Eschatological Passover, He was providing the sacrifice but, against all expectation, it was to be Himself. He did this by setting His face like flint to go to Jerusalem. when He arrived at the start of the Jewish Passover, He controlled events in such a way that He was arrested and slain during the Passover week. Indeed, John's account uses a different calendar from the synoptic writers that makes Jesus to die at the very time that the Passover lambs were slain.

Jesus and the New Exodus

From the beginning of His ministry Jesus endorsed His own status when He went into the synagogue and addressed the meeting by reading from the scroll of Isaiah (Isa. 61:1). He read:

> The Spirit of the Lord is upon me, because he has anointed me
> to proclaim good news to the poor. He has sent me to proclaim
> liberty to the captives and recovering of sight to the blind, to
> set at liberty those who are oppressed (Luke 4:18).

There was no possibility that the hearers would have misunderstand the significance of this reading, for Jesus added: "Today this Scripture has been fulfilled in your hearing" (Luke 4:21). Using the passage in Isaiah, He was announcing the New Exodus when He, as the Son of David (Matt. 1:1), the Servant of the Lord, would bring the prophet's promises to fulfilment.

Jesus and His Public Announcements.

John records a series of claims that Jesus made which are linked to both the Egyptian and Babylonian Exoduses. The first is found in Exodus 3:14-15 when

---

[31] The One called the "BRANCH" is the Messiah, the son of David—the One who will return to occupy the Temple of God (as we will see in Ezekiel). God gave to David the plans for the Temple built by Solomon which also served as the plans for those who rebuilt it in Zerubbabel's time.

Jesus and the Exodus

Moses stood before the burning bush. After being told he is to return to Egypt and deliver the Israelites from bondage, Moses asked God who he should say sent him. God replied that he should say: "I AM has sent me to you...This is my name forever, and this is my memorial from generation to generation".

This was the beginning of the Exodus narrative and was when God revealed His name. This point is hugely important in the biblical story and defines the rest of the biblical understanding about who God is.[32]

John brings together a collection of Jesus' sayings in which He uses this "I Am" formula. Scholars see these sayings to be echoing Moses' encounter with God in the burning bush (Exod 3:14 with John 8:58)

Jesus said to them, "I tell you the solemn truth, before Abraham came into existence, I am!" (John 8:58 NET)

This use of the title at the burning bush is about God assuring Moses and His people that He is more than able to meet their needs in the impending Exodus from Egypt.

John records seven sayings which echo Isaiah's record of when God again describes Himself with the designation "I Am":

> Jesus said to them, "I am the bread of life. The one who comes to me will never go hungry, and the one who believes in me will never be thirsty." (John 6:35 NET)

> Then Jesus spoke out again, "I am the light of the world! The one who follows me will never walk in darkness but will have the light of life." (John 8:12 NET)

> I am the door. If anyone enters through me, he will be saved, and will come in and go out, and find pasture. (John 10:9 NET)

---

[32] See Catrin H. Williams, "I am He": *The Interpretation of 'ANI HU' in Jewish and Early Christian Literature: 113* (Wissenschaftliche Untersuchungen zum Neuen Testament 2. Reihe, 1999).

> I am the good shepherd. The good shepherd lays down his life for the sheep. (John 10:11 NET)
>
> Jesus said to her, "I am the resurrection and the life. The one who believes in me will live even if he dies." (John 11:25 NET)
>
> Jesus replied, "I am the way, and the truth, and the life. No one comes to the Father except through me." (John 14:6 NET)
>
> I am the true vine, and my Father is the gardener. (John 15:1 NET)

The important thing to note for this study is that all but one of these sayings are linked to God's repeated promises throughout the book of Isaiah. John shows that Jesus turns to these sayings about God caring for Israel throughout the forthcoming Second Exodus. Here, in John's Gospel, Jesus makes the same promises to His disciples as they participate in the forthcoming New Exodus.

Jesus' Last Passover

But the most important evidence for how Jesus viewed the Exodus is given in the way He wanted to celebrate His last meal with the disciples. Each gospel writer includes the celebration of the Last Supper, which was the Jewish Passover meal.[33] While many sections of the Church have gone on to celebrate the Last Supper (calling it Holy Communion, the Eucharist, The Lord's Table, or The Lord's Supper, all terms referring to the same event but containing different theological meanings) as a weekly, monthly, quarterly, or even annual celebration, what must not be missed is what the "do this" instruction refers to. It is the Passover. In the context in which this instruction was given it was a command to cease celebrating the deliverance from Egypt under Moses and, in its place, to celebrate the New Exodus, which the death of Jesus was about to secure. From this, I conclude that 'The Lord's Table' is not the

---

[33] Of course, John does not record the same details of the celebration that the Synoptic Gospels give. He records a discourse that the synoptic writers chose to leave out of their accounts (Jn 14–17). The discourse focuses on the spiritual meaning of the rite. John's discourse is very much part of the same Passover event, John 13:21–38. In place of the Breaking of Bread, John has given the discourse in which Jesus says that He is the Bread of Life and He explained the need of the disciples to be nourished by this spiritual food, see John 6:25–59.

source of grace, for neither the Jews nor the Old Testament ever said it was. If it was that, then it would need to be celebrated every day of our lives. It is the occasion of remembrance and, just like God instituted it as an annual event for the Jews to remember how God had saved them on a set day each year, so the Christian celebration should be about remembering the salvation secured by Christ's death for His people. In saying this, I do not want to suggest that these extra weekly, monthly, or whenever, practices should be abandoned, but that no more significance should be read into them than the Jews would have read into their Passover celebrations.

But what Jesus said has further significance. It would be blasphemy for any man to change the Passover in such a radical way. The only One who could instruct this change is the One who originally instituted it, and that is the God of the Exodus. Therefore, by daring to reinterpret the Passover in this way, i.e., by putting Himself at the centre of the event, Jesus demonstrates that He is not only the Lord of the Sabbath but the Lord of redemption, i.e., Jehovah Himself. For Him to have changed the meaning of the feast in such a radical way if He was a mere creature, would have been blasphemy. But, because He did do this, He demonstrates that He saw Himself to be God who alone could redeem His people.

James and the New Exodus

We have seen that Jesus predicted He would build the temple in three days, meaning that He would rise from the dead after three days (John 3:19–20). He thus saw that His death would end the ministry of the temple and would bring about the promised end time temple predicted in Ezek. 40–45. Of course, He was not speaking of Herod's temple being destroyed, as the Jews thought, but the destruction of His body and the emergence of the Church, His spiritual body, out of His death. The fulfilment of the building of the new temple was at the spiritual, not material, level. This spiritual fulfilment was confirmed by James when he acquitted Peter for baptising uncircumcised Gentiles. James did this because he saw that the promise to build the tent of David, i.e., the temple that David had provided the materials for, was now truly fulfilled in the establishment of a spiritual temple to which the Gentiles have the right of entry.

> And with this the words of the prophets agree, just as it is written, "After this I will return, and I will rebuild the tent of

David that has fallen; I will rebuild its ruins, and I will restore it, that the remnant of mankind may seek the Lord, and all the Gentiles who are called by my name," says the Lord, who makes these things. (Acts 15:15–17; see also 1 Cor. 3:16; 1 Pet 2:4–10)

This statement by James (Acts 15:12–21) demonstrates that the fulfilment of the Babylonian Exodus promises, concerning the rebuilding of the temple in their New Exodus context, were spiritual realities. This typological principle of interpreting the prophecies is found consistently throughout the New Testament and, as we have just noted, Jesus Himself authorized such typological interpretation when He said He would raise the temple after three days.

So, we see that, throughout His ministry, Jesus unashamedly linked Himself to the promises of the New Exodus. He was the Bridegroom of the New Exodus, highlighted by the parables He used to teach the people of the coming Kingdom of God. In these parables, He described the coming kingdom as being like a marriage, and He put himself at its centre by saying that He is the bridegroom (Matt. 9:15; 22:1–12 and parallels). Such an audacious claim is normally overlooked as to what it contributed to the early church's understanding of the person of Jesus. This affirmation of His status was witnessed to by John the Baptist (John 3:29) and is powerful evidence of a very early advanced Christology. This is because, throughout the Old Testament and into the Jewish Intertestamental Literature, the bridal couple is always Yahweh and Israel. Yet here, Jesus unashamedly steps into the role that would be jealously defended by all Jews, that Yahweh would marry Israel. But, here, Jesus says He had come for His bride and would die to redeem her. No early believer would say that Yahweh stepped aside for the Son because they knew that Jesus, the Son, is Yahweh! Therefore, the often-made claim that an advanced Christology is evidence of the lateness of the texts is therefore inadmissible evidence of the early church's limited understanding of Christ. It cannot be upheld. Such an argument is circular, for it defines evidence in such a way as to remove anything that challenges the premise of a high Christology being held by the apostolic community, thus destroying, or nullifying the evidence on the grounds of prejudice.

Conclusion

We have examined statements and actions by Jesus to see how He viewed the New Exodus paradigm, and through this lens we have discovered Exodus truths that have previously been hidden in the text of the gospels. These often-overlooked insights confirm that we are appreciating and benefitting from The Exodus narrative. What is especially significant is that Jesus began His ministry with the proclamation that Isaiah's Second Exodus prophecy was being fulfilled at last, and it concludes with Him not only giving new meaning to the Passover celebration but also embracing the necessity of His death to make it happen. We also noted how Jesus intertwined the I Am statements from Isaiah into His own self-identification, indicating He was fully conscious of His New Exodus mission.

Chapter 17 Paul and the New Exodus

We saw in chapter 4 that Paul structured his letter around 18 quotations from the book of Isaiah. This gave us unique insight into how the Old Testament, and Isaiah especially, controlled the mind of Paul. As the Exodus was so important to the Jewish community and he has argued how it has been fulfilled in the life and death of Jesus, it would be surprising if he went anywhere else other than the Old Testament to how His death achieved this.

The most important text that Paul has written about the fulfilment of the Passover type is found in his letter to the Romans. There are echoes of the original Passover in Romans 3:21–26. I want to show you that Paul uses key words in v24, 25, which evoked the Egyptian Passover. I include the passage below, and have underlined the key terms so that I can comment on the original Greek that Paul used to show what the translated English rendering should be making clear:

> and are justified by his grace as a gift, through the (1) redemption that is in Christ Jesus, whom God (2) put forward as a (3) propitiation by his blood, to be received by faith. This was to show God's righteousness, because in his divine forbearance he had (4) passed over (5) former sins.

Paul speaks of the sacrifice of Christ as being (1 *apolytrōseōs*) 'redemption'. This redemption is 'in Christ Jesus', i.e., in what He achieved through His death. Paul says that Jesus' death was (2 *proetheto*) 'publicly displayed'. Only the Passover was publicly displayed, when its blood was daubed on the doorposts and lintels of the Jewish homes. Jesus' blood, like that of the lambs in the Egyptian Exodus, was both an atonement and propitiation (3 *hilastērion*). But unlike the first Passover, when the angel of the Lord passed over the Jewish homes and spared the firstborn, there was no passing over the sins of the children of Abraham in this Exodus. Here, the beloved Son died for all of His people. God no longer passed over (4 *paresin*) His people's former sins (5 *progegonotōn*) for in the eschatological Passover, which Jesus' death was, all their sins were judged.

This is not a debt to be settled at a future date; but there, on the cross, God in Christ dealt with the issue of humanity's sin. Just as God ordered the public display of the blood of the lamb on each Jewish house in Egypt, so the blood of His firstborn Son was displayed for all to see on Calvary. This was the time that God visited their sins in judgement. These five important and technically significant terms are not found together anywhere else other than in the Passover. This fact alone suggests that Paul's model of Israel's deliverance from Egypt foreshadowed the New Covenant Community's rescue from the domain of Sin (i.e., Satan's kingdom). In other words, Paul sees Jesus' death as the sacrifice necessary to bring the New Exodus about.

Despite the fact that these terms are only found together in the Passover setting, few have recognised the setting of Romans 3:21–25. A few have identified individual terms such as 'redemption' as being linked with the Passover, but no one, to my knowledge, has seen the significance of the five terms being used together in this description. Their understanding has been deflected from the Passover setting because Paul calls the death of Christ an atonement. In their thinking, it was the Day of Atonement that could be the only setting. But, as we have seen, this proposed Day of Atonement setting has recently been questioned because the ceremony of the Day of Atonement took place in the Holy of Holies and could not be publicly displayed as the passage demands. However, when we recognise how Ezekiel had merged the Passover with the Day of Atonement (see Ezek. 45:18–25 and explanation given in chapter 15 on pages 130ff), the problem is solved. Atonement and redemption were typified in the Passover blood-offering. As at the first Passover, Christ's Passover offering was publicly displayed. for all to see.

Other Evidence

There are other pointers to the Passover and Christ's death in Romans. In Rom. 5, Paul says:

> For while we were still weak, at the right time Christ died for the ungodly. For one will die for a righteous person—though perhaps for a good person one would dare even to die—but God shows his love for us in that while we were still sinners, Christ died for us. Since, therefore, we have now been justified by his blood, much more shall we be saved by him from the wrath of God. For if while we were enemies we were

reconciled to God by the death of his Son, much more, now that we are reconciled, shall we be saved by his life. More than that, we also rejoice in God through our Lord Jesus Christ, through whom we have now received reconciliation. (Rom. 5:6–11)

The Old Testament shows that the right time for God's intervention was always when His people acknowledge that there is salvation in no one else but Him. It was in Egypt (Exod. 2:23) and Babylon (Isa. 49:8) that Israel saw her sin and weakness and, when she cried out to God for His deliverance, He stepped in and became her Redeemer. And here, where Paul is describing how humanity has come under the control of Satan with no hope of rescue, it is in this condition of utter weakness that the right time has come for salvation. In the Egyptian Exodus, the firstborn were spared and, in the Babylonian Exodus, a mysterious servant king was to suffer to make their release possible. But here, in the New Exodus, God finally shows His incredible love in giving His Son to save those who are, by personal choice, His enemies.

Whitley has noted Passover imagery in the phrase: "Since, therefore, we have now been justified by his blood, much more shall we be saved by him from the wrath of God".[34] (Rom. 5:9) Moses encouraged Israel not to fear God as He had shown His love for them in redeeming them from Egypt. Having done that, they had no need to fear Him when they encountered Him in the theophany of Sinai. He would keep them from judgement, i.e., the wrath of God.

This Passover theme is seen to continue into Romans 6, when Paul wrote:

> What shall we say then? Are we to continue in sin that grace may abound? By no means! How can we who died to sin still live in it? Do you not know that all of us who have been baptized into Christ Jesus were baptized into his death? We were buried therefore with him by baptism into death, in order

---

[34] 'The fact that in Rom. 5:9 the blood protects us from the future wrath of God again suggests a reference to the original Passover' D.E H. Whitley, 'Saint Paul's Thought on the Atonement,' *JTS* 8 (1957) 240-255. 250

that, just as Christ was raised from the dead by the glory of the Father, we too might walk in newness of life.

For if we have been united with him in a death like his, we shall certainly be united with him in a resurrection like his. We know that our old self was crucified with him in order that the body of sin might be brought to nothing, so that we would no longer be enslaved to sin. For one who has died has been set free from sin. Now if we have died with Christ, we believe that we will also live with him. We know that Christ, being raised from the dead, will never die again; death no longer has dominion over him. For the death he died he died to sin, once for all, but the life he lives he lives to God. So you also must consider yourselves dead to sin and alive to God in Christ Jesus (Rom. 6:1–11).

The German scholar, Warnack,[35] recognised that the background to what Paul is saying in the opening of Romans 6 is the Passover. I totally agree with this because, as we will see in chapter 21, Paul clearly links baptism with the Exodus of the Jews from Egypt. Just like Moses urged the Jews to follow a life of obedience now they had been delivered from Pharaoh's control, so Paul continually appeals to the churches to abandon their former way of life under the control of Sin (Satan) and live under the rule of the God who has redeemed them.

Explicit Evidence

Furthermore, Paul could not have been clearer about his model for interpreting the meaning and achievement of the death of Christ than when he wrote to the

---

[35] Warnack, V, 'Taufe und Hellsschehen Nach Rom 6,' ALW 111 2(1954) 284-366, Also see 'Die Taufe des Romerbriefes in der Neuren Theologischn Diskussion,' ALW 2(1958), 274 - 332. Also identified by Nixon, Robin Ernest, *The Exodus in The New Testament*, Tyndale Monographs, 4.4 (London: Tyndale Press, 1963)24; Knox, Wilfred, *St Paul and The Church Of The Gentiles* (Cambridge: Cambridge U.P, 1939).91; Cullmann, Oscar and J.K.S. Reid, *Baptism In The New Testament* (London: SCM, 1952) 48 and Wright, N.T. "The Letter to the Romans: Introduction, Commentary, and Reflections" *In the New Interpreter's Bible, Volume X, Acts-1 Corinthians*, edited by L.E. Keek, 39–70, Nashville, Abingdon, 2002. p 534.

Corinthians: "Christ, our Passover lamb, has been sacrificed" (1 Cor. 5:7), which is as clear a Passover picture that anyone could wish for.

Another indication of the importance of the New Exodus for Paul's Christology is found in 1 Corinthians where Paul, sharing what he had received from his predecessors in the faith, says:

> Now I would remind you, brothers, of the gospel I preached to you, which you received, in which you stand, and by which you are being saved, if you hold fast to the word I preached to you—unless you believed in vain.
>
> For I delivered to you as of first importance what I also received: that Christ died for our sins in accordance with the Scriptures, that he was buried, that he was raised on the third day in accordance with the Scriptures. (1 Cor. 15:1–4)

Paul's evidence that the scriptures predicted that Christ would rise on the third day has been sought for centuries without any convincing answer being given. But recently, a viable suggestion has been made regarding Jesus being called the "first fruits" in v20.[36] Now the first fruits are the first part of the new harvest, and this was brought to the temple to be waved before the Lord as a wave offering. In this way, thanks were given for the coming harvest and acknowledgement was made that it was God's gift to His people. The day this wave offering was to be made was three days after Passover (Lev. 23:11–15) In other words, as we will find as we continue our study, Paul again uses typology, and this method is not an occasional intrusion into his arguments, but it is the foundation of his theological understanding and teaching. So, Jesus, the Passover sacrifice, presented the fruit of His death to the Father three days after His Paschal sacrifice had been made. He is, therefore, the first fruits of the coming harvest, which will be the resurrection of His people (1 Cor. 15:12–23). Thus, a proper understanding of Paul's New Exodus theology is vitally important for a proper appreciation of his understanding of the person and work of Christ.

---

[36] F.F. Bruce, *1 and 2 Corinthians*. (Oliphants, London, 1961), and more recently Joel R. White, 'He was Raised on the Third Day According to the Scriptures' (1 Cor. 15:4): A Typological Interpretation Based on the Cultic Calendar in Leviticus 23' *TynB* 66(2015).

The Eschatological Temple

Temple language flows through both Testaments and it is richly employed by Paul and other apostles. Although the temple had been destroyed as a punishment for Israel's unfaithfulness, it was promised that it would be restored when God delivered the people from their Babylonian captivity. The promised, restored temple would be open for all nations to worship in and its membership would not be restricted to Jews (Isa. 2:2–5; 19:1–2; Acts 11; 15:12–21; 1 Cor 3:16; 6:19; Eph. 2:19–21). All who believe are living stones in this holy temple and have been appointed priests, like the firstborn after the Exodus from Egypt (Rom. 12:1–2; 1 Pet 4:10).

In other words, the priesthood of all believers is based on the Old Testament doctrine of the Exodus. We are priests because Christ, like the lamb, has died in our place. Just as God claimed all the firstborn as a community of priests, so He claims all those who have been redeemed through the death of a far greater sacrifice as His priestly people. So, the church is the church of the firstborn (Rom. 12:1–2; 15:16; cf. 1 Pet 2:4–5; Heb. 12:23; Rev. 1:5–6). Paul tenaciously defends the equal standing of believing Gentiles with believing Jews in this New Covenant Community. In this Community, all believers are priests, and, while some are called to be leaders, there is no hierarchy amongst them. The Gentile believers are not to submit to circumcision, for Abraham himself was not circumcised when God justified him (Gen. 15:6; cf. 17:9–14). Therefore, Paul argues, salvation was not achieved by circumcision but by having the same faith as Abraham, which was exemplified by total obedience (Rom. 4:9–12; 16–25).

The Great Acceptance

Paul had come to accept that the Jews, who boasted in their covenant with God, were no better than the Gentiles, for they had broken the law. This was not because they had failed to live a high enough moral standard but because they were part of the nation who, throughout its history, had gone after other gods. This is why Israel was called the harlot and was put away in exile (Ezek. 16:37–42).

When suing for peace or seeking alliances, Israel committed herself to the gods of the nations she negotiated with. In doing this, she rejected the LORD as God and His promise to protect her if she remained faithful to Him. God had promised that He would preserve a remnant community and, together with Gentiles who believed, He would form a New Covenant Community. They were to be a people who were circumcised in heart, which is what He had always wanted. Because they had turned from sin and idolatry, they would become the true, promised bride that the death of Christ secured for Himself (2 Cor. 11:2; Eph. 5:25–26).

The New Exodus and the Spirit

As the promises of the Babylonian Exodus spoke of the Spirit's work of leading, sustaining, and equipping (Joel 2:28), there could be no true fulfilment of the Exodus until these promises were met. It is likely that Paul (then, Saul) witnessed the outpouring of the Spirit at Pentecost in Jerusalem before he became a believer. If that was so, he could have reflected on Joel's words that the Spirit's presence in power was evidence that God's Kingdom had arrived (Joel 2:28), a connection that the apostle Peter made on that day (Acts 2:16–21).

Paul probably would have seen that the reception of the gospel message resulted in this outpouring, and this would have led him to expect similar results in the missionary work he eventually embarked on (Rom. 1:18–19; Eph. 19: 2–7; 1 Thes. 1: 5–6). As predicted by the prophets, the work of the Spirit centres on the son of David, who the New Testament writers recognise as being fulfilled in Jesus (Rom. 1:1–4; 2 Tim. 2:8). The Holy Spirit, symbolized by water throughout scripture, provided cleansing and renewal for the New Covenant people of God (Jer. 2:13; Ps. 32:6–7; Ezekiel 34:30–31; 36:24–29; 37:26–28;1 Cor. 6:12; Eph. 5:21–27).

So, I found this clear dependence of Paul on Old Testament themes. By the careful recall of Old Testament promises in his letters, Paul demonstrated that Christ is the fulfilment of them all. No wonder he wrote in 2 Corinthians 1:20 that all the promises of God are Yes and Amen in Christ Jesus!

Conclusion

We have seen that the Passover in the Egyptian Exodus is a key event that holds together the threads of redemption history. In time, a Second Exodus was predicted for the nation, but there was no fulfilment of the many promises that were predicted to accompany it due to Israel's unbelief.

Despite Israel's ongoing unfaithfulness, these unfulfilled promises would be fulfilled in the glorious, future, New Exodus. This would be something far greater than any prophet of old could have imagined. We are talking about The Exodus narrative, the theme that brings all the promises of God to completion.

What this chapter has shown is that Paul's understanding of the atonement is Paschal (Passover) based. For hundreds of years Christian scholars have struggled to present a model of atonement that could receive general agreement. I suggest their failure is because the wrong concepts have been used. Graeco-Roman/Medieval models have been used in an attempt to produce an understanding that would adequately explain the relevant biblical material. However, all attempts have failed to produce any consensus that the relevant questions have been resolved. I want to suggest that the Paschal New Exodus model presented in this book has brought this search to an end.

Chapter 18 Back to Romans 6

Having covered some of the background themes, we can now return to my search for meaning in Romans 6–7. You may remember how I discovered a range of problems as I tried to preach to the congregation in the summer of 1976.

In the past when explaining this passage, I had dealt with the opening verses of chapter 6 as if Paul had begun a new topic because the remarks of chapter 5 bore no obvious relationship to them. However, as I prepared to preach Romans 6, I recognised a link between the two chapters that I had never seen before. I knew something was going on in the opening verses, which are about being baptised into Christ, but I couldn't quite put my finger on it. I had previously hoped I knew the meaning of the passage and had used it to teach enquirers about baptism, but the reality was I had always sensed it was speaking about something much deeper than I had appreciated.

Missing Out the Beginning!

In attempting to understand Romans 6:1–6, I will begin with v6! This is because while I preached a sermon on the first five verses, when I reached v6 I realized what I had missed and had to go back to it. I revisited the opening verses with considerably more understanding and confidence once I had appreciated what v6 was about. So, I shall deal with v6 here and consider Romans 6:1–5 in the following chapter. I hope that by doing it in this way, you will also gain insights that will clarify the earlier verses. One of the terms that had regularly caused me confusion and some distress in v6 was Paul's statement that the "body of sin" had been destroyed and that we no longer served sin. Surprisingly it was by carefully studying this term that clarity came that helped me considerably to appreciate the opening verses.

I had been to all kinds of meetings for the deepening of the Christian life. The messages were mostly exhortations to repent and claim what Christ had done for me as one of His people. I knew sincere folk who had responded to these appeals; but there didn't seem to be much difference in them a few weeks down the line. That was a problem for me, for the victory that was claimed didn't seem to work out in practice. I felt that a theoretical victory that did not work itself out in life was as unattractive as the idea of taking a dead dog for a walk.

While I hadn't publicly responded to the preaching at these meetings, I was challenged by their powerful presentations. Each time I had determined to be 'saintlier' but soon fell flat on my face. Now, years later, here I was once again trying to understand the meanings of being "dead to sin" and "the body of sin". But this time I had to explain it to people who could come back at me and ask searching questions as to what I had said.

Crucial Meaning

In trying to understand the meaning of "the body of sin," I began to recognise that the term is crucially important for our theological understanding and our Christian lives. This is because it controls so much of our understanding of Paul's doctrine of sin. It affects us deeply, for it dictates how we think of ourselves. Are we living the lives we are intended to live; or are we just pretending, hiding the fact that we are perpetual failures? This is an understanding that is hardly going to generate a positive image of ourselves. Believing in a message of constant failure stifles spiritual and emotional progress in serious ways.

The term is difficult to understand for it is found in no other place in the Bible. Because of this, we must be especially careful to find Paul's intended meaning.

The Proposed Solution

So, what was the solution I finally suggested to the congregation on that Sunday evening? I explained to those present that we had to stay within the controlling narrative of chapter 5 (something I had never done previously!), a narrative based on corporate solidarity. I reminded the people that what happened to Adam, happened to his family as well. In the same way, I reasoned, what happened to Jesus happened to His family as well. That is clear from Paul's statement made elsewhere, "For as in Adam all die, so also in Christ shall all be made alive." (1 Cor. 15:22).

In addition, I reasoned (and still do) that the only way to understand what "the body of sin" means is to keep it rooted in chapter 5. Any other solution would be guesswork. In that chapter, Paul argues that there are two communities, one "in Adam" and the other "in Christ". I further pointed out that the Community in Christ is elsewhere called "the body of Christ", i.e., the Church (Eph. 4:12 see 1 Cor. 12:12–13,27; Eph. 1:23; 3:6; 4:4,12; 5:23,30; Col. 1:18), the redeemed, remade bride of Christ. I reasoned that the community "in Adam" *might* be the "body of Adam", which I reasoned was the same as the "body of sin". In fact, I soon had to abandon this suggestion for I found that the Jewish teachers used the term the body of Adam and it bore no relation to what Paul was saying in these verses.[37] This caused me to look for a more appropriate suggestion.

I came to realize that there is widespread agreement amongst scholars that when Paul uses the singular 'sin' he uses it to denote Satan. In other words, the term is not about an individual's body but to a community that he calls the body of Sin (i.e., Satan) to which the nonbeliever belongs. Believers belong to Christ and form the body of Christ. They belong to the Kingdom of light, and they are the children of light (Eph. 5:8). This is not so for unbelievers. They remain in Adam. They belong to the body of Sin and are the children of darkness (Eph. 5:8; Col. 1:13).

Identifying Sin in the Narrative

So, Paul is telling the believers in Rome that they really have died to Sin, i.e., to Satan, and to the body of Sin, which is his kingdom on earth. Paul is saying that all those who have been baptised into Christ no longer belong to the body (i.e., the community) of Satan! So, with this understanding, Paul is saying that true believers have stopped serving Sin, i.e., Satan, the devil. Something has happened that has taken them from Satan's control.

The unbelieving community remains "in Adam" and, like Adam, its members are all under the judgement that is to come for rejecting their Creator and preferring Satan and his lies (Gen. 3:4).

The Consequences of Choice.

For choosing to remain in this kingdom, thereby rejecting the rightful claims of their Creator, unbelievers will one day be judged. This will mean eternal separation from the God who alone loved them. But by calling on the God they

---

[37] For further discussion see Holland, *Contours*, 85-110.

have rejected and asking in faith for His forgiveness, they can be removed from this kingdom that is under judgement and brought into the Kingdom of His Son (John 3:16–21).

If they choose to continue rejecting their Creator, then when physical death comes, every one of the blessings that God has bestowed will cease and they will be under the total rule of the one who despises all but himself. There will be no answers to prayer and no intervention from the God who still loves them but who respects their choice. At this time, they will discover the true nature of sin (Sin/Satan) and what it (he) has brought about.

The Great Divide

But the community in Christ is totally different! Sin (Satan) has no further hold on them. They have died to Satan and have become the body of Christ through their Saviour's death and resurrection. As we shall see in the next chapter, this transfer to being "in Christ" took place long before they were born,[38] when they, together with all other believers throughout history, were baptised into Christ. In this new state they experience all that their Creator God desires to bless them with. They will know the kindness and care of Him in all its immensity and will live in His presence as was always intended. This is the glorious hope of every believer!

And because this union was created in the moment of Jesus' death, it was a baptism "into death". And this death that they have shared in has cancelled every spiritual relationship they had been a part of, and that included their covenantal union with Adam, whose disobedience in the Garden created a covenant with Sin.

So, because they have shared in death through being one with Jesus as He died, their relationship with Satan was immediately ended. The believing community has died to Sin!

The Termination of the Covenant

Thus 'in Christ' is totally different from being 'in Moses'. Being 'in Moses' meant that Israel was delivered from the control of Pharaoh, being 'in Christ'

---

[38] Of course, this is not true for the first generation of believers, many of whom were alive when Jesus died.

means that the Church has been delivered from the control of Sin (Satan), for he has no further hold on her. She has died to Satan and has become the body of Christ through her Saviour's death and resurrection. In this new state, she experiences all that her Creator God desires to bless her with. Those who belong to this community experience the kindness and care of their Redeemer God in all its immensity and they will live in His presence as was always intended. This is the glorious hope of every believer!

And because this union was created in the moment of Jesus' death, it was a baptism that was 'into death'. And this death that all believers have shared in has cancelled every other spiritual relationship that we had been a part of, and that included our covenantal union with Adam, whose disobedience in the Garden created a covenant with Sin. So, because we have shared in death through being one with Jesus as He died, our relationship with Satan was immediately ended. The believing community has died to Sin!

The Great Termination

We see the termination of covenants in normal human relationships. When a married person dies, the one who remains does not stay married to their dead partner. If they meet someone else and remarry, they have not committed adultery. Jesus was asked to explain the status of a woman whose husband had died. He had six brothers, and she married the first of them under the law of levirate marriage (Mark 12:18–27). To make the story more complicated, the interrogators said she eventually married all six brothers due to more untimely deaths. The question they put to Jesus was: "whose wife would she be in the resurrection?" Jesus did not explain that it was not adultery for a widow to remarry more than once, instead he dealt with the status of people when they die. Like every other contract/covenant, death brought it to an end. The gist of His explanation was that each marriage relationship had ended, and they are like the angels in heaven. This fact is at the heart of much of what Paul is arguing (Rom. 7:1–6). Death terminates every kind of previous covenant relationship. So, this is the great divide of humanity. Being right with God is not about nationality, ethnicity, gender, or culture; not even about the religion we formally identify with, be it Muslim, Hindu, Christian, etc. Nor is it about whether we have our names on a church register or if we are members of a particular denomination. It's not even whether we hold to an orthodox statement of faith. It is whether we are 'in Christ' or 'in Adam', i.e., 'in the body of Christ' or 'in the body of Sin.' We died to God through Adam's disobedience and so were brought into a covenant relationship with Satan. This covenantal relationship with Sin has been terminated and because we have chosen to share in the death that Jesus died to release us from the kingdom of darkness, we are delivered from the body of Sin. Only this can end the relationship His elect had been in with Satan. Which community we are in determines our future eternity.

Conclusion

Paul's teaching concerning dying to sin has normally been understood to refer to individual experience. It is seen to be the key to personal sanctification and Christian growth. This emphasis has meant that the corporate nature of Paul's theology has been overlooked, and for many it has been lost. By reading Paul's letters as originally intended, as letters to churches (communities) about their corporate experience of salvation and their responsibility as the redeemed people of God, we see that the experience of salvation that Paul refers to is their participation in the New Exodus. When Christ died to redeem His people, His death was not 'merely' about the forgiveness of His people's sins, it was about their deliverance from the kingdom of darkness. Through this adjustment to the corporate perspective, we have come to see that the New Exodus, like the two Exodus events of the Old Testament, is not about the experiences of individuals but of communities. So, Paul, as a Jew, uses corporate language and imagery to explain the salvation that Jesus has won for His people. In understanding this we are progressing to a fuller understanding of the Exodus narrative.

Chapter 19 Glorious Liberation!

My thinking had turned a corner. I had started the series on Paul's letter to the Romans accepting all that I had been taught; but as I tried to explain it to the congregation, I was faced with the realization that it failed to convince me it was the correct understanding of what Paul was saying. I felt I had the essentials of the Christian faith but didn't know how the parts fitted together. I was beginning to ask questions about Paul's vocabulary, which had confused me for many years, and I needed to understand what was happening so I could teach and preach in a helpful way. The way became clearer to my mind when I reflected on what I had come to appreciate through the study I had made so far. These were that:

1. Paul was incredibly knowledgeable about the Old Testament. It seemed he could not think outside its theological framework. This surprised me, for I was used to searching all manner of non-biblical material to understand elusive meanings I had encountered in his letters. From now on, I became increasingly suspicious of this method and wanted to see how the Old Testament shaped his thinking, illustrations, and vocabulary.
2. My previous reading of Paul's letters assumed they were about the individual Christian's experience when, in fact, it was at a much higher level. It was about what God has done for His people, i.e., it was much more corporate than I had ever thought.
3. The third thing I had come to appreciate was that people didn't have their own copy of the letters Paul had written. Their content could only be learned by coming to a gathering where it could be read publicly to the entire congregation. In other words, it was their combined story that was being explained, not their individual ones.

Because of these corrections I began to see that Paul is explaining how a New Community has been brought into existence and that the great divide is whether a person is in Adam, being a child of darkness, or in Christ, being a child of God. But Paul is not focusing on the individual but on the community that the individual must belong to.

Jesus and the Exodus

So, if the corporate framework, which Paul began in chapter five and continues into chapter 6 is correct, the body of sin is not about the individual at all; it is about a community that is in opposition to the Church, which Paul elsewhere called 'the Body of Christ'. Thus, unless a person has recognised that the death and resurrection of Jesus is at the centre of God's plan to save people from sin, then they remain as part of that kingdom that 'is in Adam' and that shares in his condemnation. But if a person sees what God was doing through Christ's death on the cross and sees that faith in Jesus is the only way of salvation, and if they believe on Him and confess Him as Saviour and Lord, they no longer remain in that community that is the 'body of sin' (also called the kingdom of darkness). In other words, they are no longer under the control of Satan and under the judgement of God. Sadly, this is the state of solidarity for millions of people. If they are not 'in Christ', they are 'in Adam' and live in a realm that is under God's judgement.

The Danger of Religious Effort

No person can reverse this status by fulfilling religious duties or striving for moral improvement. Such efforts, which in themselves can be very commendable and good, can never change them from being under judgement and part of that kingdom of darkness. It is because they are decent, moral, human beings that devout, religious people are in most danger of missing God's amazing provision. This is because they put their trust in the wrong things. Their achievements, which can never change their status regardless of how hard they try, can easily become something that deceives them into thinking that what they have done will make them acceptable before God. But this can never be the answer; for if it is, then Christ's death has been in vain. If it was possible to change our status by our deeds, then it effectively tells God that He has overreacted to sin and got the problem out of all proportion. What an incredible claim for the creature to charge his/her Creator with!

Thus, the statement by Paul that the body of sin had been destroyed is anything but a fanciful view of the Church. He is not saying that the Church is a community of sinless people. True, Christians do sin, but certainly not with the impunity that they did before they became followers of Christ. They no longer belong to Sin (Satan), but to Christ. I will deal with this more fully when

I discuss the end of the Covenant.[39] In the meantime, just let your heart and mind absorb this amazing fact: if you are 'in Christ', sin [Sin i.e., Satan] will have no mastery over you (Rom. 6:14).

This is far more wonderful than being made into some sort of human being who is morally perfect. You have been taken completely outside of the control of Satan; and even if you fail, as you will, it will not remove you from the security that Christ has given you. Of course, as a Christian, you will never see this as a license to sin. Such an attitude cuts right across what you have been saved for, to be a servant of righteousness, i.e., of God (Rom. 6:11–14; Eph. 2:10–11).

Supporting Evidence

So, the body of sin does not refer to our bodies being sinful or to our 'sinful nature'. The term refers to the community that rejects God as King and choses Satan. I think this is the meaning Paul intended because it finds support in his other letters. By comparing related terms in Rom. 6:6 with the way he uses them elsewhere we get enormous help, because the meaning of these terms in his other letters is very clear as we shall see.

Paul wrote in Rom. 6:6:

> We know that our old self was crucified with him in order that
> the body of sin might be brought to nothing.

It is important we notice that the term "our old self" is linked with the term "the body of sin". This is an example of what is known as 'Hebrew parallelism', and it occurs throughout the Old Testament, especially in the Psalms (e.g., Ps. 1:5; 2:4; 2:9; 19:1). In this Hebrew literary practice, two different words or expressions are put in the same sentence as examples of the same truth. Though they are different, they carry the same meaning and illuminate each other.[40]

---

[39] See Chapter 22.

[40] 'Ever since Robert Lowth's 1753 study *Lectures on the Sacred Poetry of the Hebrews*, biblical scholars have known that ancient Hebrew writers relied on parallelism to make their poetry.

Jesus and the Exodus

There are scholars who think that the opening passage in Romans 6:1–10 was originally an ancient baptismal confession that Paul borrowed or composed for the Church. If so, it will certainly have a poetic structure and the statement is very likely to be another example of Hebrew parallelism. In other words, "the body of sin" is a repetition of the meaning of the different term "our old self" (Greek literally, 'our old man').

The Questioning of Tradition

Traditionally, the old self has been understood to be the Adamic nature that all his offspring inherited, and the new nature (Greek, literally, 'new man') is that which the believer has received. But this traditional understanding of our old self has recently been questioned, and for good reason. Paul has used the same term elsewhere three times; and in none of these places does it mean 'sinful nature'. Note very carefully what Paul says to the Ephesians:

> But now in Christ Jesus you who once were far off have been brought near by the blood of Christ. For he himself is our peace, who has made us both one and has broken down in his flesh the dividing wall of hostility by abolishing the law of commandments expressed in ordinances, that he might create in himself one new man in place of the two, so making peace, and might reconcile us both to God in one body through the cross, thereby killing the hostility. And he came and preached peace to you who were far off and peace to those who were near. For through him we both have access in one Spirit to the Father. So then you are no longer strangers and aliens, but you are fellow citizens with the saints and members of the household of God, Jesus himself being the cornerstone, in whom the whole structure, being joined together, grows into a holy temple in the Lord. In him you also are being built

---

What is parallelism? It is a structure of thought (rather than external form like meter or rhyme) in which the writer balances a series of words so that patterns of deliberate contrast or intentional repetition appear. These rhetorical devices also appear in English. L. Kip Wheeler, *Parallelism in Hebrew Poetry*, Carson-Newman University, https://web.cn.edu/kwheeler/diagram_Hebrew_Poetry.html, accessed September 14, 2023.

together into a dwelling place for God by the Spirit (Ephesians 2:13–22)

One of the purposes of the death of Jesus was to create a new people (Paul's term, "one new man") from believing Jews and believing Gentiles. In this 'new man', God created a union of equals, reconciled not only to one another but also to God Himself (v16).

Reconciled and Unified

So, being reconciled and unified, the believers form the Church of Christ, named elsewhere in scripture as the 'bride of Christ'. In other words, the new man is not the individual believer's new life from God but a corporate term which speaks of the Church.

Paul continues by speaking first of the kingdom of darkness and then of the Kingdom of light, saying:

> They are darkened in their understanding, alienated from the life of God because of the ignorance that is in them, due to their hardness of heart. They have become callous and have given themselves up to sensuality, greedy to practice every kind of impurity. But that is not the way you learned Christ!—assuming that you have heard about him and were taught in him, as the truth is in Jesus, to put off your *old self,* (Greek literally 'old man'), which belongs to your former manner of life and is corrupt through deceitful desires, and to be renewed in the spirit of your minds, and to put on the new self (Greek literally 'new man'), created after the likeness of God in true righteousness and holiness. (Ephesians 4:18–24, italics added)

Here, we see the same sort of appeal as in Ephesians 2:13–22. The term "new self" (Greek, 'new man') is used again in v24. Helpfully, it is explicitly stated that it is the new man that must replace the "old self" or 'old man' (v22). The church in Ephesus must put off the values and lifestyle of the kingdom of darkness and put on the lifestyle of the Kingdom of light, the new man.

The Greek makes it very clear that Paul is speaking about two communities; so, in v18, they are darkened in their understanding etc. He then tells the Ephesian believers (v20) that this is not what they have learned of Christ. So, these two statements, about the disobedient community and the obedient community, are not descriptions about individuals per se but are descriptions of the lifestyles of the two communities. Elsewhere, Paul says:

> Put to death therefore what is earthly in you: sexual immorality, impurity, passion, evil desire, and covetousness, which is idolatry. On account of these the wrath of God is coming. in these you too once walked, when you were living in them. But now you must put them all away: anger, wrath, malice, slander, and obscene talk from your mouth. Do not lie to one another, seeing that you have put off the *old self* with its practices (Greek literally old man with its practices) and have put on the new self (Greek literally new man), which is being renewed in knowledge after the image of its creator. Here there is not Greek and Jew, circumcised and uncircumcised, barbarian, Scythian, slave, free; but Christ is all, and in all. (Col. 3:5–11, italics added)

These three passages clearly compare the life of the unbelieving community with the life of the believing community. This is made particularly so in Colossians 3:11, where Paul says: "Here there is no Greek and Jew, circumcised and uncircumcised, barbarian, Scythian, slave, free; but Christ is all, and in all."

The Crucial 'Here'

In other words, "here" is crucial, it is the redeemed Community, the Church, in which Paul says there are no divisions. All such distinctions and divisions have been done away with; for, in Christ, believers are "all one in Christ Jesus" (Col. 3:5–11).

We have noted that Romans 6:6–7 is an example of Hebrew parallelism, where one term expands on and explains a previous term. In this case, "our old self was crucified with him in order that the body of sin might be brought to nothing" (Rom. 6:6), the body of sin is expanding on 'our old self', the unredeemed or unbelieving community. So, the body of sin is the old man, and both terms are corporate descriptions and not the individual ones they have traditionally been assigned.

Jesus and the Exodus

The Hebrew Mindset

So, reading the statement in this Hebraic way shows that Paul is not saying they have somehow attained a condition of perfection and cannot sin. He is saying that they all shared this experience at the same time; the original Greek is clearly indicating that at one precise moment they all died with Christ. Their baptism was not a collection of individual events but one common event, just as the Jews had been baptised into Moses (see below). Thus, the statement is not about individual Christian experience; it is, as we shall see, not even about their experience of water baptism. Instead, Paul is describing the experience of the community. They have been rescued from the kingdom of darkness and, therefore, sin (Satan) no longer has control over them.

The Transforming Type

The Old Testament event or 'type' that Paul has elsewhere used to explain what this occurrence looks like is found in 1 Cor. 10:1–10, where he compares Israel's baptism into Moses with the Church's baptism into Christ. They are both corporate events. So, for the final time, if the new man is the Church, which is the body of Christ, then the body of sin is the body (community) that is under the control of Sin (Satan). Just read the chapter and you will see for yourself! They are called not to serve sin but to serve righteousness. What we find here is a much bigger picture than a battle for personal piety; it is about who the community 'in Christ' will serve. It MUST NOT serve Satan.

This is a startling truth that can so easily be missed but, in fact, it is in plain sight. If we read the letter as a Greek text that has retained all the Hebraic characteristics of the LXX, i.e., its Hebraic literary structures, idioms, and grammatical characteristics, then Paul, "a Hebrew of the Hebrews" (Phil. 3:5), is saying that the condition of humanity in Adam is the same as that of disobedient Israel who was warned of God's judgement. Israel continually rebelled against Yahweh and, unbelievably, gave her wholehearted attention and obedience to other gods. It is this waywardness that is at the heart of the human condition. All are part of the body of Sin if they have not repented and been transferred into the Kingdom of light (Col. 1:12-13), the community that belongs to Christ and not Satan.

I came to see that the baptism Paul writes about in the opening verse of chapter 6 was an historic event that would never happen again. It was a corporate event. I then knew that there had been a huge change in my understanding. In fact, it equipped me to go back and review what the opening verses of chapter 6 were saying, and that is what we will examine next.

Further Evidence

I later found out that some scholars had come to the same conclusion as I had, however, there was a big difference in the way they had tackled the problem. Most who had made this discovery had studied the meaning of 'the body of sin' linguistically; I had studied it theologically. My approach had been through trying to follow the argument occurring in the passage; others had made their judgement on the word itself. Here is a selection of what they have said:

> Torrence said: "in his death, the many who inhered in him died too, and indeed the whole body of sin, the whole company of sinners into which he incorporated himself to make their guilt and their judgement his own, that through his death he might destroy the body of sin, redeem them from the power of guilt and death, and through his resurrection raise them up as the new Israel." [41]
>
> Bruce said: "This 'body of sin' is more than an individual affair, it is rather that old solidarity of sin and death which all share 'in Adam', but which has been broken by the death of Christ with a view to the creation of the new solidarity of righteousness and life of which believers are made part 'in Christ'".[42]
>
> Manson, who was professor of New Testament at Cambridge, came closest to what I have argued by questioning the traditional assumption that in the phrase 'body of Sin' the term 'of Sin' is "a genitive of quality"; he argued that it: "does not yield a very good sense." He took it to be a possessive genitive and said it is "perhaps better to regard 'the body of sin' as the opposite of 'the body of Christ'. It is the mass of unredeemed humanity in bondage to the evil power.

---

[41] T. F. Torrance, *Theology in Reconstruction*, (London: SCM, 1965) 198.

[42] F.F. Bruce, The Epistle of Paul to the Romans: An Introduction and Commentary, (London Tyndale Press, 1967), 38.

Every conversion means that the body of sin loses a member, and the body of Christ gains one." [43]

So, thankfully, I had not gone off course; other leading scholars had agreed. But what I could not understand was how these good men had come to the same conclusion and yet never saw that this corporate understanding was the key to a fresher, more meaningful, reading of these crucial chapters. They carried on with their ongoing interpretation of the following text as though this corporate discovery had no further relevance. They continued to read chapter 6 and its teaching on baptism as though it was about the experience of the individual believer, whereas the discovery of the body of sin as a corporate description ought to have sent them back to look at what Paul meant by baptism into Christ. It is the implication of this discovery that we will consider in the next chapter.

Conclusion

We have considered how a correct understanding of Paul's use of the term 'the body of sin' has shown that Paul was not flitting around using a range of conflicting, descriptive strategies. He took his corporate reasoning, begun in chapter 5, into chapter 6 and, importantly, he continued to speak at a historical, corporate level. In addition, we have seen that the body of sin is not to be identified with our individual bodies. It is true that Paul is very concerned about how we use our bodies (Rom. 12:1–2; 1 Thes. 4:3–8), but the essence of his understanding as a Jew is that he would not see them as sinful but as instruments of sin if we chose to live under Satan's rule. This discovery has taken us another step towards understanding The Exodus narrative.

---

[43] T.W. Manson, art 'Romans' in Peakes Commentary on the Bible, M. M. Black (ed), H.H. Rowley (ed) (Routledge; 1st edition. 1971) 945

Chapter 20 Baptism and Freedom from Sin

My search to make sense of Romans 6 was an adventure I will never forget. I had no idea at the start of this journey where it would lead. All my previous understanding was being challenged and I was searching for an explanation that made sense to the ordinary people who heard the letter being read to them. This was my focus, for I could not believe that Paul would deliberately write about something so important in a way that would leave people, even world-renowned scholars, totally confused. I accepted he was writing for people in the first century, but I reasoned that, as long as I understood their horizons correctly, its meaning ought to be clear.

Despite this, I seemed to be getting into a denser fog, for a door into many possibilities had opened. I had to make sense of Romans 6:1–6 and also the statements that followed. Each of these presented their own challenge!

What I was beginning to understand was how my worldview was so very different from Paul's. I was beginning to unpack concepts I did not understand before. I came to see that these Jewish (Semitic) ideas are not restricted to Paul's letter to the Romans but are throughout his writings. Even though most people see Paul's ideas as archaic, they do not realize that they are an essential reflection of our modern existence.

The Importance of Solidarity

I hope, having considered human solidarity earlier, you will better appreciate some important statements Paul makes, and see that he is not making mistakes in his arguments as some scholars have suggested.

While this concept of solidarity is not always spelt out as clearly as it is in Romans, it is still there in Paul's other letters, often just below the surface of the arguments. Its hidden influence causes some to claim that he is remote and irrelevant to the modern reader. However, when these silent influences are recognised, they transform our understanding of the message he proclaimed and provide us with new powerful insights, which make his statements incredibly relevant to us in the twenty-first century. What I especially appreciated through this journey of discovery was that, by identifying the

'Jewish Paul' in his letter to the Romans, I was enabled to understand his other letters in ways I had never appreciated before.

An Incomplete Insight

Now, while Professor C H Dodd's book gave me an important clue about the importance of solidarity, I noticed he did not keep to his own advice about following Paul's corporate thought. He expounded on the corporate meaning of Paul's teaching in Romans 5 but went on to explain his teaching in the following chapters at the individual level. This was simply inconsistent. Firstly, there were no chapter divisions in Paul's original letter, so there was nothing to presume he had changed his mindset. Secondly, if Paul had made a change of perspective from corporate to individual, he would most assuredly have made such an important point clear. It was because of understanding what 'the body of sin' and 'the old man' meant, I could see that Paul's way of arguing in Romans 5 continued into the next chapter. So, I decided I had to follow his argument by keeping to this corporate narrative.

Returning to the Beginning

Armed with this new insight, I returned to my congregation and told them to ignore my past teaching on the opening verses of chapter 6! I was now able to expound my new understanding.

As a pastor, I had taught that Rom. 6:1–10 explained how a believer's baptism, in which the candidate was plunged under the water, was a picture of death. But I was being to see, through the way Paul wrote about this baptism, that something much bigger was going on in the passage. Because Romans 5:12–21 is clearly corporate, as is the body of sin in Romans 6:6, then for Paul's explanation to fit into this flow of thought it meant Romans 6:1–5 would also need to be corporate. Now, I am not saying that the passage cannot serve the purpose of explaining water baptism, but I am saying that this is not what Paul was focusing on as he penned this passage.

Much More than Water Baptism

So, I was beginning to see that the passage was not as straightforward as being a discussion on water baptism. For one thing, the Greek grammatical construction that Paul used (the aorist tense of the verb) suggests that the baptism being discussed did not refer to an event that had been performed many thousands of times. The Greek term suggests it was *one, completed, never to be repeated*, baptism. In other words, it was a single event that all believers had somehow together shared in. Being a single event in which *the entire Church of all generations was rescued*. Elsewhere in the New Testament Jesus' death is described as His Exodus (see Luke 9:31, ESV uses 'departure', but acknowledges in the footnote that the Greek word is 'Exodus'), when He died for His people to deliver them from the kingdom of darkness. That was Jesus' own Exodus, the New Exodus, when He led all His people out of the spiritual Egypt, the kingdom of darkness.

This corporate insight is underscored again by the Greek in another way. It says: 'through *the* baptism into *the* death' (Rom. 6:3, *dia ou baptismatos eis ton thanaton* [the underlined words are the appropriate definite articles 'the']). It seemed to be emphasizing that this baptism was unique and specific; not one that was repeatedly practiced. Paul appeared to be speaking of something on a vastly different scale from that which I had previously understood.

Another problem that had worried me was the statement that they had been baptised 'into death'. I had performed a number of funeral services and had pronounced the statement "from dust to dust and ashes to ashes". I had viewed baptism to be a symbolic funeral service. But the thought that, when at the graveside, I had buried someone into death horrified me. Burial follows death; it is never intended to achieve death. But this is what Paul says - the recipients of the letter had been baptised (buried) into death!

Collaborating Evidence

These difficulties caused me to explore what Paul had said elsewhere about baptism. I turned to 1 Corinthians 10:1–13:

> For I do not want you to be unaware, brothers, that our fathers were all under the cloud, and all passed through the sea, and all were baptized into Moses in the cloud and in the sea, and all ate the same spiritual food, and all drank the same spiritual drink. For they drank from the spiritual Rock that followed them, and the Rock was Christ. Nevertheless, with most of them God was not pleased, for they were overthrown in the wilderness.

> Now these things took place as examples for us, that we might not desire evil as they did. Do not be idolaters as some of them were; as it is written, "The people sat down to eat and drink and rose up to play." We must not indulge in sexual immorality as some of them did, and twenty-three thousand fell in a single day. We must not put Christ to the test, as some of them did and were destroyed by serpents, nor grumble, as some of them did and were destroyed by the Destroyer. Now these things happened to them as an example, but they were written down for our instruction, on whom the end of the ages has come. Therefore let anyone who thinks that he stands take heed lest he fall. No temptation has overtaken you that is not common to man. God is faithful, and he will not let you be tempted beyond your ability, but with the temptation he will also provide the way of escape, that you may be able to endure it.

The key word in this passage is not "baptized", which I expected, but "example" (v11). In Greek, the word is *typos*. Some translators have chosen to translate this as 'illustration', but this is far too loose a translation for a word with technical significance. It is the same word that Paul used in Romans 5, where he says: "Not like the transgression of Adam, who was a type (*typos*) of the one who was to come" (Rom. 5:14)

In other words, 1 Corinthians 10 describes Israel's Exodus from Egypt and Romans 6 describes the Church's exodus from the kingdom of darkness. The deliverance of Israel from Egypt corresponds to the deliverance of believers through the death of Jesus. And the feature of the two Exodus deliverances, they were both corporate events when God created a new covenant community.

The Meaning of a Type

So, what is a type? It is an event in the Old Testament that is referred to by the New Testament writers when explaining a truth. It functions as a pointer to a future event that matches it; but the future event is vastly more important and is called the 'antitype'. So, antitypes in the New Testament have the distinct features of matching their Old Testament types but on a massively different scale. That is why I am saying that translating the word 'typos' as 'illustration' is to lose vitally important aspects of its meaning. This is because illustrations can come from any source; but, in biblical terms types are specific historical Old Testament events that are seen to be put there by God to point to and explain future New Testament events or truths.

Another example of an Old Testament type is Abraham's offering of his son, Isaac. That event pointed forward to the event of God the Father, offering His Son, Jesus, as a sacrifice for our sins (Rom. 4:25, where the crediting of righteousness is distinctly part of the narrative of Abraham being willing to offer his son). Therefore, for the apostles, who used them throughout the New Testament, types were hugely significant events, helping the wider church understand the much greater meaning or significance of their New Testament antitypes.

By carefully reflecting on these types, the shape of the apostles' arguments and teaching can be anticipated and constructed with more accuracy. This method of study is called 'Typology'. It was very popular in previous generations but became very speculative, with some preachers arguing that types existed in many Old Testament passages without evidence that the New Testament writers saw them being present. Some even saw types in secular history and events, and these were used to make the most fanciful of arguments! It is much safer to claim that a type exists when an apostle affirms its presence. This cautious control of Typology will protect us from making unwarranted and foolish claims, which can bring our understanding and teaching into disrepute as happened in previous generations.

In this way of understanding, we are not saying that types are prophecies; they are reflections. The early church knew that God has foretold future happenings through earlier events in salvation history. For example, we have seen how the Egyptian Exodus functioned as a type of the Babylonian Exodus, and their combined features became a type of the New Testament's New Exodus. There is a clear flow of corresponding events that move to something infinitely greater than the original types.

So, in Romans 5:14, Paul says that Adam is a type of Christ; and, in 1 Cor. 10:11, Moses, leading Israel out of Egypt, was a type of Jesus, leading His people out of the kingdom of darkness. It follows that the baptism of Israel 'into Moses', mentioned in 1 Corinthians 10:2, is drawing on the Old Testament Exodus event, and it is reflecting Paul's other usage of this Exodus type found in Romans 6:1–3: But this New Testament usage is so much more significant than the type that foretold it, for the type pointed forward to the glorious antitype of the Church being baptised into Jesus.

Comparing Events

So, what can we gain from the event when Israel was baptised into Moses that will help us understand how the Roman believers were baptised into Christ?

Firstly, we can note that no Israelite was baptised as an individual into Moses. It was the entire community that experienced this baptism, and they experienced it together in the same single event. Secondly, we can note that none of the Israelites were immersed into water. That is significant, because in the antitype of Romans 6:1–6 there is no mention of water either. So, in the type, all Israel was "baptized into Moses", whatever that meant, in one historic event. And when did it happen? It was as Moses left Egypt, i.e., during his exodus.

So how does that help us understand Paul's meaning of baptism into Christ? The type shows us that its antitype is to be understood as a corporate event, when all believers were baptised together, for it was one baptism. And when did this baptism take place? It was when Jesus died for His people at the Passover i.e., His Exodus.

Therefore, it really was a baptism into death. His people, i.e., every Christian of every generation, died with Jesus, and, because of the covenantal unity that *the* baptism had created, three days later *they were all* (we all, Rom. 6:3) *together* raised *with Him* from the grave (cf. Gal. 1:1–5; Eph. 2:4–9)!

Conclusion

We have discovered that typology is a key method Paul used to teach the church important truths. To be effective, his readers would have to understand what he was doing so they must have been familiar with typological exegesis. And this is what we find. In fact, typology was not restricted to the Jewish community because we find the same method of teaching in other ancient literature. Understanding this has helped me understand The Exodus narrative in a way I had not understood it before. It is based on a historic event and was about an entire community, i.e., Romans 6 is corporate and not individualistic.

Chapter 21 A Baptism that Rings all the Bells

My thinking was beginning to alter radically. From thinking that Romans 6 spoke about water baptism, I came to see that, when Paul is explaining baptism, he turns to the experience of Israel when coming out of Egypt. He said it was a type of when the Church was baptised into Christ. This helped me see that baptism into Christ was a single, historic, and corporate event and, most importantly, this made complete sense of the Greek tenses and grammatical construction Paul was using.

The antitype of the Egyptian Exodus event is referred to again in 1 Corinthians 12:12–13, where Paul says:

> For just as the body is one and has many members, and all the members of the body, though many, are one body, so it is with Christ. For in one Spirit we were all baptized into one body— Jews or Greeks, slaves or free—and all were made to drink of one Spirit.

Usually, this statement is understood to be saying that when a person believes, he or she is baptised into a union with Jesus. This must be reflected on again because it ignores the corporate, historic context of the passage as well as its unusual Greek grammatical construction.

The common understanding of 1 Corinthians 12:13 relies on avoiding another of those difficult Greek words that Paul has chosen to use. Strictly speaking, his words should be translated '*to form* one body' not '*into* one body'. Now the Greek word 'eis' does mean 'into', and this is rightly translated in hundreds of other places throughout the LXX of the Old Testament and the New Testament, but when it is part of a sentence that has an accusative, it becomes "to form one body."

The Inescapable Problem

This creates a huge problem for people who hold to the traditional view of baptism. If their traditional understanding is followed, the correct translation 'to form one body' would have them saying that the Church does not yet exist because it still waits for the last person to be added through baptism. Then, and only then, would the Church exist![44]

But such a position is preposterous. It clearly existed in apostolic days when the apostles wrote to communities they called 'churches' (Matt. 18:17; Acts 5:11; Rom. 16:4–5; 1 Cor. 1:2; Gal. 1:2; etc.). It was for this reason that translators, knowing the problem, chose to translate the expression '*into* one body'. The only problem with this solution is that it is not what Paul wrote!

The Decisive Moment

It was then that believing people, from all nations and generations, were joined to Christ and baptised into His death, and it was then that the Church came into existence. This is an incredible truth! Long before you and I had come to faith, this work of salvation had been done, and not one believer, of whatever generation, was missing. This could happen because God, in His foreknowledge, knew who had and who would believe in Christ. And, because it was corporate, the Church was not added to but created, and, from that very moment, it existed in its entirety.

In the Egyptian Exodus, all Israel, regardless of what generation they belonged to, was baptised into Moses and, interestingly, Jews today believe this was their experience also when, together with the rest of the nation, they 'fled from Egypt'.

In summary: in the antitype, all Christians, regardless of what generation they belong to, were baptised together into Christ by the one baptism that created the Church.

Reading in Context

I need to state the obvious again: the often-overlooked fact is that Romans 13 follows Romans 10! If we follow the argument of those chapters, we find Paul using Israel's Exodus from Egypt as a type of a greater deliverance i.e., the

---

[44] The problem of this understanding was made clear by Earnest Best in his book, One Body in Christ, (1955) *A Study in the Relationship of the Church to Christ in the Epistles of the Apostle Paul*, SCM, London, p 69. See also C.F. Moule, *The Origins of Christology* (Cambridge University Press, 1977) 71. Also R. Schnackenberg, (1965) *Baptism in the Thought of St Paul*, tr by R. G. Beasley Murray (New York: Herder & Herder, 1964), 26.

Church's deliverance from the kingdom of darkness. Just as Israel was baptised into Moses, the Church has been baptised into Christ (1 Cor. 10:3); just as Israel depended on the Passover sacrifice to keep her firstborn safe, the Church depends on God's provision of a Sacrifice at Passover to keep her safe (1 Cor. 10:16, 10:21, 11:25); and just as the Egyptians thrust gifts on the Jews to persuade them to go, and these were the materials used to build the tabernacle, so God has given His people gifts to build the Church which, in the New Testament, is the temple of God (1 Cor. 12:8–10,27–29; see also Eph. 4:7–13).

Therefore, if this understanding is correct, the statement "baptised to form one body" still remains corporate, just like the argument was in Romans 5 and 6 and in 1 Corinthians 10. It is not about water baptism but the sign it speaks of. It follows that 1 Corinthians 12:13 should be read in the context of this narrative. Baptism in 1 Corinthians 12:13 is also about the creation of the New Covenant Community, just as Israel's baptism into Moses was the creation of the Jewish nation.

If this is so, we see that Paul was correct to say that this baptism was to "create the body", for it was created in an instant and in its entirety. It involved every believer of every generation, just as every generation was included in the Fall when Adam sinned. Here, in 1 Corinthians 12:13, it is explaining what happened when God, by His Spirit, created this unity between all believers and Christ.

Seeking Supporting Evidence

If you know practicing Jews, ask what the significance of the Exodus is for them. They will tell you that it was when they became a nation. They believe that every single Jew who *had* lived, *was* living, or *would* live, was present when it took place. That really is an incredible example of the solidarity of the nation! It is an exact copy of Paul's argument that the whole human race was "in Adam". Not one person was missing from that dreadful event.

This intergenerational, national solidarity is still expressed to this very day. Every year the Jews still celebrate the Passover, the feast that was established to launch and then recall their great deliverance from Egypt 4,000 years ago in the event known as the Exodus. At the heart of the first celebration of the feast was a meal in which a lamb was eaten, and unleavened bread shared. The eldest son was instructed to ask his father, "What does this mean?" and the father had to say to him, "By a strong hand the LORD brought *us* out of Egypt, from the house of slavery". (Exod. 13:14, emphasis added).

Although the way the feast is kept has evolved over the centuries, the question and its reply continue to be at its heart. The word 'us' is repeated every year. In the context of redemption history, it is clearly intergenerational. Each family unit celebrating the event today was present with all other Jewish family units in the very first Exodus. The Exodus event was when Israel was created as a nation.

Hence, what Paul wrote is correct. He really meant that they had all been baptised, and this event had created the Church. "For in (by) one Spirit we were all baptised *to form* one body—believing Jews or Greeks, slaves or free—and all were made to drink of one Spirit" (1 Cor. 12:13).[45]

Because of this union, created by the Spirit on the first Good Friday, 50 days later at Pentecost the same Spirit was poured out during the feast of Pentecost and the Church was infused with His presence and life.

So, the argument is exactly the same as Romans 5:12–21, for all humankind, regardless of the generation they belong to, were 'in Adam' when he disobeyed, and was sent into exile from Eden and God's presence. So too, all true believers of every generation were 'in Christ' when He died for His people. Because they were made one with Him in His death, they shared in His resurrection and are seated with Him in the heavenlies (Eph. 2:4–8).

Evidence from Ephesians

Another passage where Paul says something rather unusual about baptism is in Ephesians 4. He says:

> There is one body and one Spirit—just as you were called to the one hope that belongs to your call—one Lord, one faith, one baptism, one God and Father of all, who is over all and through all and in all. But grace was given to each one of us according to the measure of Christ's gift. Therefore it says,

---

[45] Italics added to emphasise the Greek.

Jesus and the Exodus

"When he ascended on high he led a host of captives, and he gave gifts to men." (In saying, 'He ascended,' what does it mean but that he had also descended into the lower regions, the earth? He who descended is the one who also ascended far above all the heavens, that he might fill all things.) And he gave the apostles, the prophets, the evangelists, the shepherds, and teachers to equip the saints for the work of ministry, for building up the body of Christ." (Eph. 4:4–12)

Scholars are surprised that Paul mentions baptism without mentioning the Eucharist, the other appointed sacrament. No satisfactory reason for this separation has been provided. The impasse exists because all fail to note the wider context of the statement, for in the passage there are a series of allusions to the Egyptian Exodus.

The language of ascending and descending are echoes of Moses, who went up Sinai to meet with God and came down with the Law, which was God's gift to His newly formed Covenant Community people. It was while he was on the mountain that God told Moses the detailed plans for the building of the tabernacle, and, at this time, He also gave him instructions on specific roles and sacrifices linked to it.

In the Exodus event, God gave His people the resources needed for building the tabernacle where He was to dwell amongst His Spirit-filled people. In other words, Paul uses the Egyptian Exodus as a type for what Jesus achieved through His death and resurrection, i.e., His Exodus or the New Exodus.

So, it is against this historical event that the reference to baptism should be read. It does not refer to believer's baptism. Paul is dealing with the antitype of Israel's baptism into Moses. He speaks of the Church's baptism into Christ during His Exodus experience, when the community was formed by covenant to become Christ's bride (Eph. 5: 25–27). Just as Israel was given resources from the Egyptians for the building of the tabernacle; the Church has been given spiritual gifts from the ascended Lord, by His Spirit, so that His universal Church can be built. And just as Yahweh bestowed practical artisan gifts and other relevant skills on selected people to construct the tabernacle where He would meet with the people, so the Spirit has given spiritual gifts needed to build the living temple of the living God where He now meets with His people It was by baptism that Moses became Israel's head and representative before

God, and it is through the similar but much greater (one) baptism by the Spirit that Jesus became the Church's head and representative before the Father. So being "in Christ" is not a mystical experience but a covenantal (or contractual) relationship. It means being in the family of God through the work that Christ did on the Cross to secure His bridal community.

The Missing Sacrament

It is because Paul is not speaking about the sacraments in this passage that he does not refer to the Eucharist celebration. By identifying this ongoing typological setting for the statement about "one baptism", our corporate interpretation is supported and shown likely to be correct.

Reading the statement that one baptism into Christ is the antitype of Israel's baptism into Moses makes great sense. If it was a reference to water baptism it simply would not fit in with the great foundational truths that Paul lists:

> There is one body and one Spirit—just as you were called to the one hope that belongs to your call—one Lord, one faith, one baptism, one God and Father of all, who is over all and through all and in all. But grace was given to each one of us according to the measure of Christ's gift. (Eph. 4:4–7)

Water baptism just does not fit in with this list of absolute and ultimate realities. To put this practice into such a list simply downgrades the significance of these primary truths of the Christian faith. But if it refers to the one historic event, modelled on Israel's one baptism into Moses, then it makes perfect sense. This is especially so when we recognise that the chapter is a typological exposition of the entire Exodus event.

Evidence from Galatians

Finally, there is one other baptism text that fits into this theological framework, i.e., the New Exodus paradigm. In his letter to the Galatians, Paul writes:

> for in Christ Jesus you are all sons of God, through faith. For as many of you as were baptized into Christ have put on Christ. There is neither Jew nor Greek, there is neither slave nor free, there is no male and female, for you are all one in Christ Jesus. And if you are Christ's, then you are Abraham's offspring, heirs according to promise. (Gal. 3:26–29)

Jesus and the Exodus

It was a Catholic theologian, Rudolf Schnackenburg, who commented on the oddity of the tenses Paul chose to use in this statement about being baptised into Christ. He observed that Paul has described a single event (the aorist plural passive), which he also used in Romans 6; 1 Corinthians 10; and Ephesians 2, in which all Galatian believers had shared, regardless of when they became followers of Christ. In this event, it was not only the Galatian believers who were baptised, but all believers, i.e., those who had died, those who were alive, and those who were yet to be born were present in the event described. But because Schnackenburg assumed the text spoke of water baptism, he simply dismissed the Greek construction as impossible and did what so many scholars and commentators have done throughout the Church's history. He challenged the text and substituted his own scrutinized understanding of what baptism means. Schnackenburg wrote:

> "It would be possible to interpret the whole baptismal event as a unity in which the baptised are plunged; it represents Christ as a Pneuma-sphere into which they are removed. All (παντες v 26, ασοι v 27a, παντες v 28b) are immersed into Jesus Christ, without respect to national, social and sexual distinctions. But this exposition causes misgivings. The imagery would attain its complete effect only under the presupposition that all were immersed unitedly into the baptismal water, but that is hardly possible."[46]

Such an interpretation ignores the context, the Greek grammatical constructions, and the corporate nature of the theology of the letters. If these factors are given their due recognition, they open up the texts so that we see them to be speaking of a baptism that is far more significant than water baptism, i.e., it is not about adding to the Church but is about the actual *creation* of the Church. It "is hardly possible" because Schnackenburg could not challenge the tradition he represented.

---

[46] R. Schnackenberg, *Baptism in the Thought of St. Paul*, tr. By G. R Beasley Murray, (New York: Herder & Herder, 1964), 24.

The Proper Meaning of Water Baptism

Our corporate interpretation challenges the interpretation of all the texts that have been used to claim that the apostles taught a doctrine of baptismal regeneration. However, it still allows water baptism its proper, New Testament role for believers to bear witness to their faith in the crucified, risen, and exalted Saviour. The texts that support this practice are found in the gospels and Acts; but not the epistles, other than that mentioned in 1 Corinthians 1:14, where Paul says that the only Corinthians that he baptised were Crispus and Gaius.

So, to remind ourselves of what this baptism has achieved, hear the words of Paul again:

> What shall we say then? Are we to continue in sin that grace may abound? By no means! How can we who died to sin still live in it? Do you not know that all of us who have been baptized into Christ Jesus were baptized into his death? We were buried therefore with him by baptism into death, in order that, just as Christ was raised from the dead by the glory of the Father, we too might walk in newness of life.
>
> For if we have been united with him in a death like his, we shall certainly be united with him in a resurrection like his. We know that our old self was crucified with him in order that the body of sin might be brought to nothing, so that we would no longer be enslaved to sin. For one who has died has been set free from sin. Now if we have died with Christ, we believe that we will also live with him. We know that Christ, being raised from the dead, will never die again; death no longer has dominion over him. For the death he died he died to sin, once for all, but the life he lives he lives to God. So you also must consider yourselves dead to sin and alive to God in Christ Jesus." (Rom. 6:1–11)

Thus, Christian unity is not something to be created; it already exists. It was by the Spirit that God brought the Church into existence in the death of Christ her Saviour.

I had struggled for years to get to this point, so if you have found it a struggle, please don't be disheartened. If you can see that firstly, there is a very real danger of imposing meanings on the words that don't fit and secondly, that the context must control, then you have come a long way.[47] You have come even further if you have seen that Paul's perspective about baptism is the event when God brought the Church into existence in the very moment that Jesus died for His people.

Having made this discovery about baptism, which came through understanding that the body of sin in Rom. 6:6 was a community, I had been able to follow the argument of the opening of chapter six with more confidence, so that I could explain its meaning to the congregation when we met the following Sunday.

Conclusion

The proper form of baptismal initiation has divided the Church for centuries, with each section claiming to have the correct biblical practice. In the understanding I have just explained, water baptism continues to be a confession of faith, but the correct texts must be chosen to defend the practice. If you have ever doubted whether your baptism conformed to the teaching of scripture let me say that, if it was your confession, then it hardly matters if the practice followed was precisely correct. What matters is that, as a believer, you, with the countless millions of other believers, were baptised into Christ at the moment He died. This is not an invitation to be indifferent about water baptism but an appeal to get it into its true biblical perspective. And this perspective? It is the New Exodus narrative!

---

[47] For a more detailed discussion on this topic, see Holland, *Contours*, 141-154.

Chapter 22 Baptism and Justification

As previously discussed, I had great difficulty in understanding what the 'body of sin' was in Romans 6:6. Did it refer to the principle (whatever that means) of sin that controls me? Was it referring to the utter corruption of my human nature? Was it a biologically inherited concept, or a distortion of human nature, or, perhaps, some sort of damage to my DNA?

By recognising that chapter 6 was continuing the argument, begun in chapter 5, of humanity sinning and dying 'in Adam', I concluded that the term was not about me but about the community I once belonged to. This made such sense because I knew that the night I submitted to Christ I belonged to a new community, and the one I had been a part of had no appeal to me whatsoever. I rejoiced to be with others who also loved Jesus. This was my evidence that I had died to the body of sin as it no longer had control over me.

But there was another problem in the chapter that confuses almost all scholars. What did Paul mean by "one who has died has been set free from sin" (Rom. 6:7). The problem is that the Greek reads "*justified* from sin".

The Theological Litmus Paper.

Believing it would be ridiculous to think that Paul's teaching method was to leave his audience confused, it could only be that everyone in his community shared a common understanding. Therefore, discovering the inherent paradigm/pattern/narrative of Paul's messages would be essential to properly understand him. When the correct paradigm was understood and fully applied, it would enable an infinitely better comprehension of his teaching.

The most obvious example of a paradigm change in science was when Watson and Crick (along with others) discovered the double-helical structure of DNA in 1953. Their new understanding explained so many unresolved problems that philosophers and scientists had struggled with for centuries, if not millennia. It not only resolved the problems of the past but propelled massively important research into biological sciences, giving doctors many more exciting tools with which to tackle disease. That is an example of a paradigm change and what it can achieve!

Jesus and the Exodus

We have noted a series of Paul's statements that scholars have felt necessary to correct. But what if the issue is not Paul's mistake but their paradigm? If the correct paradigm is not being used to understand Paul, then nothing will fit. This is particularly important when it comes to Romans 6:7.

The following translations of Romans 6:7 acknowledge the importance of keeping to the original text that Paul wrote:

> ASV "for he that hath died is justified from sin."
> DARBY "For he that has died is justified from sin."
> DLNT "For the *one* having died has been declared-righteous from sin."
> DRA "For he that is dead is justified from sin."
> EXB "Anyone who has died is ·made free [justified; declared righteous] from ·sin's control."
> JUB "For he that is dead is justified from sin."
> NMB "For he who is dead, is justified from sin."
> WYC "For he that is dead [*to sin*], is justified from sin."

But there are many translators and commentators who avoid this correct translation. Here are some samples:

> NABRE "For a dead person has been absolved from sin."
> NASB "For the one who has died is freed from sin."
> NET "For someone who has died has been freed from sin."
> NIV "because anyone who has died has been set free from sin."
> NKJV "For he who has died has been freed from sin."
> NRSV "For whoever has died is freed from sin."
> RSV "For he who has died is freed from sin."[48]

Because the word δεδικαίωται (*dedikaiōtai*) "justified" is contrary to the argument Paul is thought to be making, many commentators and translators try to correct what they think is his unintended error. To do this, they translate the word as "freed" or something other than "justified". So, rather than saying

---

[48] For abbreviations and a list of what all 62 translators give, see *Bible Gateway,* 'Romans 6:7', https://www.Biblegateway.com/verse/en/Romans%206:7, accessed September 14, 2023.

that people are "justified", as the Greek says, they say that Paul meant to say "freed". By doing this switch, they think they have corrected his mistake.

Facing the Problems

The problems with not keeping to the Greek word that Paul chose are that, firstly, it ceases to be a translation. It's not even a transliteration (an attempt to make a word more understandable for someone who cannot follow the original language). It is an imposition; replacing the apostle's chosen word with one that does not convey the same meaning. Secondly, it has important theological consequences.

If Paul did mean "one who has died has been freed from sin", he would be saying that death with Christ comes before justification. In other words, the experience is the basis for being justified from sin. This means that the spiritual experience of dying with Christ is the basis of Christian freedom. This might not seem a problem until it is appreciated that this argument requires you achieve some sort of unity with Christ before you are freed from your sin. In other words, Christian experience precedes being justified from sin or, putting it another way, you have to attain a Christian experience to be forgiven!

Terrible Consequences

This means that your salvation is dependent on you coming to know Christ in some way that relates to His death. You have got to have died to sin first, and then you can become a Christian! Now that is where the crunch is, for the measure by which this experience can be judged as being genuine is a threat to our assurance of salvation. There will certainly be times when you ask yourself about your status before God. Was my confession genuine? Did I repent properly? Did I loathe my sin deeply enough for God to accept me? If I have died to sin, then why do I still sin? In other words, this translation puts all the emphasis on your effort when, elsewhere, Paul has written:

> For by grace you have been saved through faith. And this is not your own doing; it is the gift of God, not a result of works, so that no one may boast. For we are his workmanship, created in Christ Jesus for good works, which God prepared beforehand, that we should walk in them. (Eph. 2:8)

In other words, everything is of God. He calls us only to repent and believe, and even these responses are His gifts. He gives us forgiveness because Christ has secured it for us, not because we have earned it. One translation of the Greek word for "justified" says that salvation is secured by works, the other says it is by grace! That is why the way "justified" is translated is so very important.

Theological Consequences

So, changing the word to mean 'freed' is a massive mistake, and it has not solved the problem at all. This widely accepted solution is a denial of Paul's gospel. It leaves us with no certainty of salvation because who could possibly achieve freeing themselves from sin (Sin) before they had a relationship with Christ? Interestingly, Paul uses the Greek term for 'justified' fourteen times throughout Romans. In the remaining thirteen uses, the translators use 'justified' with no scholar ever suggesting they should be translated 'freed'.

I hope you see what is at stake here. It is the Gospel of Christ itself and your confidence in Him being your Saviour for, if it is right, you have to save yourself before God could enter the scene!

I am not going to go into the technicalities of this, but, if you want to know more, you can read what I've written elsewhere.[49]

Ignorance Revealed.

Once more, I was floundering.

I didn't want to say that Paul had made a mistake; how could I? I held, and still hold, a high view of scripture. Scripture must judge our thinking and not the other way round. But many translators, and nearly all the commentators I had read (and these included the most conservative, with very high views of scripture), unapologetically said it had to be done. "Justified" they argued, must be changed to "freed" to avoid the greater problem of saying that Christian experience led to, or is, the basis of justification. Those that faithfully kept to the term "justified" seemed to be unaware of the underlying problems

---

[49] See Holland, *Contours*, 207-234.

voiced by the others! So, how did I get out of this seemingly impossible dilemma?

I did the only thing I could. I decided I couldn't blindly follow these learned men and their writings. I had to do my faltering best to try to understand what the argument was about.

I recall pushing away the many books on the table where I was doing my studying and focusing solely on the text Paul had written. Again, I asked myself the simple question, "where's his argument coming from?" The answer was simple; Paul was continuing his explanation that began in chapter 5! I had noted that every commentary assumed in chapter 6 he was speaking of the individual, having left behind the corporate framework laid down in chapter 5.

And what was the argument laid down in chapter 5? It was that humankind is bound in some sort of solidarity with Adam, who took all his descendants (his family) into a condition of alienation from God. Through the same principle of solidarity, Jesus had functioned as the Last Adam. By dying as the Representative of His people, He ended Adam's covenant with Satan and the separation from God that it caused. It was because of Adam's disobedience that his entire family was not only destined to separation from God but also, they deliberately follow his choice.

Adam in The Book of Hosea!

This was the reasoning behind Hosea's statement about Israel's sin of idolatry being like that of their forefather, Adam: "But like Adam they transgressed the covenant; there they dealt faithlessly with me." (Hosea 6:7)

When Adam transgressed (i.e., broke the covenant with God), he immediately entered into a covenant with Satan, who achieved his goal of capturing Adam's submission by deceitfully capturing his heart. He had taken God's place, and by taking God's place as the husband of humanity, Satan became the husband of the community of all fallen people, i.e., of the body of Sin.

However, Paul is arguing that Jesus, through His death, brought an end to Sin's (Satan's) authority over His people, the ones He had died for, i.e., the Church. Adam's sin was far worse than a schoolboy prank when the forbidden fruit was eaten. It was Adam telling God he had no right to be in control of his life and that Satan would care for him in a way that He had failed to do. It was effectively a declaration of divorce, Satan being the preferred bridegroom.

I have not invented this understanding, for the history of Israel is all about her breaking her covenant with God and entering into a covenant with other gods to achieve what she thought Her Lord had failed to provide. So, Hosea could say: "like Adam they transgressed the covenant".

Covenant Making and Breaking

This line of covenant breaking and entering into a similar relationship with a new partner is seen in Israel's behaviour in Isaiah 28, where it says:

> therefore thus says the Lord God, Behold, I am the one who has laid as a foundation in Zion, a stone, a tested stone, a precious cornerstone, of a sure foundation: Whoever believes will not be in haste. And I will make justice the line, and righteousness the plumb line; and hail will sweep away the refuge of lies, and waters will overwhelm the shelter. Then your covenant with death will be annulled, and your agreement with Sheol will not stand; when the overwhelming scourge passes through, you will be beaten down by it. As often as it passes through it will take you; for morning by morning it will pass through, by day and by night; and it will be sheer terror to understand the message. (Isa. 28:16–19)

The key verse of this passage is v18, which says:

> Then your covenant with death will be annulled, and your agreement with Sheol will not stand.

The reason it is important is that it highlights how Israel repeatedly behaved throughout the Old Testament by being unfaithful to God, leaving Him, and taking another god in His place. Her covenant with death is believed to be with the Egyptian god of death, Osiris (or Seth), who Israel believes will protect her from her enemies who threaten her very existence.[50] But this is typical of Israel's ongoing unfaithfulness, which we saw, for example in the Garden of Eden (Hosea 6:8), at Sinai (Exod. 32:4), and when Jeroboam set up golden calves for Israel to worship (2 Chron. 11:14–16).

Now this passage is set in the midst of 'the stone passage' (see Isa. 28:16, which is repeatedly referenced throughout the New Testament (Matt. 21:44; Mark 12:10; Luke 20:17; Acts 4:11; Rom. 9:33; 1 Pet 2:4]) suggests that the early believers would recognise what Israel had done. She had betrayed her loving Husband and taken the god of death, who she believed would offer her better protection than her own covenant-keeping God!

Devastating Consequences

What happened in the Garden had devastating consequences when Adam took the whole of his lineage from one Kingdom into another. He deliberately, tragically, and foolishly, turned from the God who loved him and embraced His enemy, who promised Adam all that God had sought to protect him from. Effectively, Adam took Satan in place of his loving Creator. He would serve the prince of darkness's vile intentions and seek his joy in his presence!

So how did this affect the way I read Romans 6:7? I suddenly saw that Paul had not changed the way he was arguing. He was still reasoning as a Jew! He had given no indication to the church in Rome that he had shifted his perspective one inch. This seriously clashed with the thinking that he was arguing as a Greek, which is what all the scholars I had read were either explicitly, or implicitly, assuming.

Therefore, if chapter 6 continues the reasoning of chapter 5, Paul is not writing about individual Christian experience but about the historical experiences of the Church as the elect community. It is about the New Covenant Community and how God has brought it into existence!

---

[50] J. Bright, art, 'Isaiah', in *Peakes Commentary on the Bible*, M. M. Black (ed), H.H. Rowley (ed) (Routledge; 1st edition. 1971) 509, points out that death, sheol, (moth) in v15 is also the name of the Canaanite god of the underworld and fertility. He thinks that, since the pact was with Egypt, the reference is probably to Egyptian deities of similar character, such as Osiris or Seth in whose name the pact was sealed.

Jesus and the Exodus

This was not the only insight I gained into Paul's understanding of justification. Years later, I was to see that the corporate reading of his letters had the effect of further opening up his doctrine of justification. I came to see that, throughout the Old Testament, justification is spoken about in many ways; in fact, nine in all. They were used to speak of covenant creation; covenant ratification; acquittal from sin; the imputation of righteousness; the declaration of covenant membership; God being justified; Israel being justified; justification of the Gentiles; and justification of the Divine Marriage.

I was amazed to find that, by reading Paul through the corporate lens, he was following and using this same range of nine categories of justification as well, and he used them in exactly the same way as the Old Testament writers had done. It is through this lens that the discovery of the multifaceted meaning of this vitally important doctrine was identified. This discovery was yet further confirmation of Paul's indebtedness and commitment to the Hebrew Scriptures.[51]

So, what is Paul meaning when he says, "he that has died is justified from sin"? Well, what he is *not* referring to is the freedom from sin that most have understood. If Paul is continuing his presentation seamlessly from chapter 5, we must remember that his main theme is Christ and His people.

Solving the Problem

So, how do we make sense of Romans 6:7? It is by seeing that Paul is answering the challenge of how Christ can take the elect community that had once belonged to Satan and make them His bride. He will state and explain this more fully in the opening verses of chapter 7. Here, it is sufficient to say that the Saviour can take fallen and defiled people from within the community in covenant with Satan and unite them together to be His bride. He can do it because they have shared in His death and, because of this, the covenant that enslaved them has been terminated. The elect community is no longer Satan's bride; death has not only freed her but, much more importantly, it has justified

---

[51] For more details of the nine Old Testament meanings of justification and how Paul keeps to these very meanings in corresponding discussions, see Holland, *The Search for Truth*, chapters 9-12.

her. She is not guilty for entering into this new relationship, which will be consummated on the last day.

Some may still ask whether this is the likely meaning, or is it one that is being read into the passage? This is a fair challenge because many interpretations are the result of the imposition of meanings rather than coming from within the passage and its context.

My answer to the challenge of imposition in Romans 6:7 is to remind you what we have already identified. Romans is saturated in Old Testament quotations and allusions, and the book that contributes most is Isaiah. Isaiah is all about the promised Second Exodus, and this has the Divine Marriage as its conclusion when Yahweh takes a bridal community from those who are in exile (in Babylon) and adds to them all believing Gentiles to form the New Covenant community, the Church (Isa. 19:19–25; 56:1–8; 60:1–3).

Also, we have seen that the eighteen quotations from Isaiah form the backbone of Paul's letter. We see this understanding worked out in the book of Revelation. Here, Satan is doing his best to stop Christ taking His bride; with its final chapters being about the bride's presentation to her Groom. We have seen that this Divine Marriage theme runs throughout the Old Testament as well as Paul's letters. Because of this, I do not believe that the meaning I have suggested is being read into the text; rather, it is an intrinsic part.

Therefore, there is no guilt carried over from the former marriage to Satan. He cannot cry out: "she cannot marry Jesus; she is mine". Death has broken his vile relationship and Christ will not accept that there is any charge for His Church to answer.

The Vindication of Paul

So, Paul has not made a mistake. He is not speaking of individual experience but the community's (the Church's), which has been 'justified from sin'. Once we recognise the way he uses the singular for Sin (i.e., Satan), Paul is saying that Satan cannot bring an accusation against Christ and His people for entering into the new marriage relationship. Indeed, this is the thrust of what Paul will say again in Romans 8:33–34; 7:1–4. In other words, Paul is not saying we have been freed from sinning but that we have been acquitted, justified, from any charge that Sin (Satan) can make against the redeemed people becoming Christ's bride. For, as Paul goes on to explain:

What then shall we say to these things? If God is for us, who can be against us? He who did not spare his own Son but gave him up for us all, how will he not also with him graciously give us all things? Who shall bring any charge against God's elect? It is God who justifies. Who is to condemn? Christ Jesus is the one who died—more than that, who was raised—who is at the right hand of God, who indeed is interceding for us. Who shall separate us from the love of Christ? Shall tribulation, or distress, or persecution, or famine, or nakedness, or danger, or sword? As it is written, "For your sake we are being killed all the day long; we are regarded as sheep to be slaughtered.' No, in all these things we are more than conquerors through him who loved us. For I am sure that neither death nor life, nor angels nor rulers, nor things present nor things to come, nor powers, nor height nor depth, nor anything else in all creation, will be able to separate us from the love of God in Christ Jesus our Lord. (Rom. 8:31–39)

And all God's people should say AMEN!

Conclusion

Once again, we have seen that by staying in the paradigm of the New Exodus one of the long-standing problems of the exegesis of Romans 6, i.e., the reason why Paul spoke of death and justification in v7, has been resolved. Instead of referring the justification of the individual, it speaks of the justification of the Church in that she is not committing adultery in becoming the bride of a new Husband while her former husband is alive. Through sharing in the death of Christ, His death has become her death, and through that death her relationship with Satan has been ended. This is another example of how the Exodus narrative brings greater clarification to what Paul has written.

Chapter 23 The Second Marriage

We have seen that there are three difficulties in Romans 6 that tend to be overlooked or avoided when preachers (and biblical scholars) explain the teaching of Paul about dying with Christ and death to sin. They are:

1. how being "baptized into Christ" releases believers from sin.
2. the meaning of "the body of sin".
3. why Paul contradicts his own theology by saying that through death they have been justified (Rom. 6:7).

I believe these problems are resolved only by reading chapter 6 as the ongoing argument of chapter 5, i.e., the consequence of human solidarity and Adam's disobedience. In this Hebraic way of thinking, the emphasis is on the community to which individuals belong through a covenant relationship. If we continue this reasoning into chapter 6, we see that Paul was continuing to write about the Church and he was not focusing on the individual. By acknowledging this, we find that the long-standing problems in chapter Romans 6:1–3,6–7 are resolved.

But there are two final problems that need to be considered and they come in the opening and closing verses of chapter 7, where Paul says:

> Or do you not know, brothers—for I am speaking to those who know the law—that the law is binding on a person only as long as he lives? For a married woman is bound by law to her husband while he lives, but if her husband dies she is released from the law of marriage. Accordingly, she will be called an adulteress if she lives with another man while her husband is alive. But if her husband dies, she is free from that law, and if she marries another man she is not an adulteress. Likewise, my brothers, you also have died to the law through the body of Christ, so that you may belong to another, to him who has been raised from the dead, in order that we may bear fruit for God. (Rom. 7:1–4)

And, at the end of the chapter, Paul writes:

> So I find it to be a law that when I want to do right, evil lies close at hand. For I delight in the law of God, in my inner

being, but I see in my members another law waging war against the law of my mind and making me captive to the law of sin that dwells in my members. Wretched man that I am! Who will deliver me from this body of death? Thanks be to God through Jesus Christ our Lord! So then, I myself serve the law of God with my mind, but with my flesh I serve the law of sin. (Rom. 7:21–25)

What is Paul saying by these statements about the significance of death and the law? And what does he mean by "this body of death" with which he seems to struggle (v24)? These are statements which still need to be unpacked and carefully examined. So, what does Paul mean by the illustration of dying to the law in v1–3, and, particularly, how is a person married to the law? How do we die to the law, and why is it called 'the law of sin and death'?

Law and its Universality

There are many suggestions made to explain the marriage passage of 7:1–3, but one of the most recent is that Paul is teaching that the believer has died so that he or she could marry the law. But this does not make any sense. No person has ever married the law! The law orders a marriage by setting out the terms on which it can take place, and through vows; a signed certificate; and witnesses; it gives the couple the right to say they are legally married. But no couple or person has ever married the law.

Now, interestingly, while most commentators continue to miss the corporate structure of chapter 6, which is typical of Hebraic thought, and skate over the problems I have raised and sought to explain in the earlier chapters, most scholars are now accepting that Romans 7 is not solely about Paul's experience as once thought. They believe it is about a larger group of which Paul is a representative member. In this understanding, the chapter is like a corporate lament, in which representatives of the human race express their distress over the consequences of being exiled from God.[52]

---

[52] For a recent study of lament in Romans see Crisler, Channing L. and Mark A. Seifrid, (2016). *Reading Romans as Lament: Paul's Use of Old Testament Lament in His Famous Letter* (Eugene, Oregon: Pickwick Publications).

Recent Scholarly Insights

Evidence that suggests the passage is drawing on the Old Testament's picture of humanity's exile from God is given by Goodrich.[53] He has shown that Romans 7 has echoes of Isaiah 40–66, which is all about God rescuing exiled Israel from Babylon so that He could take her as His bride once again. The 'new story' that Paul is writing about is how humanity, including Israel, discovers that she is cut off from God because of her sin. In this understanding, there's not one voice speaking but many, and among them is Paul's.

Most scholars now accept the corporate dimension of Romans 7:7–25, which speaks of a community that, through the disobedience of its head, has been excluded from God's presence. But these scholars, who accept the corporality of this passage, interpret Romans 7:1-6 as being about individual Christian experience. Why this unexplained movement from the singular to the corporate and how his readers are expected to follow its meaning is not addressed.

Throughout Romans 7:7–25, Paul speaks as a religious, Jewish, representative of the community. It is not biographical in the sense we are familiar with, so we must avoid analysing his experience through its statements. They are the words of many people, with one voice taking over from another as they contribute their testimony to this moving lament.

Insights From Folk Music

Recently, I listened to a radio program on the BBC where there was a discussion on folk songs. One of the contributing folk singers explained that folk songs are a collective production. A singer may compose a song about their experience, then later another singer might adapt some of it to speak of their experience. This borrowing and adapting goes on so that the final version of the song contains many voices and tells of many experiences. I believe this is how Romans 7 works. It is a lament of humanity's history, telling how it fell to the enticement of the prince of lies and the disastrous experiences that came from that dreadful act.

---

[53] See J. K. Goodrich, *Sold Under Sin: Echoes of Exile in Romans,* 14-25, NTS 59.4 (2013), 476-95.

Now while most commentators think chapter 6 is about individuals being baptised, I have tried to show that the entire chapter is like chapter 5. It not only follows it but is based upon it. Thus, it is about a community that was unified and baptised into Christ as He died. The community parallels the one that was in Adam, which died to God through Adam's disobedience. The first community was taken from life into death, but the second community has been taken from death into life.

The Correct Context

So, chapter 7 is an account of a community that lives under the consequences of having been excluded from fellowship with God. They are dead to Him and struggling in darkness and unbelief. Some are totally ignorant of their state and live as if they have a special relationship with God. Such is the position of Paul's own people, the Jews. Clearly, they have great regard for the law of God; but they don't recognise they are like all other people who are in Adam. True, they did once have a special relationship with God, but they messed it up and lost all the blessings they had been given. The reality is that they are no longer 'in Moses' but back 'in Adam'. Even though their own prophets, God's spokesmen, had warned that God would disown them, they continued to presume arrogantly that nothing would change. "The rest of the world is in Adam," they argued, "but we are the children of promise, the children of Abraham."

However, there are some Jews who, by faith, recognise their Maker is absent and that they are being ruled by Sin (Satan). They cry out to God for His help. These people, identified as the remnant, seek to put Him before all else.

Understanding Paul's Distress

One of the reasons for turning from the traditional understanding that the passage is all about Paul's own struggle with sin is because he says he had lived without the law (Rom. 7:9). This makes no sense, because there never was a time when Paul lived apart from the law. We don't have details of his early years, but he boasted he was of the tribe of Benjamin and circumcised on the eighth day (Phil. 3:5). He was born seemingly into a Hebrew-speaking home and lived his whole life under the law, guided either by his parents or a godly guardian's example and teaching. He progressed from obeying it as a family duty to personally embracing and living by it. His desire to become a teacher of the law led him to train in Jerusalem under the famous rabbi, Gamaliel.

But while most commentators have come to see that the passage is about the experience of either humankind or Israel (or possibly, both) in Adam rather than Paul's personal struggle, few, if any, seem to have resolved the enigma of the opening illustration of chapter 7.

Failure to Follow On.

Surprisingly, what these scholars have missed is that the illustration is referring to Israel's corporate experience of the law. They read the illustration as the conclusion of chapter 6, which they've treated as being about individual Christian experience.

It is not until v 7 that most scholars recognise that Paul has 'returned' to a corporate explanation begun in 5:12ff. They've failed to see that the illustration in the opening verses of the chapter is rooted in Israel's experience of God's call. She had been saved to be the bride of her God (Isa. 62:2–5; Jer. 2:1–3; Hosea 2:1–8). Tragically, she'd been unfaithful to her divine Husband and went after the gods of the surrounding nations, throwing herself at them and revealing in the licentious lifestyles the nations practiced and promoted.

The Old Testament talks about the nation of Israel as being God's bride; and in the New Testament it is always the Church that is the bride of Christ. In neither instance is the bride an individual. Thus, to force an individual interpretation on this passage is simply unacceptable and leaves readers confused and disappointed.

The corporate interpretation has resolved the technical textual problems of chapter 6, so we should not be surprised to find it is this same perspective that continues into the opening of chapter 7. Thus, Rom. 7:1ff continues the same sort of reasoning as found in chapters 5 and 6. In fact, the corporate reading is ongoing throughout the whole of Romans!

Deliverance From This Body of Death

The final passage that has caused scholars confusion as to how to understand it is:

> So I find it to be a law that when I want to do right, evil lies close at hand. For I delight in the law of God, in my inner being, but I see in my members another law waging war against the law of my mind and making me captive to the law of sin that dwells in my members. Wretched man that I am! Who will deliver me from this body of death? Thanks be to God through Jesus Christ our Lord! So then, I myself serve the law of God with my mind, but with my flesh I serve the law of sin. (Rom. 7:21–25)

Paul seems to continue to struggle with his flesh. He describes himself as a "wretched man" (v24^a) and longs for deliverance from "this body of death" (v24^b). Despite this burden, he thanks God for what he has received through Christ (v25^a) before suddenly, and unexpectedly for the reader, acknowledging that he still serves the law of sin (25^b).

But such a reading is ignoring what we have learned. The passage is corporate, it is the lament of those who were in Adam as they spoke of their desperate plight. Its Paul voice but also that of millions of others who were awakened to their condition in Sin, i.e., in their solidarity with Adam, and from which they long to be freed. This is not a description of every person, for many love their rebellion and prefer darkness rather than light. In this reading, the body of death (v24^a) is not the physical body, for we know that Paul, as a Jew, would never describe the body as sinful. As we found in Rom. 6:6, the body of Sin is the community that exists apart from Christ, so here the body of death is not the human corpse but the godless community, the world, that does its best to nullify the power of the gospel by mocking and threatening those who have left that realm and who rejoice to be members of Christ.

Conclusion

By following the principles of The Exodus narrative, we have found that Paul's descriptions are corporate and based on the merger of the Egyptian and Babylonian Exodus types. By appreciating this we have found new solutions to old problems. First, that Paul is not necessarily speaking of the Jewish law in the opening verses, but about law in general, acknowledging that even the Gentiles protect the state of marriage through laws that their societies respect and seek to live by. Second, that death to the law refers to the law or authority that the husband had over his wife in ancient marriage arrangements – more about this in the next chapter. Third, that the passage is a lament, in which humanity reflects on the consequences Adam's Fall bestowed on his offspring. And finally, the body of death has the same meaning as 'the body of sin', i.e., it speaks of humanity in covenant union with Satan. Paul's entire letter explains God's consistency in how He has dealt with humankind, including the Jewish people. All that He does has to be truthful; and, in rescuing humanity, He never fails to be the holy God that He is.

Chapter 24 The Law of Sin and Death

Once we understand the corporateness of Romans 5–7, the problematic texts that have caused scholars to 'correct' what Paul has written are shown to need no such correction at all. Indeed, the entire section opens up as a logical, coherent argument, in which all the grammatical details scholars have felt obliged to alter are exactly what Paul intended.

A visual presentation of chapters 5–7 may help to highlight the ongoing corporate explanation:

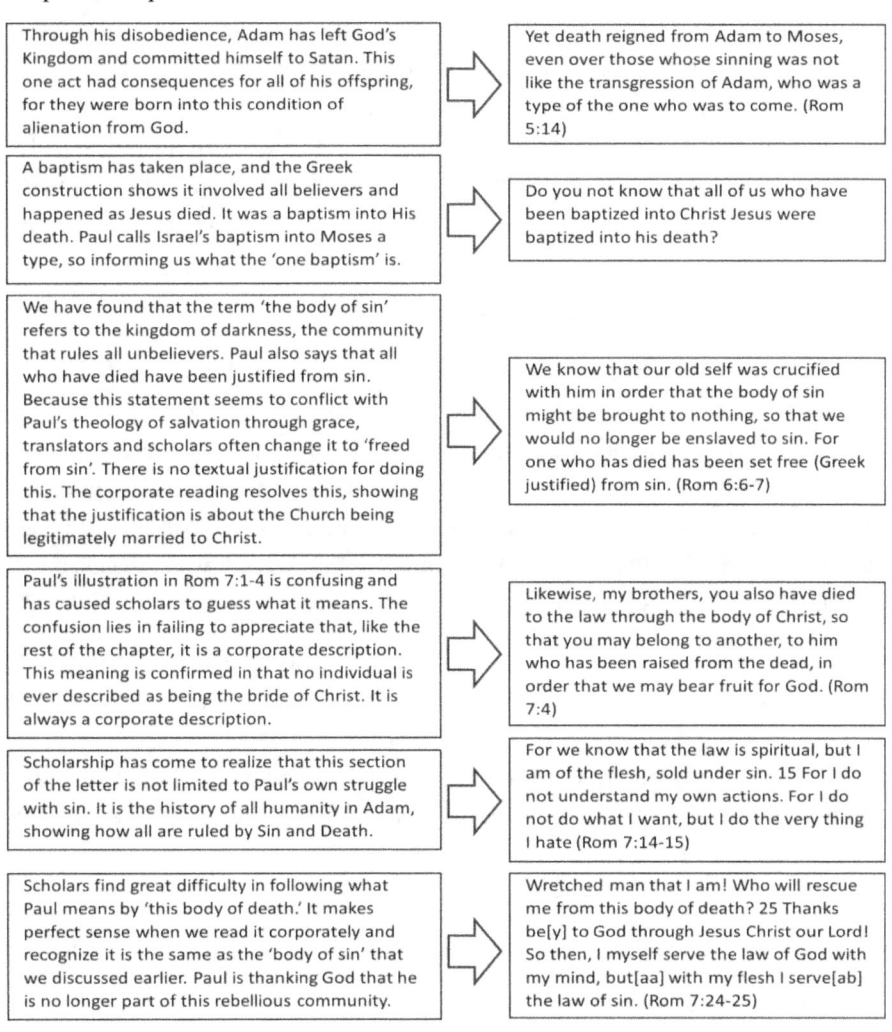

Hopefully, this diagram helps to show the flow of Paul's corporate argument. Admittedly, this has not been easy to identify because our western mindset is programmed to apply our analysis to individuals. But Paul, a first century Jew, couldn't think in such a way, for the corporate line of argument was natural to everyone who lived at that time in history, especially those who were Jews.

We have seen how in the following generations Israel embraced many other gods and served them with devotion. The nation was called 'an adulteress for she willingly chose Satan in the guise of these gods to replace God once again. Of course, there were some in Israel whose hearts had been circumcised, like the prophets. They didn't want to be under Satan's rule again but wanted to stay within the care of the God who had rescued them from Egypt. In Paul's story, Satan is the husband of those who are in Adam, but he is the former husband of those who are now in Christ! These two communities had a common ancestor in Adam, who had been in a covenant relationship with God in Eden and lost everything he had by believing Satan and betrayed the love of God.

Marriage as a Lifetime Commitment

In ancient understanding, a woman locked herself into a lifelong relationship when she married. In getting married, she was putting herself under the authority of her husband and, in some systems of marriage, he could even forbid a remarriage if they divorced. Indeed, the law, both Israel's Torah and probably the law of most nations, upheld that male status. This was the "law of the husband" that Paul refers to in Rom. 7:2.[54] As Death was also used as a pseudonym for Sin (Satan, the husband of the body of sin).

Thus, humanity in Adam is in a marriage-like covenant relationship with Satan, otherwise known as Sin and Death. The Torah itself (as do all systems of law which have family sections) upholds marriage vows and can be appealed to by any party when its precepts are not being respected. Because Satan can appeal to God's holy Law, it becomes the Law that serves this

---

[54] The ESV has 'she is released from the law of marriage. But in a footnote the translators acknowledge that the Greek is the *"law concerning the husband"* or as the AV has it, "she is loosed from the law of her husband".

wicked husband, so it is the Law of Sin and Death, i.e., the law that Satan, as the new husband, 'legitimately' appeals to.

It can be argued that Adam knew nothing about laws or covenants because the terms aren't found in the creation narrative. Nevertheless, Israel certainly did know these terms and their meanings, as well as the implications of their content, and read them back into Adamic imagery. It was Hosea who was first to explicitly use the Divine Marriage imagery, basing his entire prophecy on it and saying that Adam had broken the covenant.

So, even though there is no explicit mention of the Divine Marriage in the creation story and no mention of covenant in the opening chapters of Genesis, it does come into the understanding of the Jewish community. And the key to the backdoor of the Divine Marriage narrative is supplied by Hosea.

When Adam and Eve were excluded from the garden, the word used is the Hebrew for being 'put away'. This spoke of a man putting away his wife. The imagery comes up time and again throughout the Old Testament when the prophets warned that Israel will be 'put away' into exile if she continues to worship foreign gods. In other words, Israel was threatened with divorce.

In fact, Hosea uses this very term. When witnessing Israel's idolatry, he said: "But they have broken the agreement as Adam did; they have been unfaithful to me." (Hosea 6:7 New Century Version).[55] But because there is no mention of covenant in the creation account, some scholars suggest that 'Adam' does not refer to the garden account but to an obscure village called Adam, where they assume idolatry had taken place. The weakness of this suggestion is that there is no evidence that such practice has ever taken place in this very obscure, small, and insignificant place called Adam.

The Divine Marriage in the New Testament

Throughout this study, most of the material relating to the Divine Marriage theme has come from the Old Testament. It would be tragic if I left you with the impression that it had little reference to the Christian community, for it most certainly does. Indeed, to miss this would mean that you will have missed the glorious last chapter of the New Exodus narrative. To ensure that this

---

[55] The ISI has "But like Adam, they broke the covenant."

theme is not missed as a part of Christian biblical teaching, I give the following survey of this glorious New Testament theme:

The Divine Marriage in the Gospels

Matthew 22:1–12 records the wedding banquet. Here we see the combination of Kingdom/Divine Marriage imagery in ancient Israel, a Jewish bridegroom would wear a crown (and a seamless robe) on his wedding day.

Matthew 25:13 records that in the parable of the virgins, the servants should have watched for the coming of their master, who is described as the Bridegroom (v4). They are called not only to be ready for him but also for the bride he'd gone to fetch.

Mark 2:19 says that the disciples can't fast because the Groom is still with them. In Jewish tradition, fasting was forbidden when a wedding was in preparation. A bride is not even to mourn the death of her father, as the joy of the newly created union must not be marred.

John 2:1–12 tells of the wedding at Cana, where Jesus performs the bridegroom's role of providing the drink for the wedding. He provides the wine not only for this wedding but for the coming Divine Marriage. Only the groom and those who serve him know the true source of this wine, which is far better than what any other groom could provide.

John 4:5–29 recounts Jesus declaring Himself to be the promised Bridegroom Messiah, referencing, by allusion (v 26), His fulfilment of Isaiah 52:6: "… in that day they shall know that it is I who speak; here I am" and thus also of Isaiah 54 (as above).

The Divine Marriage in Paul

Romans 7:1–6 describes salvation as the Church marrying a new Husband.

1 Corinthians 6:20 says the believers have been bought with a price. This is not a reference to purchase from slavery, for the earlier language (1 Cor. 6:16–17) is marital imagery. Also, 1 Corinthians 5:7 says that "Christ our Passover has been sacrificed for us", so linking the Church's experience with Israel's history of being married to the Lord at Passover (Exodus). So, the

language of being redeemed, (1 Cor. 6:20), is the same as that used throughout the Old Testament of Yahweh redeeming Israel to be His bride.[56]

2 Corinthians 11:2 speaks of Paul presenting the Church to Christ as a pure virgin. Galatians 4:20–31 describes the Old and New Covenants as marriages. The Old is with Israel and the New is with the Church. The children of the Old are bound by the Law; the children of the New enjoy freedom from condemnation. The mothers are either Hagar, representing Israel under the Law, or the New Jerusalem, representing the Church (cf. Rev. 21:1–4). Paul appeals to Isaiah 56:1, in which widowed Israel is promised children:

> Fear not, for you will not be ashamed; be not confounded, for you will not be disgraced; for you will forget the shame of your youth, and the reproach of your widowhood you will remember no more. For your Maker is your husband, the LORD of hosts is his name; and the Holy One of Israel is your Redeemer, the God of the whole earth he is called. For the LORD has called you like a wife deserted and grieved in spirit, like a wife of youth when she is cast off, says your God. For a brief moment I deserted you, but with great compassion I will gather you. In overflowing anger for a moment I hid my face from you, but with everlasting love I will have compassion on you, says the LORD, your Redeemer. (Isa. 54:4–8)

In other words, the Lord will act as the Levirate (redeemer) husband and will be Israel's Redeemer.

Ephesians 5:22–33 gives an extended comparison between Christ and a human husband. It's an example of giving a deeper meaning to Genesis 2:24 to illustrate how the Church is the Bride in the Divine Marriage.

2 Timothy 2:11–13 is seen by some to be a Christian hymn, reflecting the betrothal practices of ancient Israel.

---

[56] For a fuller of this explanation see Holland, *Contours*, 111-139.

And finally, Rev. 21:1–4 speaks of the Church (the new Jerusalem), coming out of heaven as a Bride, beautifully dressed for her husband.

Thus, the Divine Marriage imagery was well known; and reading such statements in the context of this widespread understood model made perfect sense for the apostolic church.

Conclusion

So, we have attempted to follow The Exodus narrative that runs throughout the scriptures of Israel and have seen how Israel repeatedly followed the example of Adam in betraying her Creator by taking another god in His place. In doing this, she bound herself in a covenant relationship that excluded her Maker and replaced Him with other gods. In this new relationship(s), she accepted that they had 'legitimate' control in the marriage she had consented to. This is the setting that Paul uses to explain what being 'under Sin' entails. At the heart of The Exodus narrative is the promise that God will provide One who will break Satan's power that he has through God's own Law. This will bring about a new relationship that will never end (Gen. 3:15). If the Divine Marriage theme is missing from our understanding, then many passages will be inadequately understood. Texts that naturally fit into this model are often linked with adoption or slavery, with the result that the Exodus motif is further diminished. The concept of The Divine Marriage is central to understanding the New Exodus narrative. By missing this, a serious loss in Biblical understanding has occurred.

SECTION 4 Exploring Themes

Chapter 25 The New Exodus and the Firstborn of all Creation

The benefit of accepting a Hebraic reading of the New Testament is no better demonstrated than by Colossians 1:12–20. It is referred to by many as 'The Christ Hymn.' In this hymn, Jesus is called "the Firstborn of all creation."

From the earliest years of the church there were those who opposed calling Jesus 'God', and they used this passage as their key verse to prove their case. They argued that, if Jesus is the Firstborn of all creation, then there was a time when He didn't exist. He is, they conceded, the greatest of God's created beings but, because He was created, He was never God.

There are groups today that follow this argument, e.g., Jehovah Witnesses, Mormons, and Unitarians. All these groups claim to believe in God and link themselves, in various ways, to a distorted interpretation of the message that Jesus preached, while emphatically denying that He was (is) God.

Identifying Origins

Biblical scholars have grappled with the identity of the origin of the term 'firstborn' for centuries. Most have concluded that the term was used in the Greek world to speak of Wisdom and was taken up by the church to speak of Christ.

The argument used to support this claim was rather desperate. It contended that it was derived from a Jewish rabbi, Philo, who taught in the Egyptian city of Alexandria. Unapologetically, he sought to interpret the Old Testament scriptures in the light of Hellenistic philosophy. In that system, there is a term that spoke of a *'protogenesis'* being the elder son. In Philo's system of thought, the *protogenesis* was the nearest being to the unknowable God that had come amongst men to enlighten them to the truth.

Because the Greek for 'firstborn' was *'prototokos'*, a word that resembles *'protogenesis'*, Philo, along with others, assumed they had the same identity. It followed from this association that many scholars concluded that the *'protogenesis'* was the same as the *'prototokos'* and, because the *'protogenesis'* in Greek philosophy revealed the unknown god, the *'prototokos'* in Paul's argument became the incarnation of God's wisdom. By this very dubious linkage of terms with similar spellings but conflicting meanings, scholars concluded that the 'firstborn' was the incarnation of the wisdom of God.

Understanding Meanings

In all fairness, this connection was reasonable to make. After all, John tells us that "In the beginning was the Word and the Word was with God and the Word was God" and that "the Word became flesh" (John 1:1–3). It sounded like a perfect match, and the obvious origin and meaning of the term 'firstborn'; but it leaves some difficult issues unresolved. One of those issues is that *'prototokos'* simply is not the same as *'protogonos'*. You cannot, or rather you should not, play with language in such a way. Rain sounds the same as reign but the two are miles apart as far as meaning is concerned! A rule, as an instrument for measurement, is very different from a monarch's rule. Words like these cannot be merged to produce a collection of hybrid words, where the meaning of one is united with the meaning of the other to make a third new meaning.

Another reason for resisting such a merger of *'protogonos'* and *'prototokos'* is that they represent hugely different views of God. The Greek view is that he (or, maybe better, 'it') is totally unknowable. The Jewish/Christian view of God is that He is personal and self-revealing. He does not stand apart from His creation but engages with it and rules over it. The two views are diametrically opposed. Certainly, no Greek would think of the *'protogonos'* becoming incarnate; to do so would mean it had become a creature. Therefore, for the Greeks, who hold to a doctrine of dualism in which all physical things are seen as evil, physical incarnation is unfit to reveal the Logos. In their thinking, God was unknowable and would be defiled by any contact with anything that was physical.

So, we have to reject this Greek meaning of wisdom because it clashes with the Jewish understandings of the goodness of all creation and of physical things not being evil in themselves. Because of this, we have to reject the Greek origin of 'firstborn'. We need to look for a different solution.

An Obvious Solution

The answer is "it is in plain sight!" Whenever a suggestion is brought, the criterion by which it must be judged is whether it fits naturally into the passage in which it is used. So, what can we observe about the passage? It is widely acknowledged to be a hymn that praises Christ. It is also seen to have words that are believed to have Old Testament roots. As it's very unlikely that a Greek writer would use such words, it suggests that the hymn is highly likely to have a Jewish origin.[57]

Added to this, there are many scholars who see the three preceding verses (v12–14) to contain the New Exodus motif. They see that the author of the hymn (it is debated who wrote it) is modelling the death of Jesus and what His death achieved on the Exodus of Israel from Egypt under Moses. In fact, the end of the hymn also has a clear sacrificial theme as it speaks of Christ, by His death, reconciling all things together by His blood, shed on the cross (Col. 1:20). These themes have no place at all in the Hellenistic understanding of Wisdom, adding grave doubt to the claim that the source of the hymn was Hellenistic meditations on the source of Wisdom.

The Missing Designation

Another unexpected feature of this theme is while Yahweh is repeatedly called Israel's Redeemer, Jesus is never called the Church's Redeemer. What He is called is the "Firstborn of many brothers" (Rom. 8:29). And the reason why Jesus is not called the Redeemer? This is probably because the apostles knew that in The Exodus narrative any one of the brothers in a family could act as the redeemer if the older siblings refused the role, as we see in the story of Boaz and Ruth (Ruth 4:6). Another reason might be that the role of the redeemer was not vicarious, the redeemer did not die for members of his family. His intervention was social and economic but not vicarious in dying for them. In contrast to the role of the redeemer, which the firstborn could also reject fulfilling, the firstborn had no such option of abdicating his role as the firstborn. He was the one designated to die and so be the saviour of his family. Hence the reason for Jesus being called the Firstborn was that His primary role was to die for His people. But in Jesus, our faithful High Priest, He does not

---

[57] Peter Williams The director of Tyndale House Cambridge states: "Christianity arose in the cradle of Judaism, and the further back we go in time, the more Jewish all our records of Christianity are.... Scholars disagree on many matters concerning the gospels, but on one thing they seem almost universally agreed—the gospels are Jewish." Peter J. Williams, *Can We Trust the Gospels* (Wheaton, Ill.: Crossway, 2018). 22, 78.

leave the social role to others, so He is both the Firstborn and the Redeemer of His is people, but He is given the Firstborn title as this is His most important work.

What was Paul saying?

So, these clues suggest that, in Paul's thinking, Jesus died as the Passover sacrifice (2 Cor. 5:7), which delivered His people from the kingdom of darkness (Col. 1:12–14), as well as an offering for His people's sins (1 Cor. 15:3). In light of this, it would seem reasonable to suggest that Paul was saying that Christ died just as the firstborn at the Passover would have done if lambs had not been slain as their substitutes. Jesus died not only for His people's sins but also to redeem the whole of creation, for His death was to "reconcile all things in heaven and on earth and to make peace with God through the blood of his cross" (Col. 1:20). Therefore, Paul calls Jesus "the firstborn of all creation."

Now that is the most incredible thing imaginable. Only God can achieve this outcome, for the Old Testament repeatedly says that only the Creator can redeem His creation (Isa. 44:6; 65:17; Rev. 21:5). So, what does that lead us to? It is surely that Jesus is God in the flesh, which is why Paul says the fullness of God dwells in Him (Col. 1:19; 2:9). In other words, God is Jesus, or Jesus is God. Both statements are true!

Conclusion

We have seen that, historically, scholarship has sought to interpret the description of Jesus being the Firstborn of all creation by seeking to understand it as being the equivalent of a similar sounding word. But this was one that totally lacked any theological links whatsoever. Indeed, the presence of semitic themes in the hymn make it very unlikely that it comes from a Greek stable as the hymn requires a Hebrew foundation to make sense of these features in the original work. Because of this, we considered what redemptive event in Jewish history focused on the firstborn, and the obvious answer was the Passover. This setting removed all the problems scholars had with the meaning of the hymn and showed us that the Passover has huge significance in both Jewish and Christian soteriology. We have reached the point that ought to be convincing us that The Exodus narrative is the vital key to both Old and New Testament understanding of God and His redemptive work.

Chapter 26 Checking This Out

Now if this is how the first Christians viewed Jesus and His death, i.e., as being the fulfilment of the New Exodus promises, then we ought to find clear evidence to support it in the New Testament documents; and this is exactly what we find:

> Now the birth of Jesus Christ took place in this way. When his mother Mary had been betrothed to Joseph, before they came together, she was found to be with child from the Holy Spirit. And her husband Joseph, being a just man and unwilling to put her to shame, resolved to divorce her quietly. But as he considered these things, behold, an angel of the Lord appeared to him in a dream, saying, "Joseph, son of David, do not fear to take Mary as your wife, for that which is conceived in her is from the Holy Spirit. She will bear a son, and you shall call his name Jesus, for he will save his people from their sins." All this took place to fulfil what the Lord had spoken by the prophet: "Behold, the virgin shall conceive and bear a son, and they shall call his name Immanuel" When Joseph woke from sleep, he did as the angel of the Lord commanded him: he took his wife but knew her not until she had given birth to a son. And he called his name Jesus. (Matt. 1:18–25)

The use of the term 'firstborn' in the Greek of Matthew 1:25 is unexpected and redundant in the view of most scholars and translators, including the ESV. This is because the narrative has already stated that Jesus was Mary's first child, so they consider the statement that Jesus was her firstborn to be unnecessary. This is so widely agreed that most modern translations remove it. The difficulty in removing 'firstborn' is that the term is in all the earliest manuscripts; only one late text does not have it. Another problem with editing the text by removing words is that it is the wrong way round as far as textual critics are concerned. They reason that words are normally added by a scribe in an attempt to make meanings clear. However here, contrary to normal practice, a word, they say, has been removed.

But perhaps the presence of the term is not a Jewish problem but a Gentile one. The firstborn in the Jewish scriptures had a very important role. He represented his family on the night of the Passover and, if a lamb was not sacrificed in his place, he died when the Angel of Death passed through the land. Also, in Psalm 89:27, the Lord says of the Jewish king: "I have made him my firstborn over the kings of the earth".

In the opening chapters of Matthew, we have the magi coming to worship the One who was born King of the Jews and, later in the gospel, we are told that Jesus died as the Paschal (firstborn/royal) sacrifice. This fact was emphasized by the timing of His death, i.e., the Passover, and that He died under the inscription: 'The King of the Jews'(Matt. 27:37).

Following His death, Jesus told His disciples that all authority in heaven and earth was given to Him, i.e., following His resurrection He was the Lord of the whole of creation. He had rescued it from Satan's control and restored it to its rightful owner. In other words, He is 'the Firstborn of all creation'.

While most scholars have removed 'firstborn' from Matthew 1:25, they have had no textual evidence to warrant doing the same in Luke 2:7. There's not one late text to justify removing it from this passage, so scholars have left the supposedly redundant word where Luke placed it.

Luke and Jesus Status as the Firstborn

But, again, a better understanding of Jewish redemptive history provides the reason why Luke included it. He records that Jesus' parents, even though warned to flee because Herod was seeking the life of the child, went up to the temple to make a sacrifice for the purification of Mary (Lev. 12:6). This is strange, for it was no longer necessary under Jewish law to make the offering in the Temple. If it had been, then the vast majority of Jewish mothers could not have gone through purification following childbirth as they lived too far away from the temple to be able to present themselves by the specified date. But this requirement was made possible because in many places the local synagogue was called the temple.

A careful reading of Luke 2:22–26 gives information that has often been overlooked. It was not Mary who was being presented to the Lord, it was Jesus:

Jesus and the Exodus

> Now when the time came for their purification according to the law of Moses, Joseph and Mary brought Jesus up to Jerusalem to present him to the Lord (just as it is written in the law of the Lord, *"Every firstborn male will be set apart to the Lord"*), and to offer a sacrifice according to what is specified in the law of the Lord, a pair of doves or two young pigeons. (Luke 2:22–26 NET).

Thus, Luke makes it abundantly clear that the purpose of the visit was "to present Him (the baby Jesus) to the Lord." According to Hays intertextual exegesis, an Old Testament quote in the New Testament is recognised as a signpost, referring the reader back to the wider context of the citation. This context yields a far greater meaning than the quote alone.[58] Thus, we see that the thrust of the original passage is about the need to redeem the firstborn. This vitally important theme is not mentioned by Luke but he has directed his reader(s) to it:

> Everything devoted in Israel will be yours. The firstborn of every womb which they present to the LORD, whether human or animal, will be yours. Nevertheless, the firstborn sons you must redeem, and the firstborn males of unclean animals you must redeem. And those that must be redeemed you are to redeem when they are a month old, according to your estimation, for five shekels of silver according to the sanctuary shekel (which is twenty gerahs). (Num. 18:14–16 NET)

Now, while Luke says everything was done according to the law, he fails to mention the most important observance for any Jewish couple to follow. There's no mention of Joseph and Mary redeeming Jesus. If a firstborn child was not redeemed in acknowledgement that the firstborn was spared in the first Passover when the Angel of Death passed through the land, then he was taken as the Lord's property to serve as a priest, eventually serving in the Temple.

So, by not redeeming the child, Mary and Joseph were doing nothing less than presenting Jesus to the Lord to become a Priest (Num. 3:11–13). This

---

[58] See Hays, Echoes of Scripture.

failure to redeem Him cannot be an oversight on their part or Luke's as they all knew it was the most important thing any Jewish couple had to do on the birth of a firstborn son. It was God's command to all Israelites, so it is inconceivable for them to have overlooked performing this crucial ritual.

This suggestion is supported by the fact that Mary sang the song of Hannah (1Sam 2:1–10; Luke 1:46–55) when she visited the home of Elisabeth early in her pregnancy. This was a song that Hannah sang as she presented her son, Samuel, to the Lord to become a priest under Eli. In taking this song to her lips, Mary was clearly identifying her action with Hannah's act of consecration. When, as a youth, Jesus remained in the Temple without His parent's knowledge, His words to them were: "Why were you searching for me?" "Didn't you know I had to be in my Father's house?" (Luke 2:49). This was something they should have known as they hadn't redeemed Him as a baby. So His calling, which they had clearly recognised by not redeeming Him, was to be a Priest.

His being dedicated to the Lord explains Jesus' reaction when His disciples told Him that His mother and brother were outside the house. He said: "Who is my mother, who are my brethren but those who hear the word of God and obey it" (Luke 8:19–21). Because He had not been redeemed, the natural ties of His family had been severed. His brothers and sisters were fellow members of the Kingdom of God, and all who believed in Him were fellow priestly people (1 Pet 2:9).

Further Supporting Evidence

In Romans Paul writes:

> For I consider that the sufferings of this present time are not worth comparing with the glory that is to be revealed to us. For the creation waits with eager longing for the revealing of the sons of God. For the creation was subjected to futility, not willingly, but because of him who subjected it, in hope that the creation itself will be set free from its bondage to corruption and obtain the freedom of the glory of the children of God. For we know that the whole creation has been groaning together in the pains of childbirth until now. And not only the creation, but we ourselves, who have the firstfruits of

> the Spirit, groan inwardly as we wait eagerly for adoption as sons, the redemption of our bodies. For in this hope we were saved. Now hope that is seen is not hope. For who hopes for what he sees? But if we hope for what we do not see, we wait for it with patience.
>
> Likewise the Spirit helps us in our weakness. For we do not know what to pray for as we ought, but the Spirit himself intercedes for us with groanings too deep for words. And he who searches hearts knows what is the mind of the Spirit, because the Spirit intercedes for the saints according to the will of God. And we know that for those who love God all things work together for good, for those who are called according to his purpose. For those whom he foreknew he also predestined to be conformed to the image of his Son, in order that he might be the firstborn among many brothers. And those whom he predestined he also called, and those whom he called he also justified, and those whom he justified he also glorified. (Rom. 8:18–30)

The meaning of v29 is normally taken as Christ being the elder brother of God's family. But this misses the flow of the passage. Paul has described Jesus' death in terms of a Passover sacrifice, which is clearly shown in Romans 3:21–25. Just as the Passover sacrifices were publicly displayed when their blood was daubed on the doorposts and lintels, so Jesus' death was publicly displayed at Calvary. The Passover was the only sacrifice publicly displayed. It involved God passing over the sins previously committed (Rom. 3:25) and was a sacrifice for both atonement and redemption. All of these key words are pointing to the Paschal nature of Jesus' death.[59]

The Role of the Firstborn

As has been mentioned, the firstborn son was given a very important role in the Jewish family. He was its appointed redeemer; and to enable him to fulfil this role he was given double the inheritance of his siblings. This 'double

---

[59] For a fuller discussion, see Tom Holland, *Romans the Divine Marriage, A Biblical Theological Commentary* (Eugene, OR: Pickwick Publications, 2011). 48-96

portion' provided him with funds that might be needed to support the remainder of the family. For example, it would enable him to rescue a family member from servitude by paying the debt they'd incurred and could not repay. And this is what Romans 8:29 is about. Jesus is the Firstborn, or Redeemer, of many brethren. That is what Paul has been describing; for, by His death, Jesus redeemed humanity's lost inheritance by redeeming the creation it had been given in the Genesis narrative. This was an inheritance that groaned and travailed, waiting its final redemption. It had become the property that Satan dared to offer Jesus if He bowed down and worshipped him.

In Romans 8:31–39, Paul expands this thought:

> What then shall we say to these things? If God is for us, who can be against us? He who did not spare his own Son but gave him up for us all, how will he not also with him graciously give us all things? Who shall bring any charge against God's elect? It is God who justifies. Who is to condemn? Christ Jesus is the one who died—more than that, who was raised—who is at the right hand of God, who indeed is interceding for us. Who shall separate us from the love of Christ? Shall tribulation, or distress, or persecution, or famine, or nakedness, or danger, or sword? As it is written, "For your sake we are being killed all the day long; we are regarded as sheep to be slaughtered." No, in all these things we are more than conquerors through him who loved us. For I am sure that neither death nor life, nor angels nor rulers, nor things present nor things to come, nor powers, nor height nor depth, nor anything else in all creation, will be able to separate us from the love of God in Christ Jesus our Lord.

Evidence from Hebrews

Further evidence is found in Hebrews:

> He is the radiance of the glory of God and the exact imprint of his nature, and he upholds the universe by the word of his power. After making purification for sins, he sat down at the right hand of the Majesty on high, having become as much

> superior to angels as the name he has inherited is more excellent than theirs. For to which of the angels did God ever say, "You are my Son, today I have begotten you"? Or again, "I will be to him a father, and he shall be to me a son"? And again, when he brings the firstborn into the world, he says, "Let all God's angels worship him." Of the angels he says, "He makes his angels winds, and his ministers a flame of fire." But of the Son he says, "Your throne, O God, is forever and ever, the sceptre of uprightness is the sceptre of your kingdom. You have loved righteousness and hated wickedness; therefore God, your God, has anointed you with the oil of gladness beyond your companions." (Heb. 1:3–9)

In this passage, Christ is described as being God's Firstborn, who the Father has brought into the world. Earlier, He was described as the express image of the invisible God. The Firstborn cleansed His people from their sins and then sat down on the right hand of the Majesty on high (Heb. 1:3). The passage goes on to say that this One, who sits at the right hand of God, will transform creation when He rolls it up like a robe. "Like a garment they will be changed" (Heb. 1:12).

The second chapter goes on to emphasise the oneness of Christ with His people using clear Adamic imagery (Heb. 2:5–8). Once again, the same motifs found in other passages containing the description of 'Firstborn' are present, so the themes of redemption, kingship, and New Creation are used. This suggests that the New Testament's use of 'Firstborn' is a key term of redemptive history.

In Hebrews 12:23, the author informs his readers that they have come to the Church of the Firstborn. This is much more than a title setting Christ as the Head of the Christian community. In line with earlier use, it describes the Church as His property also for He has given His life for her redemption (9:11–13, 24–28).

Finally, in Revelation 1:4–8:

> John to the seven churches that are in Asia: Grace to you and peace from him who is and who was and who is to come, and from the seven spirits who are before his throne, and from

> Jesus Christ the faithful witness, the firstborn of the dead, and the ruler of kings on earth. To him who loves us and has freed us from our sins by his blood and made us a kingdom, priests to his God and Father, to him be glory and dominion forever and ever. Amen. Behold, he is coming with the clouds, and every eye will see him, even those who pierced him, and all tribes of the earth will wail on account of him. Even so. Amen. "I am the Alpha and the Omega," says the Lord God, "who is and who was and who is to come, the Almighty."

This passage is a further example of a New Testament writer speaking of Christ as being the Firstborn. He has been raised from the dead and is presented as the conqueror of death (see also Col. 1:18; Heb. 1:3; 2:14–15). This is far more than John asserting that Christ is the victorious Messiah, for He is worshipped as the One who has "freed us from our sins by his own blood". Those He redeemed He formed into a priestly people to serve God (Rev. 1:5). Clearly, Jesus is the originator of the New Creation which Isaiah, in particular, spoke about and which the book of Revelation majors on.

Conclusion

We can see from this study that the clear meaning of a major New Testament text has been hidden because it was not read as being a fruit of The Exodus narrative. Many scholars had noted that the introduction to the hymn was based on the Exodus story of redemption but, instead of allowing the introduction to the hymn to guide its interpretation, it was abandoned, and a Greek source replaced the Old Testament story of the Exodus event. There are many other examples of failures to recognise the powerful influence of The Exodus narrative in the New Testament, but none are as significant as this hymn. It has been the Achilles heel of the doctrine of the Trinity. By recognising the control that the Exodus story has on the meaning of the hymn, it ceases to be the problem it has been since the second century when Arian used it as his key evidence to deny the teaching of Athanasius. In fact, it not only ceases to be a problem for the doctrine of the Trinity, the hymn becomes its most important evidence, for only God Himself can redeem His creation, and that is exactly what the death of Jesus achieved (Col. 1:20). So, Jesus is much more than a creature, He is the Creator Himself who has redeemed His creation and conquered Satan. This vital dimension of Christology could only be established because it was the fruit of understanding the existence of The Exodus narrative.

Chapter 27 Understanding the Biblical Meaning of 'Flesh'

As we have seen, the Old Testament is clear that flesh is never used to say something is evil. It would help us to see the way this Hebrew word *basar* was used in the Old Testament and how it was translated by the Greek word *sarx* (flesh) to convey the Hebraic meanings. By such a study, we will discover that the translators of the Hebrew Bible did not abandon the Hebraic meaning.

In the Greek Old Testament (LXX), *basar /sarx* is used to designate people, so:

> And God saw the earth, and behold, it was corrupt, for all flesh had corrupted their way on the earth. And God said to Noah, "I have determined to make an end of all flesh, for the earth is filled with violence through them. Behold, I will destroy them with the earth. (Gen. 6:12–13)

The NIV has "for all the people on the earth had corrupted their ways."

The term is not restricted to humans, it is also used to speak of all airbreathing beings, so:

> For behold, I will bring a flood of waters upon the earth to destroy all flesh in which is the breath of life under heaven. Everything that is on the earth shall die. (Gen. 6:17)

> They went into the ark with Noah, two and two of all flesh in which there was the breath of life. (Gen. 7:15).

It is used to speak of the body or skin, so:

> You shall be circumcised in the flesh of your foreskins, and it shall be a sign of the covenant between me and you. (Gen. 17:11)

> So he went down and dipped himself seven times in the Jordan, according to the word of the man of God, and his flesh was restored like the flesh of a little child, and he was clean. (2 Kings 5:14)

> Let her not be as one dead, whose flesh is half eaten away when he comes out of his mother's womb. (Num. 12:12)

> But you shall not eat flesh with its life, that is, its blood. (Gen. 9:4)

> Both he who is born in your house and he who is bought with your money, shall surely be circumcised. So shall my covenant be in your flesh an everlasting covenant. (Gen. 17:13)

> They shall eat the flesh that night, roasted on the fire; with unleavened bread and bitter herbs they shall eat it. (Exod. 12:8)

It is used in a way that shows that flesh is clearly not evil, so:

> Whatever touches its flesh shall be holy, and when any of its blood is splashed on a garment, you shall wash that on which it was splashed in a holy place. (Lev. 6:27)

> And the flesh of the sacrifice of his peace offerings for thanksgiving shall be eaten on the day of his offering. He shall not leave any of it until the morning. (Lev. 7:15)

However, Numbers 9:6 shows that when the body dies it becomes ceremonially unclean and anything that touches it also becomes unclean. If this happens to a person, they have to wash and be separated for seven days (Num. 19:11) to avoid contaminating other people. But here, the uncleanness is because it is a dead body, which no doubt has begun to decay and carry dangerous pathogens. The uncleanness has nothing to do with a body that has become sinful.

It is used to speak of humankind, so:

> And the glory of the LORD shall be revealed, and all flesh shall see it together, for the mouth of the LORD has spoken. (Isa. 40:5)

It is used to denote family relationships, so

> This at last is bone of my bones and flesh of my flesh" (Gen. 2:23)

> Then the word of the LORD came to him: "This man will not be your heir, but a son who is your own flesh and blood will be your heir." (Gen. 15:4 NIV)

Laban, Jacob's uncle, is approached to see if he will allow his daughter Rachel to marry Jacob, and he said:

> and Laban said to him, "Surely you are my bone and my flesh." (Gen. 29:14)

Laban is clearly agreeing to the marriage, saying Jacob belonged to the same family community. The relationship had nothing to do with Laban being Jacob's uncle but everything to do with wider family relationships.

Later in Genesis we have the story of the brothers of Joseph, full of envy, planning to sell Joseph into slavery. Genesis records Judah saying these words:

> "Come, let us sell him to the Ishmaelites, and let not our hand be upon him, for he is our brother, our own flesh." And his brothers listened to him. (Gen. 37:27)

This familiar meaning is found in what Israel said of David at his coronation:

> Then all Israel gathered together to David at Hebron and said, "Behold, we are your bone and flesh." (1 Chron. 11:1)

This is clearly nothing to do with their bodies being joined together. They are obviously declaring their oneness with David as a result of having a common ancestor. Because of this common ancestral link, they were happy to accept him as their king and be bound as subjects to him.

It is used to speak of human weakness or frailty:

> "With him is an arm of flesh, but with us is the LORD our God, to help us and to fight our battles." And the people took confidence from the words of Hezekiah king of Judah. (2 Chron. 32:8)

Jesus and the Exodus

> Then all flesh shall know that I am the LORD your Saviour,
> and your Redeemer, the Mighty One of Jacob. (Isa. 49:26)

The passage describes the frailty of humanity, likening it to grass that is so transitory, for we are here one day and gone the next. Humankind is like this, says Isaiah. It cannot claim any existence other than what God's will and purpose determine. Israel can be sure of a more dependable existence than grass because God is not only her Creator but also her Saviour and Redeemer.

It is used to speak of the key blessing to people who are in the New Covenant, so:

> And I will give you a new heart, and a new spirit I will put within you. And I will remove the heart of stone from your flesh and give you a heart of flesh. (Ezek. 36:26).

> And it shall come to pass afterward, that I will pour out my Spirit on all flesh; your sons and your daughters shall prophesy, your old men shall dream dreams, and your young men shall see visions. (Joel 2:28)

Here is the clearest evidence possible that the Hebraic view of flesh was the very opposite from the Graeco-Roman view. For the latter, it was the source of evil; for the former, it spoke of purity and blessing. A heart of flesh was given to God's repentant people so that they could obey the terms of the New Covenant.

I hope that from this brief analysis you will see that the word '*sarx*' has some very positive meanings in the Greek Old Testament. In fact, one of the great blessings of the promised New Covenant was that the people would be given hearts of flesh. Its meaning cannot possibly be a sinful heart; rather, it is an obedient heart that senses its weakness. It is a heart that loves God and wants to serve Him.

These are the Hebrew meanings for 'flesh' in the Old Testament. Not one of them comes close to the Greek meaning of something that is intrinsically evil or is an expression of sexual perversion.

To judge if Paul's use of 'flesh' lines up with his Hebraic heritage, we need to work through all of his letters. Also, as the word *sarx* is also found elsewhere in the New Testament, it would be wise to note what the other writers are doing with the term. To do this requires examining a large number of texts, so this will make a demanding chapter.

To avoid loading the reader with an obligation to read this evidence and causing some to lose the flow of the main arguments I am trying to make, that Paul's thoughtforms are essentially Hebraic rather than Greek, the evidence will be put as an appendix on the publisher's website.[60] When Paul speaks of being in the flesh is saying that they live according to the lifestyle set by Adam's disobedience. While this lifestyle can include sexual immorality it is not necessarily the predominant feature, for strictly religious observance itself can be a work of the flesh (Col. 2:18; 23; Gal. 5:19–21).

In these passages, Paul is using the term as an expression of human solidarity in the family of Adam, similar to how the Israelites addressed David when they joined him at Hebron saying they were his 'bone and flesh' (1 Chron. 11:1).Thus, for Paul, being 'in the flesh' means being under the curse that Adam's disobedience brought about; being 'in Christ' is the opposite, and speaks of having all the blessings Christ has secured through His death for His people. Unredeemed humanity is in the flesh; redeemed humanity is in the Spirit. Both terms are essentially relational and covenantal, and 'flesh' in Hebrew thinking in these passages has very little to do with sex or the body.

Conclusion

We have seen that when Jews refer to 'flesh' they mean something quite different from the Greek meaning. The former meaning has a corporate focus that the Greek one does not contain, and it has a much greater range of meanings. This demonstrates how the translator of any literature must be alert to the cultural and historical differences between the work of the original author and him/herself. All too often the translated version loses the distinct features contained in the original text. (One such example is the loss of the Hebraic emphasis on corporateness.) The culture of the translator can control the translation to such a degree that misunderstanding is built into the new text and the reader is denied its true meaning. It is partly through this loss of the Hebrew meaning through its translation into Greek that The Exodus narrative

---

[60] See www.apiarypublishing.com/jesusandtheexodus/flesh_in_the_new_testament/.

has been missed, as has its importance as a guide in our interpretation of the New Testament.

SECTION 5 Checking Out History

Chapter 28 Recovering Apostolic History

All that I have shared in this book has been based on careful research. Following a range of publications, which have been reviewed by world-leading scholars, there have been no serious challenges to my proposals, apart from one issue. This one challenge that has been made is the impossibility that Paul was as committed to the Jewish tradition as I have argued. This claim is made because most scholars agree that first century Judaism was thoroughly Hellenised. They believe this is established through inscriptions and texts found in Palestine, which show heavy indebtedness to Greek thought. Scholars argue that, because of this, it was not possible for Paul to have avoided being influenced by Hellenism.

While it is true that the Roman occupiers enforced Rome's standardization regarding laws and commercial practices, it does not prove that everyone enthusiastically embraced its culture. Clearly, resentment over Roman control simmered away in most of the population and the preference for most Jewish people would have been to follow their own ancient culture and practices. I can verify this from my own experience as an Englishman living in Wales. Almost all Welsh people speak English, but a growing portion are returning to their national language of Welsh as a way of asserting their separate identity. This has historical precedence going back into ancient history and is happening throughout the world to this day. The Jews of the first century were no less proud than any other group, indeed they were far prouder of their national identity than most. In the light of this it is unreasonable to treat this period as one when Jews welcomed the culture of their unwelcome occupiers. In other words, we must let the Jews of the first century be themselves and resist the trend to be academic anarchists by destroying other histories in order to create the required 'evidence' to support our modern intellectual fads.

The Evidence of Borrowing

The case for the Hellenisation of the church rests on three assumptions:

Firstly, there is 'evidence' that Hellenistic material was used by the apostles who wrote the New Testament. This is a powerful point; but only until the examples that are presented as evidence are examined in detail. For example, the dominant belief of Jesus being the 'Firstborn of all creation' in Colossians

1:18 is that it reflects the Greek belief in the unknowable god, who is described as 'the wisdom of the cosmos'. But, as we have seen by following the narrative of the Passover though the Old Testament and then into the New Testament, it has been shown that the Hellenistic solution is a false understanding that has cloaked the proper Hebraic meaning of the title 'Firstborn', a title in which the Church greatly rejoiced.

I have examined other examples where most scholars assume that the Church used Greek ideas/illustrations as understood by the wider Romans world in the first century and have shown that these Graeco-Roman based solutions to the meaning of texts have produced more problems than they are supposed to have solved. However, a careful study of the Old Testament provides far more satisfying Hebraic solutions.[61]

Also, the argument that because Paul wrote in Greek is proof that he was Hellenised hardly merits a reply. Millions of immigrants have learned their host country's language in order to partake in employment opportunities etc., but they would be insulted if they were charged with betraying the culture of their home nations. Often, they are the most ardent of national observers.

The Evidence of a Straw Man

Secondly, it was widely argued that Paul was appointed to be the apostle to the Gentiles because of his supposed education in their culture. Because of his education in Hellenism, he was supremely equipped to commend the gospel to these people who were afar off, for he could communicate in both their language and culture. But again, this is based on unsupported evidence. We have found from Romans 5–7 that Paul backed his message by referencing the Old Testament scriptures and not once by appealing to Greek culture. We saw how Old Testament material pervades all his preaching throughout the Acts of the Apostles. The single appeal to a poet in Acts 17:23, which many appeal to as evidence for Hellenisation, fails to secure the claim for a Hellenised Paul. Almost everyone can, even though they might not know its source, quote a line from Shakespeare. It would be utter folly to argue the person had a thorough knowledge of the bard's work based on the quote of a single line of his texts.

---

[61] For other examples of confusion see Holland, *Search for Truth*, 47-126

Jesus and the Exodus

Those who argue that Paul Hellenised the Christian message are faced with the problem that none of the presentations he made in his evangelistic work as recorded throughout Acts (apart from his very brief citation of a Greek poet in Athens to get attention) has any Greek content. In contrast to this, they are bathed in Hebraic texts and arguments. This inconsistency highlights the paucity of the claim that the church had become Hellenised, requiring the use of Hellenistic texts to interpret Paul's message. Those who continue to argue for a Hellenised Paul must answer the question: "Why did he change the content of his letters when he was evangelizing by using the same Hebraic message that Peter had used at Pentecost?" The answer is simply that Paul never was Hellenised, and he never sought to Hellenise the church.

There is no suggestion that Paul made any attempt to construct either a philosophical or theological case for his message, which was all about the resurrection of Christ.[62] It was this that caused a large portion of the crowd listening to him in Acts 17 to turn away to seek some other presentation that they hoped would be more relevant to them. To argue, as some do, that the quote was the introduction to a much longer oration which engaged with the teaching of the philosophers is nothing but speculation and should not be considered as serious evidence.

Abandonment of the Sacred

Thirdly, it is argued that, because the Church moved away from its Jewish roots by rewriting its message in imagery acceptable to Gentile minds, it resulted in an explosive expansion of its numbers. But there is no evidence, other than that cited above and shown to be seriously off-target, that this expansion happened because of the Jewish message being Hellenised. The claim that the expanding Gentile churches were led by men who preached an adapted Hellenised message has no evidence to support it. It is based on the imagination of scholars, drawing their evidence from the development of secular, parallel movements. They have overlooked the phenomenal, supernatural element of early Jewish Christian history. They have embraced the largely irrelevant conclusions of sociological studies, which can say nothing about a movement that has been born in the context of the fulfilment

---

[62] See Holland, *Search for Truth*, 47-155.

of Israel's hopes in the coming of God's Servant and His death to bring humanity out of Satan's control.

In ignoring this dimension, that the sociological understanding was based not on facts but on prejudices that reject the spiritual dimension of the Christian Gospel. They, therefore, have no relevance in contributing to a true account of those early years of the Church's history.

Testing History

Could the message of Christ have had the effect that the New Testament suggests? Firstly, we need to appreciate the impact that the coming of Jesus had. Not only had the Old Testament scriptures spoken about it, but John the Baptist declared to Israel that Jesus was the promised Messiah. The crowds that flocked to see and hear Him were huge, and this went on for an unspecified length of time. John's preaching clearly had a massive impact, even attracting the attention of the leaders in Jerusalem.

Likewise, Jesus' teaching and healing ministries repeatedly drew huge crowds of many thousands, many of whom travelled considerable distances to hear Him. It is hard to imagine a community that did not know something about the Prophet from Nazareth. The sudden appearance and explosion of the 'Jewish sect', later called the 'followers of the Way', caused the message about Jesus to spread like wildfire. Even in Jerusalem the Jewish leaders expressed fear that the whole world was going after Him (John 12:19).

The Power of the Resurrection Event

After Jesus' resurrection, the witness of the apostles to His resurrection persuaded many thousands of Jews to become His disciples. Soon news of the resurrection broke out of Judea and reached synagogues throughout the Roman world. This spread of the message would have been inevitable as pilgrims returned home from Jerusalem after the events of the Passover in which Jesus died with the news that the crucified Jesus had risen from the dead. Their testimony was later added to by Jews who witnessed the day of Pentecost in Jerusalem and heard the powerful preaching of Peter. He explained the significance of the different tongues that were being spoken by the apostles, resulting in 3,000 responding and submitting to baptism.

Jesus and the Exodus

There was clearly a lot of confusion, both inside and outside the movement (Acts 19:1–4; 1 Cor. 15: 12–19; 1 Thes. 5:6–14). To correct this, the apostles wrote letters to the fledgling churches and travelled extensively to explain the significance of the teaching, death, and resurrection of Jesus.

Tracing the History of the Church's Expansion

The converts won by Peter's sermon on the Day of Pentecost were all devout Jews who never saw themselves to be responding to a new religion. They were embracing the fulfilment of the promises that the Old Testament had repeatedly made of a restoration of Israel to her God. It was through the witness of these new believers when they returned to their own communities that the message was taken out from Jerusalem. A third wave of 'gospel witness' followed when the authorities manipulated a wave of persecution against the Church, causing many believers to flee to places where they felt safer. This led to believing communities being born. These came into existence before Paul became a follower of Jesus. An example of these communities was the one in Damascus to which he travelled in order to arrest its believers. It was when Paul was on the way to Damascus that he encountered the risen Christ.

Clearly, one of the greatest events brought about by the gospel was the transformation of Paul (then, Saul of Tarsus) from fanatical opponent of the movement to becoming one of the Church's most committed and effective preachers of the gospel. It is beyond dispute that Paul had massive influence, not only on the mission to the Jews (Acts 9:22) but also to the nations.

Jewish Evangelism

Although Paul was called to be the apostle to the Gentiles, it would be a serious mistake to think that he neglected the Jewish community. This was far from true. He stated the agenda of his missionary work when he wrote to the church in Rome: "For I am not ashamed of the gospel, for it is God's power for salvation to everyone who believes, to the Jew first and also to the Greek" (Rom. 1:16). In fact, he saw that, if the Jewish community could be won, it would be hugely significant for winning the Gentiles (Rom. 11:12). His actual ministry to reach the Gentile world did not happen for some years after becoming a disciple of Jesus (Acts 11:25–26; 13:1–4).

Even though Paul's ministry focused on reaching the Gentiles, he continued to attend local synagogues. These places of instruction and worship, scattered throughout the Roman Empire, regularly had Gentiles, called 'God-fearers', in their congregations. They had turned from their pagan gods and had come to listen and learn about the God of Israel from the Jewish scriptures. These were the Gentiles Paul wanted to reach, for not only were they identifying with the descendants of Abraham and their God, but they were the low-hanging fruit that was ripe for picking!

The Message That Won Gentiles

In these synagogue services, it was normal for a visiting rabbi to be invited to bring a message; and Paul was treated no differently. He was urged by the people to tell them about the message he was preaching concerning Jesus and the Way (Acts 9:2). The God-fearers had no problem with what he was expounding, for they saw it was supported by what the Jewish scriptures taught. What they were hearing was the 'primitive' gospel message as preached by Peter on the Day of Pentecost. Gentiles heard this very Jewish message and believed (Acts 13:43–44). What was especially welcoming for them was to be told that God did not require their physical circumcision to become one of His people. Evidence that their hearts had been circumcised meant that they already had what circumcision symbolized.

Thus, the early churches were established in the same gospel that was first preached to the Jews after the resurrection of Jesus. There had been no adaptation or development of the message to engage the Gentile world as is claimed by many scholars. It was the preserved Jewish message that was the foundation of the numerous congregations being formed. Indeed, the only debate concerned how the Law applied to the Gentile converts. This is strong evidence that Paul was not adapting his message for the Gentiles, for, if he had, the Jewish 'Law-lovers', who hated him for accepting uncircumcised, believing Gentiles, would have also charged him with departing from the Jewish message they so tenaciously held to; and this they never did.

The Return to the Mother Church

When Paul eventually returned to Jerusalem after his third missionary journey, he was greeted with the statement: "You see, brother, how many thousands there are among the Jews of those who have believed. They are all zealous for the law" (Acts 21:20). These converts, who were all zealous, never once suggested that Paul had abandoned the message they had come to accept. All the leaders of the Jerusalem church were concerned about was that he was being accused of having abandoned the Law regarding the need for circumcision. They had heard a false report that Paul was teaching the Jews of the diaspora that they should abandon circumcision.

The apostles were satisfied that Paul was giving no such instruction but that he had simply taught that Gentile converts should not be circumcised (Acts 21:21–24). To show that he did not teach that believing Jews should abandon circumcision, he instructed his co-worker, Timothy, to be circumcised. He reasoned it right to do this as Timothy's mother was Jewish and she had not circumcised Timothy when he was born (Acts 16:1–3). Thus, he advised Jews to be circumcised so as not to cause offence to other Jews, but not to depend on it as the means of salvation.

Paul Living Out the Law

To make his position clear regarding his respect for the Law, Paul followed the advice of the Jerusalem leaders, who suggested that he could defuse the situation by joining men who were going to purify themselves. This was the evidence that he continued to follow the Law. Again, if Paul taught the Gentiles a different message from what the apostles were teaching in Jerusalem, "those zealous for the law" would surely have raised this as a reason for bringing a charge against him. The fact that *no charge was ever made against Paul* for tampering with the agreed message of the scriptures is evidence that none could be made. The message he preached to the Gentiles was in complete harmony with what was preached in Jerusalem, for they had accepted that Peter was right to baptise Gentile converts, even though they had not been circumcised (Acts 11:15–18).

The Message Preached

To answer the claim that Paul Hellenised the gospel, we need to follow the letters he wrote and the sermons and lectures he gave to see if they endorse the theological development that many believe took place throughout his teaching. The messages of Paul and the other apostles are recorded throughout the book of Acts. They were all based on appealing to Old Testament proof-texts, where typological exegeses was used to show how the cited texts related to the events that had recently taken place, so Acts 2:25,29,34.

Other examples of typological exegesis are found in Acts 4:25; 7:45; 13:34–36. By this method, a statement that David made or something he experienced functioned as a pointer to a much greater fulfilment that had taken place in the suffering or victory of Jesus, the Greater Son of David. The gist of this exegesis is: "if this happened to David, how much more will it be true in the experience of his Greater Son!" Such typological exegesis was not new to the apostles' audiences, for it is found throughout the Old Testament, and Jesus Himself used it.

We can draw from this that whatever Paul taught; it satisfied the concerns that the Jewish converts had for the Law. This shows how we should challenge all hermeneutical proposals that violate this respect for the Law. These people must have believed that they could say that Christ has fulfilled the Law in a way that did not diminish their respect for it. There could be no slipshod exegesis of their ancient texts and, surely, they would not have allowed Hellenism to contaminate their sacred traditions. On this issue of keeping to the traditions of their faith, Paul set an example for the non-Christian Jewish leader Akiba, because, as we shall soon see, decades after Paul, he was faced with the temptation to Hellenise his teaching.

I appreciate that the charge will be made: "but you are abandoning all the research of modern scholarship". My reply is: "I am simply seeking to understand how the early church understood their texts. To achieve this, I am disregarding all sources that lack essential evidence that they influenced the first century church.[63] Such a method is fundamental to any historical research and, if it is not followed, the results are likely to be seriously flawed."

Challenging Church Growth

I have written a very positive account of the early church's explosive growth in the first century, an account that many would challenge. The trouble is that there is little, if any, independent evidence giving details of this phenomenal growth. Some think the account in Acts is exaggerated but their judgement is not based on evidence, only instinct.

---

[63] This is the same practice that courts use when seeking to judge if a plaintiff is guilty or innocent. In other words, its importance as a correct method for seeking truth is established in that the entire judicial system is built on it.

Recent Evidence

We are fortunate that we do have access to a similar event that allows us to make a responsible judgement on the likelihood of Acts giving us a trustworthy account of what happened during those heady early days of the Church. The 1904–05 Welsh revival gives statistics of rapid church expansion in a matter of months, which was witnessed to and reported on by professional journalists. Estimates vary from 100,000 to 150,000 people becoming part of this powerful movement, and all within a tiny principality. There were those who were sceptical about the significance of this movement, but they could not deny that it spread like wildfire, spilling out to other nations as well. Such recent evidence cannot be dismissed, even though the genuineness of some of the professions of faith can be questioned. What the event demonstrates is that such times of revival cannot be assessed by cold logic as to what are 'reasonable numbers.' The entire movement was followed and reported on by the secular press, which acknowledged the power of the movement in changing tens of thousands of lives, even if it would not assent to the truth of the message preached.

But the number of converts was far higher than those recorded by the Welsh Press. Dr Noel Gibbard researched the spread of this movement and found that it ignited similar revivals throughout Europe, Russia, North and South America, India, and Korea.[64] It led to leaders of the Welsh Revival and its key supporters being invited to either travel to these places or receive delegations from them to observe, meet and learn. They came to witness the extraordinary event and then they travelled back to their homelands, reporting with great excitement what they had witnessed and encouraging their own compatriots to pray to God for a similar visitation. So, the numbers of converts in these distant locations were much greater than what had happened in Wales, where it all began.

Other revivals have been experienced throughout history and in different locations. Almost two centuries earlier, the Great Awakening (1720–1740's), under the leadership of the Wesley brothers and George Whitfield, had huge

---

[64] N. Gibbard, The Wings of a Dove: The International Effects of the 1904-05 Revival (Bridgend: Evangelical Press, 2004).

impact on Great Britain and North America, when vast numbers became followers of Christ. While there are some secular records of these events, none had the amount of independent media coverage that the Welsh revival had, and it is these records that ought to remove any scepticism that vast numbers can come to faith in a very short length of time.

Mass religious movements were experienced throughout Europe in the sixteenth century, when the preaching of Luther and Calvin brought about a huge change in belief as well as liturgical practices and lifestyles. These were all mass religious movements that had a great effect on millions of people, as well as subsequent generations and history.

Conclusion

We have considered the huge impact that the gospel had on the people of Israel and the surrounding nations, and we have seen that it did not need to be recast to win the Gentiles. We have argued that the scepticism many scholars have toward the accuracy of Luke's account of early church growth is not justified. It is certainly not normal in secular terms, but its explosive growth is far from being an isolated event in the history of the church. There are other documented and independently verified accounts of recent church expansions like those recorded in Acts.

Throughout all the accounts of growth given in Acts, the message of the apostles remained the same: God had given up His Son as a sacrifice for sin, calling people to come out of darkness to become His forgiven people. Thus, The Exodus narrative continued and still does to this day.

Chapter 29 Introducing Rabbi Akiba

In considering a rabbi who was born some twenty years after the death of Paul, we need to ask what relevance he has to our study.

Firstly, the life of Akiba is the key evidence for the rewriting of Paul's biography. By claiming the apostle was a zealot when a student rabbi, scholars have opened the door to justify disregarding the traditional reading of Paul's early years and bringing in a totally new study of Paul's letters, an understanding that is called 'the New Perspective on Paul'.

In this new reading, they claim that Paul was not only a student of Gamaliel but that, at the same time, he studied under Hillel. Hillel was the spiritual leader of those who stood against Roman rule. Being part of this group, known as the zealots, Paul, they claim, would have engaged in activities that led to violence. Membership of this movement, they say, introduced him to zealot literature and traditions that would later influence his teaching as an apostle of Jesus. Some New Perspective scholars say this material also influenced Jesus and His understanding of the need for His death.[65]

But careful study on Akiba has shown that the New Perspective scholars' reliance on him is unfounded. However, contrary to expectations Akiba provides actual historic facts which support my case that Paul did not have to rewrite the gospel to reach the Gentiles and so grow the church. Apart from the hugely different messages that both men preached, Akiba shared the same interpretive method I am claiming Paul followed. We will see shortly that Akiba rejected Hellenism and was ultra-conservative in his commitment to the Old Testament scriptures, a position that drew tens of thousands of followers.

Also, we have evidence from the massive following he drew of the impact of the interpretive method Akiba used when expounding the Hebrew scriptures. We can use this information to suggest that the first century church could have been effectively led by a man who did not embrace Hellenism, as I am claiming was Paul's position. If Akiba was able to build a following using

---

[65] See N.T. Wright, The Resurrection of the Son of God, Christian Origins and the Question of God, Vol 3 (London: SPCK, 2003) 147.

discarded interpretive methods, then there is no reason why Paul could not have done similarly. Thus, if Akiba could achieve such growth in his movement at a time when Rome was actually at war with the Jews, then Paul could certainly have achieved similar, if not greater growth. This is a very reasonable claim considering Paul's message was about the promised, crucified and risen Messiah, who God had attested by many miracles in the presence of thousands of neutral observers.

Thirdly, those who argue for the rewriting of Paul's early history argue that Akiba became the religious leader of the Bar Kokhba revolt (132–136 CE). Tradition has it that Akiba became disillusioned with the pacifist mentor he had committed himself to. By joining the zealots, he turned from his pacifist position and instructed his remaining disciples to defend themselves (many had already been killed by the Romans). The Romans had turned indiscriminately on all Jews supposing they all supported the revolt, which led to many thousands being slain to put the rebellion down.[66]

The Fatal Flaw

But rather than this change of allegiance being historically true, it has been recognised that the evidence of the association of Akiba with Bar Kokhba is very tenuous.[67] This connection is challenged because we know from Roman records that Akiba was eventually put to death by Rome because he disobeyed her edict that banned preaching in public[68] and not because he was a zealot. This was the charge on his indictment papers at the trial that sentenced him to death and is probably only one of a few reliable historic documented facts that we can link Akiba to. This fact must trump all existing speculation about him.

---

[66] Akiva's teacher was Nachum Ish Gamzu, see 'Rabbi Akiva', Jewish History.org, https://www.jewishhistory.org/rabbi-akiva-2.

[67] This is acknowledged by Wright, *What Saint Paul Really Said, Was Paul of Tarus the Real Founder of Christianity*? (Oxford: Lion, 1997) 118 who is a leading advocate for saying that Paul put himself under two opposing mentors at the same time.

[68] For further issues suggesting the claim that Akiba was a zealot is flawed see *Search for the Truth* pp 430-433.

If he had been a zealot, then surely that would have been the main charge against him, but there is not a word regarding this in the charge.[69]

Akiba and His Role in Teaching Israel

The following is an extract from an article written by a leading Jewish scholar, Louis Ginzberg. He is writing about the aforesaid Akiba (also known as Akiva), who is still recognised as one of the greatest Jewish rabbis of all time. Ginzberg wrote:

> [Akiba] feared that the Jews, by their facility in accommodating themselves to surrounding circumstances—even then a marked characteristic—might become entangled in the net of Grecian philosophy, and even in that of Gnosticism. The example of his colleagues and friends, Elisha ben Abuyah, Ben 'Azzai, and Ben Zoma strengthened him still more in his conviction of the necessity of providing some counterpoise to the intellectual influence of the non-Jewish world.[70]

Ginzberg could not be clearer. Akiba [Akiva] was alarmed that some rabbis had accommodated themselves to the Roman occupation, and this included accepting its alien philosophy. From this overlooked statement, we see that Paul (if my construction is correct) was not the only rabbi of the first two centuries who avoided engaging with Hellenism. We know that Akiba had studied the Christian writings to equip himself with the information he needed to refute Christian claims that had influenced so many Jews to become followers of Christ. It is possible that it was through his engagement with Paul's writings he saw the benefit of not losing the Jewish message through engagement with the philosophers. Thus, while Akiba could not have influenced Paul, Paul could have influenced Akiba. That there was an audience for the works of teachers who shunned Hellenistic influences is supported by Hengel, who is regarded as being amongst the most authoritative writers on

---

[69] For a fuller critique of the claim that Akiba was a zealot see Holland, *Search for Truth*, pp 430-433.

[70] Ginzberg, Louis, 'Akiba-ben-Joseph,' *Jewish Encyclopedia*, Vol: 305, https://www.jewishencyclopedia.com/articles/1033-akiba-ben-joseph.

Jesus and the Exodus

the history of the zealot movement. He has pointed out that many first century Palestinian Jews rejected the culture that the Roman occupiers brought with them.[71]

So Akiba turns out to have had the same outlook I am claiming Paul had. He also kept himself apart from Hellenism. Interestingly, this conservative position as a teacher of the Jewish people did not nullify Akiba's ministry. Rather, it promoted it, for he had between 12,000 to 48,000 disciples.[72] Clearly, his 'narrowness' was not a problem for drawing followers. In fact, it might have been his greatest asset.

Akiba's Influence

If we explore the extent of the influence of Akiba's disciples, we will gain a much clearer understanding of how widespread this traditional Jewish reading of scripture was maintained. Akiba's disciples were rabbis, who had or would have gone on to have their own congregations. The minimum size of a congregation to maintain a rabbi was ten families, based on the principle of each family contributing a tenth of its income to pay a salary for his service. If we take Ginzberg's lower number of disciples, then 12,000 Jewish leaders were directly under Akiba's teaching. They were committed to repeating what they learned. This was not an option to consider, it was a condition of being a disciple of any rabbi and, certainly, a condition of being a part of the reforming movement that Akiba led.

The Size of Akiba's Reforming Movement

If each of these followers of Akiba and their wives had two children (a low figure for Jewish families at that time), then the number of people being instructed in their families would have been 528,000. We can deduce this by assuming that there were 11 families in each synagogue (including the rabbi's), then it would give a congregation of 44 (including the rabbi). If we assume that the 12,000 student-rabbis under Akiba's instruction went on to lead congregations, then we have 528,000 people (44x12,000) coming under

---

[71] M. Hengel, The Zealots, Investigations into the Jewish Freedom Movement in the Period from Herod 1 until 70AD (Edinburgh: T.& T. Clark 1989).177

[72] Ginzberg, Lois, "Akiba-ben-Joseph," *Jewish Encyclopedia.*

Jesus and the Exodus

Akiba's teaching. Thus, using Ginzberg's more limited calculation, we can assume that one in ten of the Jewish population of five million would have been part of this reforming movement that the conservative teacher, Akiba, led.

There may be some who think that this number of disciples (12,000) could relate to the people who followed Akiba and not just to his rabbinic students. But the following quote makes clear that this number was of rabbinical students, among them being four future distinguished teachers that came from the school. You will no doubt notice that the author has cited the much higher number of disciples compared to what I have used, so, if he is correct, my estimate of Akiba's influence will be twice what I have suggested.

> Rabbi Akiva did not keep his learning to himself but had many students and disciples, more than any other single teacher. As you know, he had no less than 24 thousand students at one time. Some of the greatest Rabbis of the next generation were among his disciples, as, for example, Rabbi Simeon ben Yochai, whose Yahrzeit is observed on Lag B'Omer. Together with another great Sage, Rabbi Chanina ben Chakinai, Rabbi Simeon went to Bnei Brak to learn Torah from Rabbi Akiva, and they stayed there for thirteen years![73]

An Unexpected Appointment

Following the failed Bar Kokhba revolt (132–136 CE), which sought to overthrow Rome's authority in Palestine, Rome identified a group from within the Jewish community which they could trust to be a peaceful representative of the nation. They chose the rabbis because they had a history of nonviolence. They had no interest in politics, only in the study of their ancient texts.[74] It

---

[73] 'Rabbi Akiva: His Life and Teachings', Chabad.org, https://www.chabad.org/library/article_cdo/aid/112059/jewish/Rabbi-Akiva-His-Life-and-Teachings.htm.

[74] "The strength of the rabbinate lay in its ability to represent simultaneously the interests of the Jews and the Romans, whose religious and political needs, respectively, now chanced to coincide. The rabbis were regarded favourably by the Romans as a politically submissive class, which, with its wide influence over the Jewish masses, could translate the Pax Romana (the

Jesus and the Exodus

should be noted that this appointment by Rome, which made the rabbinic movement the official representative of the Jews, is the strongest evidence that the rabbis were not a significant part of the zealot movement, as argued by those who promote the New Perspective on Paul. In fact, it was this appointment that provided the rabbinic community with its authority, transforming it from a small faction within first century Judaism to become the holder of power until this day.

So, ironically, Akiba, who was put to death by Rome, was a massive influence on the movement that Rome eventually went on to appoint to represent the Jewish people. Naturally, Akiba's group drew Jews to its ranks. Akiba had a distinct traditional position that rejected all Graeco-Roman influence on their sacred texts, and this, no doubt, was a massive draw for those concerned Jews who were anxious to cling to their heritage without provoking Rome. So, all these new disciples who associated with Akiba were favoured by Rome and they were entirely comfortable that they were honouring their God. There was no compromise that their consciences had to struggle with as they embraced Akiba's conservative reading. Their status was similar to what the Jews had previously enjoyed of being authorized by Rome as a licensed religion, enjoying privileges that others did not have. This newly bestowed status on the rabbinic movement would have drawn devout Jews into this new fold where they could practice their faith with the approval of the emperor. Such an incentive would have been a powerful reason for many attaching themselves to the uncompromising teaching of Akiba which assured them of the historic relevance of their faith.

Conclusion

In reading the letters of Paul from a Hebraic, corporate perspective, I have argued for a reading which implies that this is how the early believers understood his letters. This essentially Hebraic way of thinking is exhibited throughout the Old Testament. Tragically, this sort of reading was eventually lost because of the individualistic reading of scripture that emerged in the

---

peace imposed by Roman rule) into Jewish religious precepts. To the Jews, on the other hand, the rabbinic ideology gave the appearance of continuity to Jewish self-rule and freedom from alien interference.", *Encyclopedia Britannica*, Rabbinic Judaism (2nd–18th century), https://www.britannica.com/topic/Judaism/Rabbinic-Judaism-2nd-18th-century.

second century. This was due to the appointment of leaders who had received their education in the Greek academies and whose individualistic model of interpretation came into the Church's method of reading. This move to an individualistic interpretation of the apostles' letters was accelerated even further with the emphasis on individual salvation as preached by the reformers in the sixteenth century and then with the influence of the Enlightenment in the eighteenth century.

In order to trace the development of The Exodus narrative, we must recognise and appreciate how reading methods have changed over the last two thousand years. They have masked, and then caused to be lost, the rich Hebraic heritage that is present throughout the apostles' writings as they drew on the Hebrew scriptures for their evidence. In this way, the presence of The Exodus narrative was missed, and other methods of reading took its place. It is a loss that has deprived the Church of one of the most unifying themes in scripture. It has left many coping with an inadequate understanding as they struggle to grasp the unspeakable riches of the gospel they had come to believe.

Chapter 30 Conclusion

The purpose of this book is to call on those who have the huge privilege and responsibility of teaching the Bible's message to the people of God to take seriously the same Jewish scriptures that Jesus said cannot be broken (John 10:35) and that Paul was speaking about when he wrote:

> All Scripture is breathed out by God and profitable for teaching, for reproof, for correction, and for training in righteousness. (2 Tim 3:16)

Also, to follow the example of the Bereans, of whom Luke wrote:

> Now these Jews were more noble than those in Thessalonica; they received the word with all eagerness, examining the Scriptures daily to see if these things were so. (Acts 17:11)

So, summarising what we have learned:

The church of the first century did not become increasingly Greek in her thinking. This happened in the second century, when she lost touch with her Jewish heritage and produced teachers who were trained not in the schools of Jerusalem but in those of Athens.

The letters of Paul to the churches are not to be read as written to the individual Christian but to the communities to which they were sent. Paul was not primarily writing about individual experience but about that of the community.

The Greek words Paul used when speaking of spiritual matters are bathed in their Hebrew meanings that the Old Testament Greek translation was intended to preserve. His quotations from the Old Testament were not haphazardly chosen. They were deployed with the intention of bringing their history and theology into the subjects he was writing about. This results in a huge increase in theological insight.

We are not the slaves of God. We are the servants of God, with all the privileges and blessings that this status brings.

Typology is a vital literary/theological tool. Rather than Paul occasionally using this teaching aid, he constructs his letters so that the whole Old

Testament functions as one huge type, guiding him in his understanding of what God has done in Christ to secure the salvation of His people. By reading Paul's letters both typologically and corporately we discovered that his doctrine of justification has nine aspects, matching the same nine aspects found in the Old Testament.

Paul sees that Adam's disobedience is the reason why humanity is separated from God and that, like Adam, everyone has gone on to sin.

Paul is never haphazard in his grammar or vocabulary. If we think he has been, it is incumbent on us to examine the interpretative principles we are using.

Paul retained his culture. This is seen, for example, in the way he uses the word *sarx* (flesh) to represent the Hebrew word *bashar*.

Paul was never a zealot as is claimed by an increasing number of New Testament scholars.

The contemporary reading of the history of the early church has assumed that the world of the first century church was so controlled by Hellenism that the sort of reading I have presented could not have taken place.

Paul never shows any reliance on Graeco-Roman sources, nor does he expect his readers to know Intertestamental Literature.

The only source Paul drew upon when writing his letters was the Old Testament, which he had known since childhood.

Paul builds the doctrine of salvation entirely in Paschal (Passover)/New Exodus terms.

The death of the lamb in the Egyptian Passover was both a sacrifice for redemption and for atonement.

The death of a lamb could not save the firstborn in the final Passover, only the death of God's beloved Son could achieve this.

Because He had spared the firstborn on the night of the Passover, God claimed them as a priestly people, so allowing the firstborn to remain with their families.

Jesus and the Exodus

The Levites stood in for the firstborn following the Passover, so becoming the priestly tribe. Their presence in and around the tabernacle was an ongoing reminder of atonement having been made.

Paul's carefully chosen Old Testament texts provide a structure for his arguments and teaching.

The expression 'firstborn of all creation' is not a reference to the Greek concept of unknowable wisdom but, as the immediate context and entire content of the hymn indicate, the expression refers to Jesus being the One who died for His people and His creation's redemption.

Paul's doctrine of salvation is corporate. The experience of the individual fits into this larger picture.

The long-overlooked theme of the Divine Marriage explains many passages that have been misunderstood.

The 'body of sin' is not a reference to an individual's body. It is a corporate term that speaks of the kingdom of darkness.

Paul sees that Adam's disobedience is the reason why humanity is separated from God and that, like Adam, everyone has gone on to sin.

The early church's doctrine of atonement was Paschal based.

Sin is the breaking of the covenant that man was created to enjoy.

When Paul speaks of sin in the singular, he is speaking of Satan.

Union with Christ is the work of the Spirit, who created a covenant union between Christ and all His people as He died for them. It is a historic covenant-making event never to be repeated again. Individuals enjoy that union when they confess Christ as their Saviour.

The Law was given to bless and guide Israel. Because she disobeyed and took other gods, it is obliged to find her guilty and sentence her to come under God's judgement.

Paul's ethical teaching comes from the Old Testament.

Christ is the Bridegroom of the Church, and salvation is about restoring humanity to union with its Creator.

Jesus and the Exodus

When Paul writes about baptism, apart from in 1 Cor 1:14–17, he is referring to the death of Jesus. This was when God's Spirit created a union between Jesus and all those He was dying to save.

Through the death of Jesus, the hold that Satan had over all who now believe in the crucified Christ was permanently severed.

If the arguments given in the preceding chapters of this book are correct, then scholarship and the Church have wandered far from the understanding and experience of the New Testament church. She had not been infiltrated by Greek thinkers in the first century and had not lost her Jewish roots. Her fledgling congregations of Jews and Gentiles were taught by Jewish believers in the echo-chamber of their Old Testament scriptures, which God had given through His servants, the prophets. The recovery of The Exodus narrative resolves numerous theological problems.

If you have enjoyed learning from this book, then *Hope for the Nations: Paul's Letter to the Romans* by Tom Holland is for you. See the next page of this book for details.

Hope for the Nations: Paul's Letter to the Romans

Tom Holland has demystified the language of the letter of Romans so that all can access this incredible treasure of Christian truth. Clearly and powerfully written to bring the truths that have brought peace to countless millions of people throughout history. For all who want to understand the Christian message, this is must-read.

BUY NOW from any good bookshop/retailer or from
www.apiarypublishing.com

Our Reviewers Testify to the Value of This Unique Commentary. Available as softback, hardback, or eBook.

Tom's commentary (Romans Hope for the Nations) invites readers to break away from fixed ideas and journey to new places. It is informed, scholarly, rich in exegetical insights, yet easy to understand. Tom argues for a reading of Romans that is tied to the Old Testament Scriptures, rooted in Isaiah, is Christ centred and communally focused. I highly recommend it for pilgrims seeking to know God more.

– **Dr Murray Lawson**; President of Scripture Union Canada

Dr Holland takes the reader deeper into the world of the Roman Church and the culture into which Paul wrote this magnificent epistle. Others have sought to do this without an appreciation for or a confessional commitment to the inerrancy and the infallibility of Romans being the very Word of God. Tom Holland's work stands out in that he believes that. The material, thus, comes forward as both scholarly and confessional. I commended this well researched and well written book to the Church and believe that the reader will benefit from it as I have in my own reading. I trust and pray that the material will find a wide audience, for it is indeed most deserving of such attention. And it now takes its rightful place in that considerable library section on Romans but stands out through both confession of true faith and courageous scholarship. Congratulations to Dr Tom Holland and the publisher for this valuable and timely contribution to studies on Romans.

– **Michael A. Milton**, Ph.D.; Chancellor and CEO and the James M. Baird Jr. Chair of Pastoral Theology, Reformed Theological Seminary.

Tom Holland's study demonstrates how a deeper understanding of the Old Testament and particularly of its prophesied new exodus can illumine Paul's theology of the person and work of Christ in profound ways. Here one will find scholarship that is not only solid and faithful, thorough and yet accessible – in short, scholarship in the service of the church.

– **Prof L. Michael Morales**; PhD., Professor of Biblical Studies, Greenville Presbyterian Theological Seminary, Greenville, USA.

The book is full of gems of knowledge and wisdom for the taking. Issues that I personally struggled with were helpfully explained time and time again. My copy of the book is filled with my notations on new insights.

You can listen to preacher after preacher and teacher after teacher on Romans and never really understand the "big message" or see the "big picture" of what the author is trying to share. Getting a hold of a scholarly work rewritten for non-scholars yet communicating the secrets of historical and contextual hermeneutics to bring alive God's Holy Word allows you to stop and think and question and reflect. Tom Holland does just that for you. I very highly recommend it to all. I will be looking for more of his books.

The author's bottom line (and his own desire for writing) is given away in the very title of this book – there is indeed "Hope for the Nations" of both Gentiles and Jews.

- **Ken B. Godevenos**; Accord Resolution Services Inc., Toronto, Ontario.

As a layperson I found this book totally fascinating, and written in a style that is straightforward, yet at the same time profoundly challenging to my previously held views on the book of Romans. The author brought out ideas that forced me to reconsider many of the standpoints I had read in other commentaries. Also, his reasoning behind the corporate reading of Romans is logical and entirely convincing, producing a potentially new understanding of the points that Paul is making. This book is a joy to read (I have read and re-read it), and I wholeheartedly recommend it to anyone who wants a fuller understanding of this important epistle.

- **Roy Harries**; Posted on Goodreads

Dr Tom Holland proves in his compelling new book, scholarly interpretation of the volume (Romans) has been fraught with misconceptions. Dr Holland attempts to correct these points of confusion and, in the process, challenge every level of readers' Biblical beliefs. Dr Holland has produced a highly readable analysis, [and] asks the reader to rethink familiar passages in Paul's Letter to the Romans in fresh ways. He corrects many widespread misunderstandings of Paul which have obscured the powerful message of the Biblical text, and his argument for a corporate reading permits the Reformer's forensic sense of justification to be maintained even in the light of the covenantal context of the New Perspective on Paul. Tom Holland's Hope for the Nations is both truly biblical and thoroughly theological. Church leaders, scholars and students alike will find their views on the well-known text challenged and transformed.

- **M.W. Johnson**

BUY NOW from any good bookshop/retailer or from
www.apiarypublishing.com

Bibliography

Best, Earnest, One Body in Christ, (1955) A Study in the Relationship of the Church to Christ in the Epistles of the Apostle Paul, SCM, London.

Bright, J., art, 'Isaiah', Peakes Commentary on the Bible, M. M. Black (ed), H.H. Rowley (ed) (Routledge; 1st edition. 1971).

Bruce, F.F., 1 and 2 Corinthians. (Oliphants, London, 1961).

Bruce, F.F., The Epistle of Paul to the Romans: An Introduction and Commentary, (London Tyndale Press, 1967).

Chadwick, H., All Things to All Men (1 Cor. IX:22), NTS 1 (1955).

Crisler, Channing L. and Mark A. Seifrid, (2016). Reading Romans as Lament: Paul's Use of Old Testament Lament in His Famous Letter (Eugene, Oregon: Pickwick Publications).

Cullmann, Oscar and J.K.S. Reid, Baptism in The New Testament (London: SCM, 1952).

Dodd, C.H., The Epistle of Paul to the Romans (London: Collins, 1946).

Dunn, J.D.G., "Paul's Understanding of the Death of Jesus" in Reconciliation and Hope, Essays presented to L. L. Morris on his 60th birthday, ed. R. Brooks (London: Paternoster, 1974).

Gibbard, N., The Wings of a Dove: The International Effects of the 1904-05 Revival (Bridgend: Evangelical Press, 2004).

Gillingham, Susan, PSALMS 90-106: BOOK FOUR AND THE COVENANT WITH DAVID, European Judaism: A Journal for the New Europe Vol. 48, No. 2 (Autumn 2015), pp. 83-101 (19 pages) Published by: Berghahn Books

Ginzberg, Louis, 'Akiba-ben-Joseph,' Jewish Encyclopedia, Vol: 305, https://www.jewishencyclopedia.com/articles/1033-akiba-ben-joseph.

Goodrich, J.K., Sold Under Sin: Echoes of Exile in Romans 7:14-25, NTS 59.4 (2013).

Harmon, Matthew S., She Must and Shall Go Free: Paul's Isaianic Gospel in Galatians. BZNW (New York: de Gruyter, 2010)

Hays, Richard, Echoes of Scripture in the Letters of Paul (New Haven: Yale University Press, 1989).

Hengel, M. The Zealots, Investigations into the Jewish Freedom Movement in the Period from Herod 1 until 70AD (Edinburgh: T.& T. Clark 1989).

Hengel, M., "The Effective History of Isaiah 53 in the Pre-Christian Period", The Suffering Servant: Isaiah 53 in Jewish and Christian Sources. Edited by Bernd Janowski and Peter Stuhlmacher. Translated by Daniel P. Bailey. (Grand Rapids: Eerdmans. 2004).

Hengel, M., The Atonement: The Origins of the Doctrine in the New Testament, (Philadelphia: Fortress, 1981)

Hill, David, Greek Words and Hebrew Meanings Studies in The Semantics of Soteriological Terms, (Cambridge: Cambridge University Press, 1967).

Holland, Tom, Romans the Divine Marriage, A Biblical Theological Commentary (Eugene, OR: Pickwick Publications, 2011).

Holland, Tom, Tom Wright and the Search for Truth, 2nd edition, (Apiary Publishing, London, 2020).

Holland, Tom., Contours of Pauline Theology: A Radical New Survey of the Influences on Paul's Biblical Writings (Fearn, Ross-shire: Christian Focus Publications, 2004).

Knox, Wilfred, St Paul and The Church of The Gentiles (Cambridge: Cambridge U.P, 1939).

Manson, T.W., art 'Romans' in Peakes Commentary on the Bible, M. M. Black (ed), H.H. Rowley (ed) (Routledge; 1st edition. 1971).

Moule, C.F.D., Fulfilment-Words in the New Testament: Use and Abuse, NTS 14(1966).

Moule, C.F.D., The Origins of Christology (Cambridge University Press, 1977).

Nixon, R.E., The Exodus in the New Testament, (London: Tyndale Press, 1963).

Nixon, R.E., The Exodus in The New Testament, Tyndale Monographs, 4.4 (London: Tyndale Press, 1963).

Petterson, Anthony R., "Zechariah and the second Exodus theme of Isaiah," Haggai, Zechariah, Malachi (Downers Grove: IVP, 2015).

Satterthwaite, Philip E. (ed); Hess, Richard S. (ed); Wenham, Gordon J. (ed), The Lord's Anointed: Interpretation of Old Testament Messianic Texts, (Cambridge: Tyndale Fellowship for Biblical Research, 1995).

Schnackenberg, R., Baptism in the Thought of St Paul, tr by R. G. Beasley Murray (New York: Herder & Herder, 1964).

Torrance, T.F., Theology in Reconstruction, (London: SCM, 1965).

Troels, Engberg-Pedersen, Paul and The Stoic, (Edinburgh: T&T Clark, 2000).

Warnack, V, 'Taufe und Hellsschehen Nach Rom 6,' ALW 111 2(1954).

Wheeler, L. Kip, Parallelism in Hebrew Poetry, Carson-Newman University, https://web.cn.edu/kwheeler/diagram_Hebrew_Poetry.html, accessed September 14, 2023.

White, Joel R., 'He was Raised on the Third Day According to the Scriptures' (1 Cor. 15:4): A Typological Interpretation Based on the Cultic Calendar in Leviticus 23' TynB 66 (2015).

Whitley, D.E H., 'Saint Paul's Thought on the Atonement,' JTS 8 (1957) 240-255. 250

Williams, Catrin H., "I am He": The Interpretation of 'ANI HU' in Jewish and Early Christian Literature: 113 (Wissenschaftliche Untersuchungen zum Neuen Testament 2. Reihe, 1999).

Williams, Peter J., Can We Trust the Gospels (Wheaton, Ill.: Crossway, 2018).

Wright, N.T. "The Letter to the Romans: Introduction, Commentary, and Reflections" In the New Interpreter's Bible, Volume X, Acts-1 Corinthians, edited by L.E. Keek, 39–70, (Nashville, Abingdon, 2002)

Wright, N.T., The Resurrection of the Son of God, Christian Origins and the Question of God, Vol 3 (London: SPCK, 2003).

Wright, N.T., *What Saint Paul Really Said, Was Paul of Tarus the Real Founder of Christianity?* (Oxford: Lion, 1997).

Ziesler, J., *The Meaning of Righteousness in Paul: A Linguistic and Theological Enquiry*, Society for Testament Studies Monograph Series, (Cambridge: Cambridge University Press 1972)

Author Index

Best, Earnest 184, 266
Bright, J. 199, 266
Bruce, F.F. 157, 174, 266
Chadwick, H. 41, 266
Crisler, Channing L. 205, 266
Cullmann, Oscar 156, 266
Dodd, C.H. 29, 178, 266
Dunn, J.D.G. 141, 266
Gibbard, N. 249, 266
Gillingham, Susan 44, 266
Ginzberg, Louis 253, 254, 255, 266
Goodrich, J.K. 205, 266
Harmon, Matthew S 58, 267
Hays, Richard 58, 225, 267
Hengel, M. 41, 127, 254, 267
Hill, David 61, 71, 267
Holland, Tom 1, 3, 9, 10, 11, 12, 13, 14, 15, 17, 19, 41, 59, 61, 91, 109, 163, 191, 196, 200, 215, 227, 242, 243, 253, 262, 263, 264, 265, 267

Knox, Wilfred 156, 267
Manson, T.W. 174, 175, 267
Moule, C.F.D. 96, 184, 267
Nixon, R.E. 141, 156, 267, 268
Petterson, Anthony R. 127, 268
Reid, J.K.S. 156, 266
Satterthwaite, Philip E..... 127, 268
Schnackenberg, R. .. 184, 189, 268
Seifrid, Mark A. 205, 266
Torrance, T.F. 174, 268
Troels, Engberg-Pedersen .41, 268
Warnack, V 156, 268
Wheeler, L. Kip 170, 268
White, Joel R 157, 268
Whitley, D.E H. 155, 268
Williams, Catrin H. 148, 268
Williams, Peter J. 221, 268
Wright, N.T. 3, 41, 156, 251, 252, 267, 268, 269
Ziesler, J. 71, 269

Scripture Index

Old Testament

Genesis

2:10	73
2:23	239
2:24	217
3:4	163
3:14–15	97
3:15	218
4:14–15	103
4:23	103
6:12–13	237
6:17	237
7:15	237
9:4	238
12:3	100
15	97, 135
15:4	239
15:6	158
15:12–16	97
15:13–14	100
17:10	97
17:11	111, 237
17:13	238
29:14	239
37:27	239

Exodus

2:23	155
3:14-15	148
4:22	101
4:22–23	135
4:24–26	98
7–11	105
12	105
12:7	103
12:8	238
12:37–38	100
12:48	98
13:14	188
13:21	101
16:35	101
17:6	101
19:33–34	137
20:2–4	99
20:3–6	136
20:7	136
20:8–11	136
20:12	136
20:13	136
20:14	68, 136
20:15	136
20:16	137
20:17	68, 137
21	137
22:16	137
23:1	137
23:6	137
24:8	120
26	101
32	98
32:1–6	104
32:4	201
32:25–29	101
34:6–7	85
40:1–5	105
49:25–26	105

Leviticus

6:27	238
7:15	238
12:3	114

12:6	228
14:1	137
15:1	137
19:9	137
19:23	137
20:6	137
20:13	137
20:22–23	138
23	272
23:11–15	157
25:8–34	103
25:35	137

Numbers

1:53	106
3:11–13	106, 230
3:39	106
3:43	106
3:46-47	106
8:19	106
9:6	238
12:2	99
12:12	238
18:14–16	229
18:15–16	106
19:11	238
35:22–29	103

Deuteronomy

4:20	99
10:16	111
19:4–10	103
19:14	137
20:1	137
20:10	137
24:1–4	113
24:5	137
24:16	85
25:5–10	103
30:6	114
30:11–20	123
32:23–25	133

Joshua

5:3–4	97

Ruth

3:13	103
4:1–8	103
4:4	103
4:6	223

2 Samuel

7:1-16	48
7:1–17	43

2 Kings

5:14	237
23:21–23	142

1 Chronicles

11:1	239, 241

2 Chronicles

11:14–16	201
21:13	100
32:8	239

Psalms

44	80, 81
44:22	80
78:38	107
89:27	121, 228

Isaiah

1:21	100
2:2	114, 115
2:2–5	158
6	76
6:9–11	76
9:7	114
11:2	146
11:10	114
11:11	95
11:11–12	48

12:3	114	52:1–6	116
19:1–2	158	52:1–12	116, 117
19:18–24	48	52:1-15	120
19:19–24	115	52:5	112
19:19–25	203	52:6	216
25:6	114	52:7	81, 116
28	200	52:7–12	117
28:16	200	52:8–10	105
28:16–19	200	52:11	121
29:18	114	52:12	116, 120, 121
32:2	114	52:13	113
32:15	114, 115	52:13–15	119
33:16	114	52:14	119
34:1	115	52:15	119, 120
34:8	105	53	81, 121, 122, 123, 124, 125, 127, 132, 271
35:4	105		
35:5–6	114	53:1–4	121
37:23	112	53:1–12	115
40:1	128	53:4–6	122
40:1–2	123	53:4–9	123
40:1–5	49	53:9	123
40:1-10	80	53:10	124
40:3	145, 146	53:11	123
40:5	238	53:12	113
40–66	80, 132, 207	54	129, 216
41:14	115	54:1-14	80
41:18	114	54:4–8	217
42:1	114, 146	54:5	105, 115
42:1–4	113	54:18	115
42:6–8	111	54–66	129
42:7	146	55	129, 130
43:3–4	105	55:1	114
43:9	115	55:3–5	130
43:14–15	105	55:12–13	130
44:3	114, 115	56:1	217
44:6	224	56:1–8	203
49:1–7	113	59:21	115
49:8	77, 155	60	131
49:26	240	60:1–3	131, 203
50:4–9	113	60:11	114
51:11	105	60:19–22	131
52	117	61:1	147

61:1–3	132	36:24–29	159
61:1–5	114	36:26	114, 240
61:6	115	36:27	114, 115
61:9	115	37:20-28	49
61:10	124, 132	37:26–28	159
61:10–11	114	40–45	150
62:1–5	100	45	142
62:1–9	115	45:8	140
62:2–5	209	45:17	147
62:4–6	132	45:17–22	140
62:5	124	45:17–25	114
63:14	115	45:18–25	154
65:7	112	45:21–25	141
65:17	77, 224		

Hosea

2:1–8	209
2:14–20	100
2:14–23	100
2:16–20	115
6:7	199, 215
6:8	201
9:1	100
14:1–7	100
14:1–9	115

Jeremiah

1:5	76
2:1–3	209
2:13	159
2:20	100
4:4	114
19:5	112
30:9	114
31:9	135
31:14	114
31:29–30	85
31:31–33	114
31:34	115
49:19	128

Joel

2:28	115, 159, 240

Micah

6:6–7	109

Haggai

1:2	129
1:3	129

Ezekiel

1	159
11:19	115
16:30	100
16:37–42	158
20	98, 135
20:4-20	104
20:25–31	108
34:12	128
34:22–24	114
34:24	147
34:30–31	159

Zechariah

6:12	140, 147
6:13	128
7:10–11	115
9:9–13	128
12:7	128
12:8	128

12:10 .... 109, 128, 135	13:7 128
12:10–11 127	14:4–11 128
12:12 128	**Malachi**
13:1 128	
13:2 129	3:8 129

New Testament

Matthew

1:1	147
1:18–25	227
1:25	227, 228
3:2	146
3:3	146
3:14	146
9:15	151
18:17	186
21:44	201
22:1–12	151, 216
25:13	216
27:37	228

Mark

1:2–3	146
2:19	216
12:10	201
12:18–27	165

Luke

1:46–55	230
2:7	228
2:22–26	228, 229
2:49	230
3:4–6	145, 146
4:18	147
4:21	147
7:22	146
8:19–21	230
9:29–31	96
9:31	179
9:51	76
13:22	76
13:31	76
18:31	76
20:17	201

John

1:1–3	222
1:23	146
2:1–12	216
2:19	147
3:16–21	164
3:19–20	150
3:19–21	86
3:29	151
4:5–29	216
6:35	148
8:12	148
8:58	148
10:9	149
10:11	149
10:35	263
11:25	149
12:19	248
14:6	149
15:1	149

Acts

2:16–21	159
2:25	252
2:28–30	122
2:29	252
2:34	252
4:11	201
4:25	252
5:11	186
7:45	252
9:2	250
9:5	79
9:15	76
9:22	249
9:29	76
11	158
11:15–18	251
11:25–26	250
13:1–4	250
13:5	60
13:14	60

13:34–36	252
13:43–44	250
13:44	62
13:44–51	63
13:47	76
13:48	60
13:50	76
14:1	60
14:19	76
14:22	78
15:12–21	151, 158
15:15–17	151
16:1–3	251
16:29–34	62
17	246
17:2	60
17:10	60
17:11	263
17:13	76
17:16–34	61
17:23	246
18	63
18:4	60
18:5–8	63
18:7	64
18:19	60
19:1–4	249
20:22	76
21:10–14	76
21:20	251
21:21–24	251
22:17	76
22:18	76
23:17–21	76
24:10–22	64
24:24–25	64
24:25	64
26:32	64
28:23	65

Romans

1:1–4	159
1:1–6	133
1:1–17	29
1:7	37
1:14–17	65
1:16	249
1:18–19	159
1:18–32	29
2:1–29	29
3:1–20	29
3:21–25	154, 231
3:21–26	153
3:21–28	29
3:23	91
3:25	231
4:1–25	29
4:9–12	158
4:25	80, 181
5	29, 154, 178, 180, 187
5:1–11	29
5:2	80
5:3–5	80
5:6–11	155
5:9	155
5:12	80, 85, 90
5:12–19	77
5:12–21	29, 178, 188
5:14	180, 181
5–7	67, 213, 246
5–8	68
6	20, 78, 155, 156, 161, 172, 180, 182, 183, 191, 204, 205, 272
6:1–3	182, 205
6:1–5	161, 178
6:1–6	161, 177, 182
6:1–10	170, 178
6:1–11	156, 193
6:3	179, 182
6:6	169, 172, 178, 193, 195, 210
6:6–7	172, 205
6:7	195, 196, 201, 202, 203, 205
6:11–14	169

6:13	80
6:14	169
6–7	37, 161
7	206, 207
7:1	209
7:1–4	203, 205
7:1–6	207
7:1–6	165
7:1–6	216
7:2	214
7:5	67
7:7–25	207
7:9	208
7:14-25	270
7:21–25	206, 210
8	80
8:1	80
8:3	67
8:17-18	80
8:18	80
8:18–30	231
8:22–34	80
8:26	80
8:29	135, 223, 232
8:31	80
8:31–39	204, 232
8:33–34	203
8:36	80
8:37	80
9:33	201
10	81, 186
10:14–15	81
10:15	116
11:12	249
12:1–2	158, 175
13	186
15:4	40
15:16	158
16:4–5	186
16–25	158

1 Corinthians

1:2	186
1:14	192
1:14–17	266
3:16	151, 158
5:7	157, 216
6:16–17	216
6:19	158
6:20	216, 217
7:22	75
10:1–10	173
10:1–13	179
10:2	181
10:3	187
10:10	187
10:11	181
10:16	187
12:8–10	187
12:12–13	163, 185
12:12–31	39
12:13	75, 185, 187, 188
12:25–26	79
12:27	163
12:27–29	187
15:1–4	157
15:3	224
15:4	272
15:12–19	249
15:12–23	157
15:22	162

2 Corinthians

1:13	24
1:20	49, 96, 159
3:7–11	76
5:7	224
5:14–17	77
5:17	77
5:21	77
6:2	77
6:3	77
6:16–18	78
11:2	159, 217

Galatians

1:1–5	182
1:2	186
1:15	76
2:17	80
3:5	80
3:13	40
3:23	40
3:26–29	191
4:1	75
4:20–31	217
4:21–31	58
5:19–21	241

Ephesians

1:23	163
2	191
2:4–6	29
2:4–8	188
2:4–9	182
2:8	197
2:10–11	169
2:13–22	171
2:19–21	158
3:6	163
4	188
4:4	163
4:4–7	190
4:4–12	189
4:7–13	187
4:12	163
4:18–24	171
5:8	163
5:21–27	159
5:22–33	217
5:23	163
5:25–26	159
5:25–27	189
5:30	163
6:1–9	39
6:5	75

19:2–7	159

Philippians

1:29-30	80
2:12–18	39
3:5	173, 209

Colossians

1:12-13	173
1:12–14	224
1:12–20	221
1:13	163
1:15	135
1:18	163, 234, 246
1:19	224
1:20	223, 224, 235
1:24–27	79
2:9	224
2:10	29
2:18	241
3:1–25	39
3:5–11	172
3:11	172
4:16	38
18:23	135
23	241

1 Thessalonians

1:5–6	159
2:14	78
2:14–15	78
4:3–8	175
5:6–14	249

2 Thessalonians

1:5-6	79

1 Timothy

4:13	38

2 Timothy

2:8	159

2:11–13 217
3:16 263

Hebrews

1:3 .... 233, 234
1:3–9 233
1:12 233
2:5–8 233
2:14–15 234
6:18 123
12:23 .... 158, 233
12:24 120

Revelation

1:3 38
1:4–8 234
1:5 .... 135, 234
1:5–6 158
5:9–10 120
21:1–4 .... 217, 218
21:5 224

www.ingramcontent.com/pod-product-compliance
Lightning Source LLC
Chambersburg PA
CBHW071304110526
44591CB00010B/767